Institutions of Rural Development for the Poor

Decentralization and Organizational Linkages

DAVID K. LEONARD &
DALE ROGERS MARSHALL, Editors

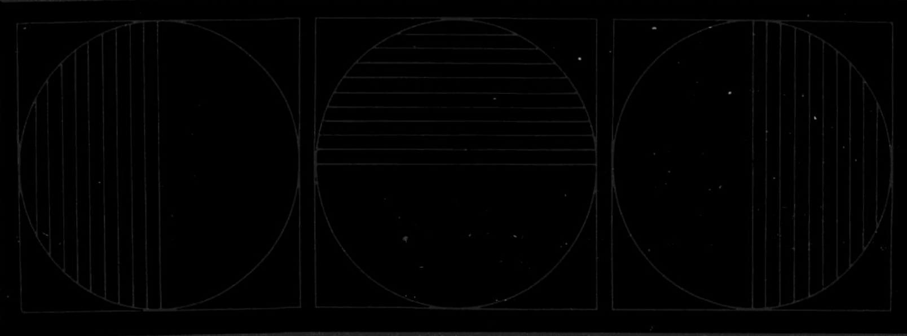

iiS
INSTITUTE
OF INTERNATIONAL
STUDIES
University of California, Berkeley

TABLE OF CONTENTS

Preface
David K. Leonard & Dale Rogers Marshall ix

I. ANALYZING THE ORGANIZATIONAL REQUIREMENTS FOR SERVING THE RURAL POOR
David K. Leonard 1

The Organizational Requirements 2

The Structural Implications 3

The Parameters for Organizational Design 7

Program Vulnerability to Inequality 8

The Responsiveness of Local Leaders 15

Support from the Center 20

Technical and Administrative Requirements and the Distribution of Capacity 24

Modes of Decentralization 27

The Dimensions for Analyzing Decentralization 28

A Typology of Decentralization Oriented to the Poor 30

The Array of Linkages 35

Control Linkages 36

Assistance Linkages 36

Conclusion 37

References 38

II. LESSONS FROM THE IMPLEMENTATION OF POVERTY PROGRAMS IN THE UNITED STATES
Dale Rogers Marshall 40

The U.S. Grant System 41

The Context for the Poverty Programs 43

Dual Forms of Decentralization: Parallel Linkages from the Center to Local Recipients 48

TABLE OF CONTENTS

Control Linkages 54

Assistance Linkages 57

Technical Assistance 59

Representation 62

Conclusion 64

References 67

III. GOVERNMENT, COOPERATIVES, AND THE PRIVATE SECTOR IN PEASANT AGRICULTURE
Stephen B. Peterson 73

Unimodal Development and its Policy Implications 73

The Decentralization of Rural Economic Infrastructure 76

What is the Role of Cooperatives in Rural Development? 78

Supplies 79

Marketing 84

Credit 90

Production 99

Production Cooperatives with Individual Land Parcels 101

Production Cooperatives with Joint Land Management 107

Conclusions on the Choice Between the Cooperative and Private Sectors 111

The Linkage Lessons of the Cooperative Experience 114

References 122

IV. ALTERNATIVE LOCAL ORGANIZATIONS SUPPORTING THE AGRICULTURAL DEVELOPMENT OF THE POOR
Stephen B. Peterson 125

Small-Farmer Groups: Organizing the Rural Poor 126

The Fundacion del Centavo: An Example of Preferred Design 131

Institutions of Rural Development for the Poor

RESEARCH SERIES
No. 49

Institutions of Rural Development for the Poor

Decentralization and Organizational Linkages

DAVID K. LEONARD &
DALE ROGERS MARSHALL, Editors

INSTITUTE
OF INTERNATIONAL
STUDIES
University of California, Berkeley

Library of Congress Cataloging in Publication Data

Main entry under title:

Institutions of rural development for the poor.

(Research series / Institute of International Studies, University of California, Berkeley, ISSN 0068-6093; no. 49)

Includes bibliographical references and index.

1. Rural development. I. Leonard, David K. II. Marshall, Dale Rogers. III. Series: Research series (University of California, Berkeley. Institute of International Studies); no. 49.

HN17.5.I53 1982 307.7'2 82-15651
ISBN 0-87725-149-5

TABLE OF CONTENTS

Single-Function Versus Multi-Function Local Organizations 135

Incentives for Organizations Versus Organizing the Rural Poor 140

Linkage Sequences 142

Conclusion 149

References 150

V. LINKING THE VILLAGE TO MODERN HEALTH SYSTEMS
Sven Steinmo 151

Centralized Health Delivery Systems 154

Hospital Systems 154

Task-Force Interventions 158

Models Using Auxiliaries 159

Clinic-Based Systems 162

Village-Based Systems 167

The Medex System 177

Linkages 180

Community Participation 184

References 189

VI. CHOOSING AMONG FORMS OF DECENTRALIZATION AND LINKAGE
David K. Leonard 193

The Character of Intermediate and Local Elites 194

Congenial Elites, Inclusive Organizations and Devolution 194

Conflict and Alternative Organizations 195

The Nature of the National Government Agency 200

National Support 200

Irresolute Central Support 201

The Distribution of Technical and Administrative Capacity 204

Technical Assistance Linkages 205

Linking Apportioned Functions 206
Redundant Linkages 209
Administrative Simplification 213
Overwhelming Constraints 213
The Allocation of Functions by Organizational Priorities 216
Assistance Linkages 220
Conclusion 222
References 224

INDEXES 227
Author Index 227
Subject Index 231

NOTES ON CONTRIBUTORS 237

TABLES

1. THE VULNERABILITY OF SELECTED PROGRAMS TO LOCAL ELITE MONOPOLIZATION OF THEIR BENEFITS 10
2. EXAMPLES OF FORMS OF DECENTRALIZATION SERVING THE POOR 32

Preface

Over the last decade improving the welfare of the poor majority has become a priority concern of the international development community. This commitment to rural areas and to less advantaged populations has presented major implementation problems. Because new approaches to rural development are being attempted, new organizational arrangements frequently are needed to implement them. Guidelines for the design of these new organizational structures have been scarce.

This book is written from the perspective of program designers and deals with critical administrative questions they must address. It specifies how they might decide which national and local organizations to involve in a program, how functions might be allocated among them, and what linkages could be created between them. Thus it analyzes various centralized and decentralized administrative systems and suggests how elements of each can be combined in specific settings so that their advantages and disadvantages compensate for each other.

Successful implementation depends both upon commitment to program goals and upon the capacity necessary to achieve them. Diverse kinds of programs make different types of demands upon these two essential organizational attributes. The benefits of some programs are much easier to divert from the poor majority for whom they are intended, and so require greater organizational commitment to the poor. Similarly, some programs use more resources or require more complex and scarce skills than others do.

Program design, then, depends upon the distribution of commitment and capacity in the social system. Identification of these attributes requires analysis of both central and local organizations. The national political system as a whole provides the context for action but central agencies still will vary among themselves in their dedication to delivering particular types of services to the rural poor. Can an agency with the right combination of commitment, administrative skills and resources be found?

Local leaders may or may not be responsive to the interests of the poor majority in specific program areas. If they are, then the regular forms of local government and organization, which are inclusive of all segments of their populations, can be used to reach the rural poor. If the leaders are not responsive to the interests of the disadvantaged, consideration must be given to alternative organizations which limit their constituencies to the poor. In either case, but especially in the latter, serious attention must be given to whether the organization has the capacity to implement the program by itself.

Depending on the answers given to the preceding questions we suggest the design option that will optimize the chances of long-term program success. The appropriate design may involve turning implementation over to a central agency, or reliance upon local government or cooperatives, or a rejection of all forms of public organization and the use of the private market and philanthropies. More often, however, it will require some combination of local and central responsibilities and the construction of linkages between them. We give a good deal of attention to these linkages—the mechanisms through which organizations influence one another. These linkages include financial aid, technical assistance, regulation, representation and informal influence. The appropriate degree of assistance and control in the linkages of the center to the local organization follow from the same analytic principles outlined above and suggestions are made concerning them.

Our general thesis is that rural development is best served by the partnership of committed and competent central and local organizations. The ideal, then, is a type of decentralization which is based on the strength of committed organizations at both the national and the local levels and a productive interaction (or linkage) between them. Such optimal conditions all too frequently do not obtain, however. Depending on the circumstances, either centralization or local autonomy or private initiative may better serve the interests of the rural poor. There is no "one best way" to improve the welfare of the poor majority. The task before us is to understand how and when to use each type of administrative design and the associated linkages.

The design principles that are offered in this book have general relevance. They have been developed with specific reference, however, to programs of agricultural development, primary health care, labor-intensive public works, and elementary education. When we began our work together, our focus was on decentralization and inter-governmental linkages. We shifted to a sectoral program approach for two reasons. First, a general inter-governmental relations approach tends to focus on distributions of power and resources as ends in themselves rather than upon the benefits they are supposed to create. Particular linkages are then seen as enhancing or hindering local democracy and the issue of whether or not services are getting to the poor gets lost. The second problem with a general inter-governmental relations approach is that it tends to downplay critical functions such as agriculture and health, which frequently are not handled by local governments.

In pursuing the sectoral approach we realized that the linkage problems of various functional areas differ somewhat from one another. We present an analysis of linkages in agriculture and health and draw on studies of elementary education and public works. We have chosen these areas because they feature most prominently in the current development efforts aimed at improving the welfare of the rural poor. The functional analyses are followed by an attempt to draw more general lessons.

Although this book is phrased as a series of prescriptions to the development practitioner, it is very much a piece of empirical social science and can be read as such with only a slight change in emphasis. As our colleague Martin Landau notes, a policy proposal is an hypothesis—it is a statement that certain actions are likely to result in certain desirable consequences. In constructing our "actionable hypotheses," we have analyzed over thirty cases of various types of national service systems in the developing world, as well as examining the more general literature on development administration. Our conclusions have been further strengthened by a review of the very extensive literature on inter-governmental linkages in the U.S. poverty programs. Although the United States is not a developing country, many of the problems of providing benefits to the poor are sufficiently universal to make its experience highly suggestive. This exploration of linkage lessons from the U.S. War on Poverty precedes the functional analyses.

This book is the result of a collaborative research effort and the product is an integrated whole, not a series of separate essays.

Throughout its development we worked closely with one another and for several months met weekly to share ideas. In addition to the authors, Jose Garzon, Richard Edelstein and Victor Magagna participated in our collective effort and produced working papers on which we have drawn in writing the book.

The research as a whole was funded by the United States Agency for International Development under a Cooperative Agreement with the University of California (AID/DSAN-CA-0199). We are grateful to our colleagues in the Project on Managing Decentralization and to its staff for the support they gave to our efforts. Various portions of this book have benefited greatly from extensive comments on earlier versions by Preston Chitere, John Cohen, Janice Jiggins, Bruce Johnston, David Korten, John Montgomery, Walter Oyugi, Judith Tendler, Norman Uphoff and others. Finally the editors and authors wish to express their great appreciation to Leslie Leonard for her extensive and thorough editorial assistance.

David K. Leonard
Dale Rogers Marshall

Chapter I

ANALYZING THE ORGANIZATIONAL REQUIREMENTS FOR SERVING THE RURAL POOR

David K. Leonard

Rural development has never been easy. Like the agriculture to which it is tied, rural growth has always taken hard work and intelligent implementation in the face of local variability and an unpredictable environment. Now development is even more difficult. The current challenge is to provide services for the world's poor majority—the marginal farmers and landless who make up the bulk of the developing countries' rural population. The farmer who begins to cultivate on rich bottom land must eventually extend operations to the rocky slopes if the enterprise is to reach its full productive potential. Even more so must development be brought to the world's poor majority, for not only production but life itself depends on the expansion. Still, growth is harder to achieve with poor resources, whether it be the soil or the cultivator that is poor. The environment is harsher; the fragility is greater; the margins for error are narrower. President Julius Nyerere once remarked that while the United States was trying to reach the moon, Tanzania was striving to reach its villages. It appears that Tanzania had the harder task and one more critical for development.

Growth in per capita income is no longer accepted as development. Dudley Seers, for example, argues that development is best indicated by reductions in (i) absolute poverty (most importantly malnutrition); (ii) unemployment; and (iii) inequality. He readily agrees that in the long term, growth in Gross National Product (GNP) is necessary to such development but insists that it is not sufficient (Seers, 1972: 21-25). Even those who use productivity as a definition of development point out that it is different from economic growth and produce substantial evidence to indicate that it is more likely to occur in societies in which the "Basic Needs" of which Seers speaks have been met (Uphoff and Ilchman, 1972).

We presume that the achievement of development so defined will require public programs and interventions. Under free market conditions, the early stages of economic development produce a dramatic widening of socio-economic differentiation (Migdal, 1974). Because the welfare and productivity of the majority of the population is thereby neglected, national development is unnecessarily slowed (Johnston and Clark, 1982; Uphoff and Esman, 1974; Uphoff and Ilchman, 1972). Intervention by the state can make these inequalities still worse and therefore it is not always desirable. If development is to be broad-based, however, appropriate public programs are required. We need better knowledge about when and how those programs can be made effective in reaching the rural poor.

To provide development for the rural poor, then, implies a variety of programs: land reform; extension of agricultural technologies that are appropriate to the resource endowments of poor farmers; improved markets and input supply for the crops the poor grow; rural primary health care services; labor-intensive rural road construction; the building of sanitary water systems and other rural public works; etc. These sorts of rural service programs are not necessarily new. In the past they often have been structured in such a way as to give special advantage to rural elites, however. Assistance has been given for crops which only the well-endowed could grow, for example, or subsidized inputs have been monopolized by the better-off. Such programs left the condition of the poor majority unchanged or even worsened relative to their richer neighbors. What is needed now are programs that will right this historic imbalance of services and development against the poor majority.

THE ORGANIZATIONAL REQUIREMENTS

Such rural development programs are quite demanding in their organizational requirements. First, the implementing agency must have a special *commitment* to the delivery of program services to the rural poor. In social systems it is unnatural for benefits to be dispensed equally, much less redistributed toward the disadvantaged. Some inner or outer dynamic must motivate the organization to overcome the momentum of inequality.

Second, the implementing agency must have or be able to find the *resources* and *technical skills* for the program. As the intended clientele is disadvantaged, it will not have these itself.

Third, the implementor needs *adaptability*. One component of the rural development problem is that our knowledge of how to achieve it is incomplete. Project implementation constantly produces unexpected consequences. Rural development requires major doses of incrementalism; one learns as one proceeds what works and what does not. Those managing the project must be able to adapt to the lessons of its experience (Johnston and Clark, 1982: Chapter 1).

Fourth, implementation of rural development programs usually entails the incorporation of community *participation*. A considerable body of literature stresses the advantages of closely involving local peoples (Uphoff, Cohen, and Goldsmith, 1979; Uphoff and Esman, 1974; Ralston, Anderson, and Colson, 1981). (i) It is necessary to mobilize local resources. (ii) It facilitates the collection of the information that is needed to adapt a program to local conditions. (iii) As rural development frequently involves the promotion of social change, active involvement of the community is generally necessary in order to bring about its transformation. (iv) Local participation may begin to build the public demand structure for a service which will lead to its continued funding.

THE STRUCTURAL IMPLICATIONS

The foregoing organizational requirements for the successful implementation of rural development have several structural implications. The importance of commitment to the delivery of program benefits to the poor requires that the allocation of implementation responsibilities be structured by the presence or absence of this attribute in different parts of the social system.

The need for technical skills and resources in rural development most often implies some degree of centralization. The rural areas in general usually have a weak tax base and need an infusion of funds from national sources if anything significant is to be undertaken. The involvement of the center also is essential if there is to be any redistribution of resources from well-off regions to the poorer ones.

On the other hand, the adaptive and participatory requirements of rural development dictate decentralization. Even if participation means nothing more than consultation and negotiation, discretion is needed at the field level to institute the bargain that is appropriate to each locale (Heiby, Ness, and Pillsbury, 1979: 7). Problem-solving and learning are inhibited by centralization as well. An organization operating in an environment characterized by change and incomplete knowledge must have decentralized management in order to cope (Thompson, 1967: 72-73, 86-87); otherwise, adaptation will be too little, too late, or inappropriate.

The decentralization required for rural development is not necessarily incompatible with central government involvement. Decentralization is a difficult concept to define and we will come back to it later. For the moment it is sufficient to note that the important thing for rural development is to have the resources and authority for timely adaptation to locally-specific conditions in the field, not in the capital. Such authority can be exercised in a variety of ways, including the involvement of national government. The operative agency could be, for example, a field office of a central ministry or a local organization with national financial assistance.

In most circumstances the organizational arrangements appropriate for rural development will not be based on a choice between either central or local involvement but on a combination of the two. The problem will be to specify exactly what kind of combination, with what division of responsibilities and with what relationships between them.

In their review of the rural development experience of sixteen Asian states, Norman Uphoff and Milton Esman concluded that one of the prerequisities for rural development is a strong system of local organizations together with effective links to compatible national agencies which can support them (1974: xi-xii). A few examples may help to illustrate the point. The preparation of coffee for the market requires a small processing and drying factory. Large estates will have their own but the operation of one is impossible for a smallholder. The Kenyan experience suggests that the optimal "factory" serves about two thousand small growers. Any economies of production that would come from a larger unit are more than offset by transport costs for the growers. Such factories have become the basic unit of cooperative organization in central Kenya and are managed independently of one another. Nonetheless, these primary societies have difficulty retaining competent accountants and so they turn to the district cooperative union for these services. Similarly, the international marketing of the coffee produced is far beyond the resources of even a district union. This function is performed by a national cooperative organization. Coffee smallholders thus are served by a three-tier cooperative system, each level with its distinctive competence and linked to the others in a complementary manner.

Another example concerns the interdependence of the community health worker and the M.D. in rural health care. There are a variety of economic and social reasons why paramedical personnel are generally more appropriate than doctors as the basic providers of health services and education in the developing world. Yet these community health workers will tend to be ineffective if they are not closely supported by M.D.'s in the larger medical system. Each has an appropriate role and scale of operation (Chapter V).

Effective primary education systems also depend on at least three levels of organization. At the level of the classroom the participation of parents is a tremendous asset in motivating the children and assisting them with learning. The construction and maintenance of school facilities also is usually done better and more quickly when it is handled at a local or intermediate level. On the other hand, the development of curricula, the setting of qualifying examinations and other functions closely related to the professional aspects of education are almost always best handled at the national level.

Finally, the construction and maintenance of rural roads involves links between community organizations and intermediate levels of subnational government. The local group is needed to organize voluntary labor for construction and to oversee and/or provide maintenance. It also can make extremely helpful contributions at the planning stage in order to ensure the optimal fit between local use and road layout (Tendler, 1979). On the other hand, the engineers to design the road and the earth-moving equipment to do the heavier construction work must be found in a supra-local organization. Rural works projects function best when each is in communication with and in support of the other (Garzon, 1981).

The preceding examples simply re-emphasize the ideal of partnership of central and local organizations in rural development. Thus we will focus both on the division of responsibility between them and on the nature of their inter-organizational linkages. We are concerned with the transactions between local participatory organizations, the national government, and the subnational governments and field offices which mediate between them. *Linkages are the mechanisms by which one organization is tied to or attempts to influence another.* Note that as we use the term, linkages are synonymous with inter-organizational relationships. This definition is narrower than that of economists, for example. Thus although we are concerned with organizations that mediate between the state and the poor, it is not they or their relationships with the poor that we refer to as linkages. Instead we are concerned with the links these organizations have to the state—financial and technical assistance, regulatory controls, influence, etc. Our linkages are *organizational linkages,* and although we use the term "linkages" by itself for convenience, in this book it always has this restricted meaning.

Organizational linkage mechanisms cannot be explored adequately unless attention is also given to: (1) the organizations being linked and their commitment to rural development, and (2) the kinds of programs which will benefit the rural poor. Thus our analysis of linkages includes a focus on program content and the types of local and national organizations most likely to be congenial to those programs. Our major concern is to give a more systematic treatment of the problems of linkage than is currently available in the development literature.

Why organizational linkages? Are they more important than appropriate national policies? No; they are shaped by those policies. Do they matter more than congenial national or local organizations? Again, no; these are the units they work with. Appropriate policies made in a national ministry have to be implemented, however, and congenial local organizations have to be provided with resources—or even to be created. Implementation entails linkages. As perplexing as the policy issues of development have been, those of implementation have been even more frustrating. At this very basic level, development practitioners have had very limited guidance in dealing with local organizations. They have created schemes of local technical assistance, training, financial aid, regulation, and representation with little more than instinct to guide them. The results have varied among dangerous dependence, throttling control, reckless discretion, and so on. It is time that we began to answer questions such as: "Just what is it that a national or international agency can *do* to create or sustain a cooperative which services the poor?" "What kinds of services and regulation should the outside agency provide for a community-based health care system?" "What kinds of representative structures do the rural poor need in order to obtain from the center the minimal resources they need to maintain their health or roads or agricultural production?" The issue is not just what the desirable end result is, but what actions should be taken toward that end. These are organizational linkage questions.

THE PARAMETERS FOR ORGANIZATIONAL DESIGN

Once a policy or program objective has been conceived that requires work with local units, it has still to be implemented. This involves very important questions of design. The program must be given specificity; national agencies and local organizations must be selected as the implementors; and linkages must be created between them. It is important to give careful and wide consideration to the available alternatives, for the success or failure of the program will depend on the choices made. Occasionally the analyst will be in a local organization and be looking for assistance from the optimal national agency. More often, he or she will be in a government bureau trying to find the best type of local group to work through. Both of these analysts have to take as given one of the implementing organizations—their own. Policy analysts also look out from the offices of presidents, planning ministries, and international donors, however, and these have a much greater degree of choice in designing the structure of implementation. It is vital that they use the choice fully and wisely. The selection of the wrong type of agency or organization spells failure for a project. Frequently the analyst takes a narrow, short-term view and considers the performance of the agency or organization only so long as it is closely linked to and monitored by a donor or the president's office. The project functions well for a time and then begins to malfunction in ways that should have been foreseeable. Our analysis is directed at averting such failures.

The choice of an organizational strategy for the implementation of a program depends both on the nature of the program and on the social character of the task environment in which it is to be placed. The distribution of benefits to the rural, poor majority is difficult to achieve. In the normal working of social structures, the poor rarely receive even an equal portion of the benefits society creates. The most effective strategy for overcoming this handicap and providing the poor with needed services depends on the interaction of the program and social structure. Some types of programs are harder to administer or lend themselves more readily than others to the appropriation of benefits by a minority. Similarly some social structures are more likely than others to permit local elites to take advantage of programs for themselves.

The success of program implementation depends on the following parameters or contextual variables: (i) the program's vulnerability to inequality; (ii) the nature of local elites and their interests; (iii) the nature and variability of interests among national agencies; and (iv) the distribution between national and local organizations of the capacity to meet the program's technical and administrative requirements. We will analyze each of these factors in turn. They are not determinative by themselves, however. Each variable creates certain propensities that may or may not be realized depending on the effect of the others. The presentation of these factors sets the analytic framework for this book, and it will be used frequently in the chapters that follow. In the conclusion we will pull together the ways in which they interact with one another and suggest the decentralization strategy and the type of inter-organizational linkages that tend to be more appropriate for programs for the poor majority in a particular context.

Program Vulnerability to Inequality. The first step to take in devising an implementation strategy for a program is to analyze its vulnerability to inequality.[1] A wide distribution of benefits is inherent in some types of programs, while elite advantage is extremely easy in others. Inequality is an endemic social condition and develops

[1]Our thinking in this section has been influenced by a manuscript draft by Judith Tendler and by correspondence with Bruce Johnston.

readily in most settings. Perfect equality is unobtainable, if the experience of existing social systems—socialist as well as capitalist—is any guide. Nonetheless there are significant differences among programs in the likelihood with which inequity will develop. Table 1 provides a listing of those programs which seem to us to be more and less susceptible to serious inequalities in the distribution of their benefits. Whether or not a program that is vulnerable to inequity will in fact produce it in any particular setting will depend on the operation of the other three contextual variables. The importance of identifying vulnerable programs is not to avoid them but to know when they can be undertaken only with the support of other favorable conditions.

As a rule programs are more vulnerable to inequality to the degree that they have one or more of the following attributes:

(i) The individual or family, rather than the community, is the unit of consumption. For example, it is much easier for local elites to gain disproportionate benefit from a water system piped to individual dwellings than from one piped to communal-use points. Most services are consumed on a non-communal basis, however. Individual consumption units take on their greatest significance when combined with one of the other following attributes.

(ii) Demand far exceeds supply. For example, the numbers wanting to attend highly selective educational institutions or to receive subsidized credit will always exceed supply. It is possible to assure equal or even preferential access for the disadvantaged to such goods, but it is always difficult. Elite efforts to obtain such scarce services make them perennially vulnerable to inequality.

(iii) Service quality can be improved at the expense of quantity. Because elites are the ones most likely to obtain scarce services they have no motive to lower service standards in order to assure wide access to them. Instead their interests are best served by pressing for higher quality and letting the clientele reached shrink. Curative veterinary and human medicine illustrate this type of vulnerability to inequality particularly well. It is common to find expensive treatments being available for a few, while funds run out for inexpensive, basic treatments for the many.

Table 1

THE VULNERABILITY OF SELECTED PROGRAMS TO LOCAL ELITE MONOPOLIZATION OF THEIR BENEFITS

Less Vulnerable	More Vulnerable
AGRICULTURE	
Water abundant irrigation	Water-short or tightly managed irrigation
Unsubsidized, competitive credit	Subsidized credit
Competitive input or marketing facilities	Monopolized input or marketing facilities
Group extension for crops for which inputs are abundant	Extension to individual farmers Extension for input-scarce crops
Improvement programs for crops on which the poor specialize	Improvement programs for crops on which the well-to-do specialize
Programs that will bring profitable new crops or production technologies to all farmers in a defined area	Programs that will bring profitable new crops or production technologies to a portion of the farmers in a wide area
Programs that introduce profitable labor-intensive technologies	Programs that introduce capital-intensive technologies
Mass, preventive veterinary medicine	Restricted, preventive veterinary medicine Curative veterinary medicine
EDUCATION	
Mass primary education	Restricted or streamed primary education
Mass secondary education	Restricted or streamed secondary education
Adult education	

Table 1 (continued)

Less Vulnerable	More Vulnerable
Vocational training for low status occupations	Vocational training for high status occupations
HEALTH	
Public sanitation and most other forms of promotive medicine	
Mass innoculations and other types of active preventive medicine	Passive preventive medicine (i.e., provided on consumer demand only)
Active but voluntary family planning assistance	Passive or involuntary family planning programs
Nutritional additives (e.g., iodine in salt)	
Mass feeding (subsidized food, famine relief, mass child feeding)	Selected target-group feeding
Simple curative medicine for villages in a low mobility society	Curative medicine for villages in a high mobility society High quality, curative medicine
PUBLIC WORKS	
Communal water points	Piped water systems for which the individual consumers bear the capital cost of initial connection
Road construction and maintenance when all residents are involved directly or indirectly in the market economy	Road construction or maintenance when only a minority will be engaged in marketed production
Labor-intensive public works projects with local labor recruitment	Capital-intensive or externally contracted public works projects

(iv) Other, scarce inputs are necessary in order to utilize the service effectively. Roads or agricultural extension in an area in which the available market crops require inputs beyond the means of the majority of farmers will serve to benefit and strengthen the better-off. Another example of high vulnerability to inequality is free university education accompanied by fee-paying primary and secondary systems.

(v) The service provider passively awaits client demand in distributing benefits. In most circumstances, the most advantaged members of society possess considerable advantages in information as well. Thus passive suppliers of services are almost certain to have disproportionate numbers of the well-to-do among their clients. An organization with benefits to offer the poor therefore most often needs to be active in promoting its services for them.

(vi) The service involves coercion or the creation of monopolies. When the state creates a monopoly in a service area or when it uses coercion to achieve its objectives, those who have political power (either local or national) are most likely to benefit. In most instances this will be the advantaged members of the society, who will then gain unearned benefits beyond those that their wealth is already buying them. Of course when state power is used on behalf of the poor and is effective, coercion and monopoly may have a beneficial, redistributive effect. It takes much greater effort on the part of the state to use these tools to help the poor than it does for elites to turn them to their own advantage, however.

Programs which are less vulnerable to inequality in the distribution of benefits have one or more of the following characteristics:

(i) Indivisible, wide-spread benefits. Many services are public goods—once they are provided in a community all who reside there can utilize them. Some of these public goods will improve the welfare of all segments of the community. The best example of such a public good is village sanitation. Everyone in a village is vulnerable to disease until all have and use proper sanitation facilities. Once they are in place the rich and the poor alike will experience less disease. Another example of this type of public good is a road to a community in which all residents can or already do participate significantly in the external market economy. All then will spend less time getting to the market and/or will receive higher profits for their goods from middlemen who find it easier to reach them. On the other hand, if most families are engaged in subsistence agriculture only and cannot shift to cash crops easily, the few who are engaged in the market will reap a disproportionate benefit which might even have a negative impact on the village's poor. This would occur if the increased profits of the better-off enabled them to put pressure on the less-advantaged to sell off their land. It is important to remember that many public goods offered in the development process are *not* inherently beneficial to the poor.

(ii) Benefits are linked to the use of a resource the poor have in abundance. When a program makes heavy demands on capital or education and provides high returns to those with these resources, the gap between the rich and the poor is likely to widen. Conversely, activities that increase the demand for labor will provide direct benefits to the poor in the form of jobs and quite possibly the indirect benefit of higher wages as a result of the increased demand. Labor-intensive public works projects therefore will have wide-spread benefits for the working poor—at least for their duration. (If a crash works program were to create a temporary labor-shortage and induce employers to purchase labor-saving equipment, workers might have difficulty getting jobs when it ended. Thus the most beneficial works projects create an extended demand for labor.) Similarly, technical innovations in agriculture that make the increased use of labor profitable are almost certain to benefit the poor, even if it is the wealthy who are first to adopt the change. Thus Bruce Johnston has argued with us that research investments in more labor-intensive agricultural technologies and machinery are indirectly highly beneficial to the poor. Programs that promote economic growth and productivity through the increased use of labor are doubly desirable because they improve income distribution while increasing the society's investable surplus.

(iii) The service deals with problems or opportunities that are more common to the poor. Some diseases are more common among the poor and interventions aimed specifically at their prevention or cure are not so likely to be diverted to the rich. For example, efforts to prevent cholera will disproportionately benefit the poor, for they are the ones who lack the needed sanitation facilities and uncontaminated water. In a different vein, some foods are more commonly consumed and grown by the poor. Efforts to improve the productivity of these crops will probably be targeted on the poorer producers with little extra effort. In East Africa, for example, wheat is a capital-intensive, luxury crop while sorghum and cassava are consumed by poorer subsistence farmers. Programs to assist with the latter crops are almost inevitably redistributive.

(iv) Supply exceeds demand. If the market is flooded with a commodity, the poor then will be able to get it. This effect can be achieved in two, complementary ways. The first is if there is a natural, upward limit on demand. A woman needs only one contraceptive at a time; a child must be provided with primary education only once; smallpox vaccinations are required but once in three years; etc. The second method of creating surplus supply is for a non-profit organization (usually a government) to subsidize the production and distribution of the good or service to the point of saturation. The two methods intereact. The saturation point usually is not reached without subsidy and it cannot be reached unless there is some kind of natural point at which demand drops off sharply.

(v) Units of service provision significantly exceed the demands of local elites. The earliest units of service to a community are usually "lumpy." If the service is to be provided to one person then it can be provided to a goodly number for very little additional cost. A primary school teacher for ten elite children will be able to instruct twenty non-elites as well. A clinic for the half-dozen well-off families can easily provide care for large numbers of poor ones. Especially in the early stages of development, local elites may be instrumental in acquiring services that can accommodate the demands of many more than themselves. These service increments will benefit at least some of the poor. Elite demand, however, will be concentrated on the first unit of service. Even if that unit does not accommodate the needs of all, local elites are not likely to press for the additional units required.

These guidelines on the vulnerability of a program to inequality indicate the kind of analysis which a program designer must make to increase the likelihood of reaching the rural poor.

Nonetheless, just because a program is vulnerable to monopolization of benefits by local elites does not mean that inequality will inevitably result. The character of the local social structure, of the national, local and intermediate organizations involved, and of the linkages between them will determine the outcome. Vulnerability is a sign of danger; as it increases, the other elements of implementation design must be more carefully crafted. Conversely, as vulnerability declines, weaknesses can be tolerated elsewhere in the implementation structure.

The Responsiveness of Local Leaders. Will the leaders of local organizations press for the distribution of benefits to their rural poor or will they seek to divert them to local elites? Just how responsive are local leaders to the needs of the poor? If local leaders have a weak commitment to the poor, programs that are vulnerable to inequality will tend to become welfare for the better-off. If there is a high degree of responsiveness to the less-advantaged, those same programs will provide a wide spread of benefits with few outside controls. Such a congenial local leadership structure can be achieved in three different ways: (1) the leaders share the interests of the poor themselves; (2) there is significant competition for leadership positions from those who seek to represent non-elite interests; or (3) alternative organizations are used which limit their membership to non-elites.

The responsiveness of leaders to the interests of the poor is assured most easily (but all too infrequently) when they share those interests. This need not mean that they are identical to their constituents. Leaders are atypical. All organizations are led by individuals who differ in significant ways from their followers. Leaders generally are more educated, wealthier, and so on, than the average member of their organizations (Almond and Verba, 1963: 380-81; Migdal, 1974: 232; Ralston, Anderson, and Colson, 1981: 24-28). If the most advantaged members of a community are excluded from leadership, then the next most advantaged group will be disproportionately represented among those who run things (Harik, 1974: 76-77; Schurmann, 1966: 445-51). Those guiding the affairs of a community's organizations thus most frequently are local elites in some degree—and not just because they are leaders. This inequality is a near universal and as such need not concern us. The issue is not necessarily whether organizations are run by local elites but whether those leaders share the interests of their followers.

An elite may differ from others only in degree, rather than in kind. The existence of stratification in a community or group does not establish that there necessarily are class differences. The greater the extent to which the members of a community share a common mode of existence, the greater the similarity in elite and non-elite interests.

The distinction between differences in degree and differences in kind is most clearly demonstrated by the interests surrounding agricultural production. Bruce Johnston (Johnston and Kilby, 1974; Johnston and Clark, 1982) is one of many who argue the crucial advantages of unimodal over bimodal patterns of agricultural development. In a unimodal system farmers have broadly similar amounts of land, produce much the same crops and are equal in their integration into the market. A bimodal pattern, on the other hand, is characterized by two distinct modes of agricultural production. A minority of farms are large and geared toward the production of market crops, generally for export. Meanwhile the great majority of farmers are small, produce different, subsistence-oriented crops and frequently provide labor for the export producers.

The local elites in a bimodal agricultural system have quite dissimilar agricultural interests from the landless, near-landless and small farmers in their communities. They have a qualitatively different resource base, produce different crops, are involved in a different market and have an employer relationship with the rest of the community. Although these local elites most often lead their communities (either openly or indirectly), they do not share the agricultural interests of their poor majority.

A local elite is most likely to have common interests with the poor when they have a broadly similar set of circumstances in common. On agricultural matters Uphoff and Esman have suggested that this occurs when the richest 20 percent of the rural population have no more than six times the income of the poorest 20 percent (1974: xvii). Within this range of difference, producers are able to profit from similar cropping patterns, marketing arrangements, production technologies and so forth. (Uphoff and Esman developed the 6:1 ratio by analyzing sixteen national systems in Asia. It seems to us to be possible that an even smaller ratio—but certainly not perfect equality—would be needed to produce commonality of interest in some cropping systems if we calculated the ratio at the community level. It is very unlikely, however, that richer and poorer farmers would be operating under similar production conditions at any ratio larger than 6:1. It would be useful to have further research done on this point at the community level.)

It is hard to overestimate the importance for development of commonality of interest among rural dwellers. Where it exists, the general, community-wide (or inclusive) local leadership structures can be used relatively easily and supported fairly freely. Where it does not exist, there will always be the danger that the direction of benefits toward the poor will be subverted and that their lot may be made even worse with development.

Nonetheless, it does not follow that local elites who differ in interests from the majority of their communities in one area will differ in all. A local landlord might have deeply conflictual interests with the area's poor majority on many agricultural matters and yet share with them a need for a health clinic (Uphoff, Cohen, and Goldsmith, 1979: 68). An agency oriented toward the poor would eschew his leadership in the first area but welcome it for the second.

The degree of inequality in a community's social structure interacts with the character of a program to indicate the compatibility of local elite and poor interests. Where either local inequality or the vulnerability of a program to inequality are low, local elite leadership is suitable for poverty-alleviating projects. Where both are high, programs oriented toward the poor majority are probably best carried out without local participatory structures or with organizations that confine their membership to the poor (alternative organizations).

The second and third strategies for achieving congenial local leadership apply to those arenas where the interests of the local elite conflict with those of the poor majority. In such situations the former's dominance generally must be challenged if significant benefits are to reach the latter. There are two, frequently complementary, ways in which this can be done. One (i.e., the second strategy) is the existence of significant competition for leadership positions from those who seek to represent non-elite interests (Uphoff, Cohen, and

Goldsmith, 1979: 68). Then, even if local elites continue to be over-represented among the community's influentials, they will have to be more responsive to the interests of the poor majority in order to maintain their positions. For responsiveness to the poor to be achieved in elite-run systems three conditions must be met: (a) there is competition for leadership; (b) the support of the poor is a necessary component of most strategies for achieving leadership; (c) at least one serious candidate for leadership appeals directly to the distinctive interests of the poor. The last condition is more likely to be met if the less-advantaged are organized, and that leads us to the third strategy.

The national government usually has to link its efforts to those of local organizations if it is to promote development effectively. The links need not be to community-wide groups like local governments, however, because they tend to be elite dominated. Instead the government can link with (and perhaps assist in forming) alternative groups which are more homogeneous in their membership and which exclude those elites and others who have dissimilar interests (Uphoff, Cohen, and Goldsmith, 1979: 116, 193, 208). The leaders who emerge in these groups may be among the more advantaged of their members—and thus different in degree. If relative homogeneity is attained, however, the interests of these leaders will not differ in kind from those of their followers.

Alternative organizations representing the interests of disadvantaged groups are generally necessary if local elite dominance of inclusive local governments and organizations is to be challenged effectively. Thus the third method of dealing with local elites with distinct interests generally is a prerequisite to the second, competitive, option.[1]

Alternative organizations need not directly enter the wider local arena as competitors, however. They can and very often should exist solely to service the needs of their own members and constituents. They then will be seen as "non-political" and less threatening by local elites.

Still, alternative organizations of the poor and powerless are likely to come under indirect dominance by local elites if they do

[1]These and our other points on alternative organizations draw heavily on Marshall's analysis of the U.S. War on Poverty in Chapter II, as well as on Schurmann's (1966) discussion of land reform and collectivization in China.

not have supporting linkages with some outside body (Adams, 1981: 229-35; Schurmann, 1966: 494, 498). The less-advantaged are far more difficult to organize as a separate group in a rural environment than workers are in an urban one. They live farther apart from one another, work alone or in small groups, reside closer to the elite, and have much more social interaction with them. The ties of the less-advantaged to rural elites are more personal. Furthermore, the rural poor can aspire to upward mobility through land ownership, a condition similar to, if smaller than, that of the local elite. Urban workers, on the other hand, rarely find upward mobility through businesses that even remotely resemble those of the elite. For all these reasons, solidarity and organization of the less-advantaged are more difficult to achieve in the countryside.[1]

Because of the difficulties they face, local alternative organizations of the rural poor generally need outside support if they are to survive. The sustenance to survive under pressure might come from a trade union, a church, a political party, or a government agency. In many cases central linkages with alternative organizations are not just a convenient channel for the distribution of national services; they are essential to the protection of the groups from local elite dominance.

Of course income is not the only basis of division within rural communities. In many societies other forms of differentiation are far more significant. Conflicts of interest can be found along the lines of ethnicity, religion, caste, kinship, sex and mode of production (e.g., pastoralists vs. agriculturalists) as well. Whenever such differences become a significant basis for the distribution of benefits, they deprive a community of homogeneity of interest. To the extent that these differences coincide with income, they have the same effect as income inequalities. Their presence often makes it easier to organize the disadvantaged separately from their elite leaders, as there are additional sociological reasons for the separation.

When ascriptive differences cross-cut income ones and are a basis for benefit distribution, however, they pose a special problem for local organizations. Whether there are differences in interest between the poor and the elites or not, the ascriptive conflicts over distribution will disrupt local organizations—both inclusive and alternative—and

[1]Several of these points are drawn from a draft manuscript by Judith Tendler.

tend to keep them weak. In Kenya, for example, kinship politics has seriously disrupted the functioning of many cooperatives in the small-farm areas. Although rich and poor belong to all the factions, the ability of these cooperatives to operate effectively and to serve the interests of small producers has been hurt by the resulting distributional conflicts (Hyden, 1973).

A lack of homogeneity of interest in a community that cross-cuts income and is based on ascriptive divisions is not a cause for promoting new local organizations. The ensuing conflicts are likely to be largely neutral with respect to the special interests of the poor. The consequence of their existence will be an inherent weakness in the community's organizations—a weakness that is a factor in deciding how to use them for rural development. The state generally will be unable to devolve as much responsibility to such local organizations or will have to maintain tighter controls over them than would otherwise be the case.

We have found the interaction between program content and local elite interests to be very important. The nature of the interaction is one of the major influences on what types of decentralization are to be preferred and what types of organizational linkage are to be developed with them. Where local leaders are responsive to the interests of the poor, then inclusive, relatively autonomous forms of local organization and government are to be preferred. Where such responsiveness is missing, alternative local organizations of the rural poor generally are needed together with strong external support.

Support from the Center. The needs of the rural poor usually will not be met if local organizations are left to their own, separate devices. Development strives to be catalytic—to produce forces that are more than the sum of the combined parts. Still, development is not alchemy—it cannot create something out of nothing. If the pace of change is to be at all adequate, linkages must be forged between base-level organizations and supra-local entities which have resources and power. Such support for progressive action by localities might be found in a state or national government agency, an international donor or a non-governmental organization (e.g., a union or a foundation). Obviously the potential support is larger the greater the resources and power of the organization. For this reason we focus on linkages to the nation-state; typically it controls the largest quantity of resources and has the greatest power to alter the conditions that stifle progressive change. This is the "center" which most often structures decentralization. Even the nation-state offers a plurality of agencies with which a local government or organization might be linked, however.

These "centers" can vary in their resources and commitment to the rural poor. Obviously the greater the resources committed to their cause the better for the poor majority. Still, commitment is the most important and problematic variable. We focus our analysis on this dimension of national government agencies.

The national political system provides the basic context which shapes the behavior of individual politicians and civil servants and within which rural development policies are formulated. Nonetheless, there probably will be differences in the progressiveness of agencies within that framework. For any particular proposed program activity it is important to ask, "Can a national agency be found to administer the program which has a positive commitment to these particular benefits' reaching the rural poor?" If not, can such an agency or subordinate unit be created in this political context? Simple willingness that the poor benefit is not enough; firm purpose is needed. Problems or resistance are almost always encountered in attempts to improve the lot of the poor, and these obstacles will not be overcome without the resolution to spend energy and resources on them.

Whether and where one will find an agency with a positive commitment to the poor in a program area depends very much on the particularities of national politics and institutional development in the country concerned. An analysis of the commitment of national systems to their poor would require a major discourse on political economy. Such an effort is beyond the scope of what we can attempt here. It is a general theme of political science and is treated in numerous general (e.g., Uphoff, 1980) and country-specific studies. Most program designers will have a reasonable idea of the general status of their country on this question.

Nonetheless, within the context of a political system, whether supportive of the poor or not, particular national agencies may be more or less progressive. This source of variation is much less widely analyzed. The major factors determining agency stance are its external alliances and its professional and institutional patterns of socialization. Over time, agencies acquire customary clienteles, upon which they rely in the ubiquitous battles for budgetary resources and for assistance in doing their work. If a particular program evokes opposition among an agency's historical clientele, its administrators are unlikely to pursue it vigorously, even if the activity has support in the larger political system. Thus when the Ministry of Health in Guatemala first encountered opposition from the national medical association to its plan for paraprofessional rural health care, it simply dropped the idea (Long and Viau, 1974). Similarly, agricultural extension services which have developed strong symbiotic relations with well-to-do progressive farmers in the promotion of export agriculture have real difficulty in creating new networks oriented toward less-advantaged, subsistence production (Thoden van Velzen, 1977).

Equally powerful are the internal patterns of recruitment and institutionalization which determine the professional orientation of an agency's decision-makers (Chapter V). Professional training and organizational experience tend to instill a commitment to the value of certain types of activities, methods of doing them, and ways of analyzing when and where to do them. These technologies, methodologies and decision-making modes often have significant implications for benefit distribution. For example, most contemporary Western medical practice is oriented toward and attaches high prestige to high technology, hospital-based, curative medicine. Agencies dominated by these types of doctors will find it difficult to give priority to the types of promotive, preventive, and paramedical medicine which mean the most to the health of the rural poor. This is the case with ministries of health in many developing countries, where agencies have been deeply involved with hospital and medical school administration. On the other hand, health practitioners trained in public health have a different orientation from the rest of the medical profession and value precisely the types of service which the disadvantaged most need. Where an agency has traditionally had its dominant functions in public health and has had relatively little to do with mainstream medical practice, its recruitment patterns and organizational socialization are likely to produce an orientation which effectively helps the poor. This is what has occurred with the Public Health Service in the United States.

A similar illustration is provided by the engineering profession. A civil engineer's training is best used and his prestige is most enhanced by large, capital-intensive projects. The labor-intensive road building projects which best benefit the poor are technically undemanding, are professionally unrewarding, and may even involve specifications that are "substandard" in the industrialized countries toward which engineering education is oriented. Agencies dominated by engineers who have not been resocialized will tend to upgrade and recapitalize labor-intensive public works projects (Tendler, 1979: 42-44; Garzon, 1981).

These examples demonstrate that the national political context, although very influential, is an insufficient predictor of the extent to which an agency will give real energy to getting program benefits to the rural poor. Depending on the way in which a program fits into the professional and institutional orientation of an agency, the response may be more or less progressive than the national "average." The particular character of the program in question, the way in which it relates to the national political framework and the institutional character of the agency all come together to determine whether or not a national organization can be found with the necessary commitment to deliver benefits to the rural poor in this program instance.

The foregoing discussion has focused on agencies of a national government. In principle other "centers" might be subjected to a similar form of analysis. We wish to call attention at this point, however, to the danger of treating international aid agencies as interchangeable with domestic organizations for the purposes of providing supporting linkages to local governments and organizations. A major attribute of the donors is that their commitments to a program area are usually relatively brief (five to ten years). To the extent that local organizations and governments develop strong links to and dependency on an international donor, the continuity of the program is highly vulnerable. A link to a domestic "center" is needed as well if the program and its benefits are to be institutionalized. We argue that the types of links which should be constructed depend on the characteristics of the central and local organizations being linked. If the eventual domestic agency at the center and the international aid agency have different linkage attributes and if those which fit the donor prevail, an inappropriate set of links will have been institutionalized. The local organization may have become dependent on a set of financial or technical supporting links that cannot be sustained by the domestic "central" organization when the donor leaves. Or the local unit may have been forced to accept a set of well-intentioned controls from the international agency which becomes destructive when an unsympathetic national agency takes them over. Precisely because the linkage to the donor will be temporary, it may easily be inappropriate for the long run. Hence our insistence on focusing our analysis on national agencies in the linkage relationship. Eventually their character, not that of the donor, will determine the nature of the working relationship with local governments and organizations.

The nature of the implementing agency at the national center thus is another critical variable in determining the type of decentralization and the nature of the linkages to be favored for a program. Where a supportive "central" organization exists, the structure of implementation should build on it. Where it is missing, local autonomy is necessary.

Technical and Administrative Requirements and the Distribution of Capacity. To implement a program effectively an organization must be more than well-intentioned; it must also have the capacity to translate those intentions into reality. Administrative capacity, be it at the center or in a local organization, is an elusive concept, for it involves more than the presence of skilled personnel. True, the organization has to be able to recognize the existence of problems and opportunities that affect it and to identify the solutions that will be appropriate to them. It also must have the ability to manage the personnel and materials required for implementing the solutions. These abilities involve technical and managerial skills.

In addition, however, the organization has to produce a decision to act, to sustain the legitimacy of that decision against internal and external challenges, and to mobilize the human and material resources needed to execute the program decided upon. These attributes are "political." As we noted in our discussion of support from the center, they derive from the interaction of leadership and institutional history. Leadership is the art of using and manipulating the organization's institutional heritage to make decisions, legitimate them and mobilize resources for their execution (Ilchman and Uphoff, 1969). Poor leadership may have difficulty acting even within the confines of its institution's history; good leadership is able to expand on it creatively. In either case, an organization will lack the capacity for certain types of actions and have adequate capacity for others.

ANALYZING THE ORGANIZATIONAL REQUIREMENTS

Programs or program components have a number of critical features which must be matched with the capacities of an organization if effective implementation is to be achieved. The first is technical. If a program is based on a particular technology the organization will need to have personnel with that technical skill, be able to obtain them, or be assured of access to them through technical assistance. This attribute is important and obvious. Consequently it frequently dominates consideration of appropriate organizations for program implementation. Sometimes this emphasis is unfortunate, for if the skill is generally available in the society it is one of the easier capacities to add to an organization. The attention given to it then may preclude attention to other attributes which are harder to provide.

The second attribute is that of scale. For reasons of efficiency or technology a program may need to be operated with a certain size of unit. An irrigation system built around a hydro-electric dam has a vast scale of operation compared to one using a tube well and pump. A hospital requires a much larger clientele to be efficient than does a clinic. The organizations constructing macadam arterial roads must be much larger than those providing maintenance or building dirt feeder roads. The implementing organization must be able to operate effectively at the particular levels of scale required, be they large or small. Many organizations are simply too small or limited in geographical scope to undertake projects with large-scale requirements; others lack the capacity to operate at the village level required by some technologies. Frequently a program has some components that have large economies of scale and others that are best managed by small or local units. Then one needs either to find a single organization with both capacities or to share the components between small organizations and a large one, with linkages between them.

The third attribute is the complexity of the administrative process required. Programs that call for a single set of tasks to be executed by a group of workers under the immediate supervision of a single superior are simple administratively. Those that involve several work units that are independent and uncoordinated with one another are somewhat more difficult, but still fairly simple. Those which require the closely coordinated action of several different operations, either in sequence or simultaneously, are administratively complex. A much higher level of managerial expertise and experience is needed for the latter than for the former types of programs. (For more on the complexity of coordination and its organizational implications, see Thompson, 1967: 54-61).

The fourth program attribute is the contributions that it requires from extra-organizational actors. A smallholder tea program will need to have feeder roads built and maintained in order to get the leaf to the factories promptly. If the implementing organization is an agricultural one, will it obtain the necessary services from a public works department? A promotive health program would need the cooperation of villagers to have latrines built and used. Note that the tea program depends on the use of influence over a government agency, while the second relies upon standing with the village community. The ability of the organization to elicit the appropriate forms of cooperation is a part of its administrative capacity.

The fifth attribute is related to the preceding and might even be seen as an extension of it. This is the magnitude of resources, largely financial, needed for the program. The more money needed to run a program, the greater the ability of the organization to raise uncommitted funds must be. If the program is managed by a national agency with international donor financing, will that agency successfully fight for an increased share of the national budget when the overseas aid ends? If the program is a pilot one, does the organization have potential access to funds, not just for the first stage but for the expansion as well? If the program is to be run by a local organization but financed by a central agency of some kind, is there the possibility of a meaningful local matching contribution? As will be argued later in this book, either local commitment or independence tend to be lost if there are no matching funds.

There are further attributes of specific programs which draw upon administrative capacity. The preceding list covers the most important ones, however, and is sufficient to illustrate the kind of analysis that is needed in assessing administrative requirements.

Administrative capacity virtually always falls below the ideal—in all parts of the world and at all levels of the political system. The issue therefore must be capacity as measured by minimal and relative standards, not absolute ones. If an organization cannot be found or created with the minimal capacity to administer the program acceptably or to absorb the technical assistance necessary for it to do so, then the program should simply not be implemented and another less demanding one should be found.

If two or more minimally adequate organizations exist, the question then will be which one to use. Since, as we will argue later, administrative weakness is easier (but not necessarily easy) to repair than commitment, the decision will usually be made on the basis of the other criteria advanced in this chapter. Once the decision about the local recipient has been made, the issue of the distribution of responsibilities between the central and local organizations will arise. Relative administrative capacity for the various specific facets of the program would then play a major role in determining the allocation of tasks. (Just because a local organization or government has administrative problems does not prove that a central one is any better, although national governments tend to behave as if it were so.) The relative administrative strength of the central and local organizations will also influence the kinds of linkages that should be built between them.

When an administratively weak local organization is attractive by other criteria as a program implementor and where a supportive "central" organization is administratively strong, the deficiency might be overcome with supportive linkages. If even these requisites are missing or if the local organization is too weak to absorb such technical assistance, another less demanding program must be found or governmental action abandoned in this area.

MODES OF DECENTRALIZATION

In the preceding pages several factors have been analyzed which have implications both for the structures of decentralization adopted and the types of inter-organizational linkages that are developed to serve them. Prior to discussing these implications in the following chapters, we need to lay out the major structural alternatives.

First, we require a more precise explanation of what is meant by centralization and decentralization. The Oxford English Dictionary defines centralization as a concentration of administrative powers in a single head or center. The concept has been used in this way for almost two centuries and its meaning is quite stable. Decentralization is the opposite of centralization—the undoing of centralization (Landau and Eagle, 1981: 1). Unfortunately this antonym lacks the clarity of "centralization."

Martin Landau and Eva Eagle suggest that "A perfectly decentralized system is one in which each member is authorized to make decisions on the basis of information which comes to him alone" (17). In practice such a condition never obtains. Even in a market economy of small enterprises most members would lack the authority or resources to make many of the decisions suggested by the information they receive. For example, they cannot respond to a profitable, but expensive investment opportunity they perceive without a loan—and thus must transmit their information to those with capital and defer to their ultimate authority on this matter. In the real world perfect decision autonomy and hence pure decentralization do not exist.

As Stephen Cohen and his associates observe, "to decentralize" is not to reach an end state but is the *process* of moving toward it. The term loses clarity because there is more than one path along which a system can move toward the unobtainable condition of pure decentralization. There are several non-comparable dimensions along which decentralization can take place. For example, "administratively France is more centralized than Britain; politically, through the party system, Britain is more centralized than France." Thus, "Decentralization is not one thing; nor is it even a series of degrees along a single spectrum or scale. For comprehensibility and utility in policy circles, the overarching abstraction 'decentralization' must be split into a host of separate, occasionally conflicting entities" (Cohen et al., 1981: 5-6).

The classical distinction between "devolution" and "deconcentration" is a recognition of the futility of analyzing decentralization along a single dimension. The former refers to the process of empowering autonomous units of local government; the latter, to the granting of authority to field units of a central government hierarchy. These two forms of decentralization are conflicting. Devolution involves a weakening of the local authority of central government; deconcentration generally involves strengthening it through an increase in the discretion of its agents.

The Dimensions for Analyzing Decentralization. There are numerous dimensions along which grants of authority can be analyzed. Thus the variety of forms of decentralization threatens to become unmanageable if we try to be comprehensive. To impose a limit one must specify the purpose for which the typology is being created and elaborate only those dimensions that are useful to it. Our purpose here is to analyze organizational forms that are helpful in bringing development to the rural poor. We therefore have devised a typology of decentralization that will serve that end. It will not have universal utility, although we have used terms that have an already established meaning wherever possible. The typology is based on four dimensions.

First, we argued earlier in this chapter that rural development programs depend on having the resources and authority for timely adaptation to locally-specific conditions present in the field, not the capital. We also expressed our interest in local participatory organizations. "The field" and "local organizations" are not the same thing, however. With the growth in the size and developmental responsibility of the modern state the structure of local governance now usually involves at least three actors—the central government, intermediate structures, and local participatory organizations. The last include village councils, neighborhood self-help groups and local action organizations. These units serve up to 1000 families, usually in the range of 100. The intermediate structures are the town and county councils and the field offices of the national administration, which used to be thought of as the base of the structure of government. The decline of traditional face-to-face groups, their replacement with more flexible and formalized participatory organizations, and our awareness of their importance for development have all contributed to a new interest in the way these truly base-level units interact with the rest of the system. Thus our typology includes local-level as well as intermediate organizations.

Second, in order to do justice to poverty-oriented programs we must differentiate between structures of local participation and governance which are inclusive (and thus potentially open to the whole population in an area) and those which are exclusive and serving the poor part of it. Following the American convention, we call these latter structures alternative organizations. (For present purposes we are interested in only those organizations limited to the poor; a comprehensive typology would include, for example, ones limited to doctors, to farmers of a particular type, etc.)

Third, a distinction between those governmental organizations which are generalist (multi-functional) and those which are specialized (restricted range of related functions) is needed. When the political system as a whole is more committed to the interests of the poor than are the specialized agencies or professionals working in a program area, then a structure which subordinates the latter to generalists at the local level is more likely to be progressive. When the converse is true, a specialist autonomy will be preferable. On a different issue, multi-functionality generally increases complexity; so when administrative capacity is weak, specialist organizations with a limited range of functions will be attractive.

Finally, the option of minimizing the involvement of all forms of collective organization and relying upon the market or philanthropies—privatization—must be considered. We presume that if the historic imbalance in the delivery of services to the poor is to be righted, action will be necessary by progressive governmental or representative organizations. There are circumstances, however, in which redistribution is not the relevant issue; instead the challenge is to minimize governmentally-caused inequality or incompetence in the delivery of services. Privatization is relevant to such situations.

A Typology of Decentralization Oriented to the Poor. Thus we see four dimensions of decentralization that are relevant to rural development: (1) What type of organization is involved at both the intermediate and the local level? (2) Are the mediating organizations representative, private, or agencies of the central government? (3) Are the governmental bodies generalist or specialist? (4) Are the representative entities inclusive or alternative organizations limited to the poor? The answers to these four questions lead to the identification of eight major types and a total of twenty-four sub-types of decentralization.

The full range of possibilities is presented in Table 2, together with an example of how each form of decentralization might look in serving the poor. The traditional typologies of decentralization refer to the character of the intermediate organizations. We will follow that convention and not attempt to invent names for the forms as they relate to the varieties of local participation.

The inclusive, generalist, intermediate representative bodies are the classic form of local government, with a full electorate and a wide range of functions. When they are promoted, it is called *devolution*. Beneath them and relating to them may be inclusive groups, such as neighborhood organizations, or alternative community groups, such as those of minorities, or perhaps an unorganized citizenry.

Decentralization to inclusive, specialized, intermediate representative organizations we can call *functional devolution*. In the United States, school boards are such units. Beneath them have grown alternative, poverty-oriented participatory groups working in the schools and pressuring the elected boards. They now supplement the traditional, inclusive Parent-Teacher Associations. An example of functional devolution with inclusive local organization is the cooperative union. In many developing countries such unions service the more face-to-face primary societies and are governed by indirectly elected committees.

Intermediate bodies that limit their services to the poor are a form of *interest organization*. An example of such a body relating to alternative local organizations is India's new Organization of the Rural Poor (International Confederation of Free Trade Unions, 1977). An example of an alternative organization without local face-to-face groups would be a trade union of agricultural laborers. Intermediate organizations limited to the poor would serve whole communities only in quite poor, undeveloped areas, so cases in the intermediate/alternative–local/inclusive boxes are infrequent empirically. One example would be an organization of a geographically concentrated, poor ethnic group. The village branches of such an association would include all those living there.

If the center is to reach the villages and if it does not use other bodies, it must serve as its own intermediary, relating to the various types of village organizations or to the poor themselves directly. When this is done at all effectively some degree of decentralization is involved. The variability of the conditions in the rural areas and the need for flexible response to them makes centralization, with no discretion for field staff, impracticable if any positive impact is to be achieved.

When authority is retained by the national government but is decentralized to one of its field agents we speak of *deconcentration*. This delegation of authority is an administrative action and does not alter the ultimate structure of control, for the center retains the power to appoint its field agents. Thus deconcentration is quite different from devolution, in which a shift in the locus of final command is involved (Cohen et al., 1981: 19).

Table 2

EXAMPLES OF FORMS OF DECENTRALIZATION SERVING THE POOR

Intermediate Representative Organizations			Local Participatory Organizations		
		General Type of Decentralization	Inclusive	Exclusive (Alternative)	None
Inclusive	Generalist	Devolution	*a*) Local government w/neighborhood groups	*b*) Local government w/pressure groups of poor or minorities	*c*) Local government w/an unorganized citizenry
Inclusive	Specialist	Functional Devolution	*d*) Cooperative unions w/primary societies	*e*) US school dist. boards w/school site advisory committees (SAC) of poor parents	*f*) Local utility authority w/an unorganized citizenry
Exclusive (Alternative)		Interest Organization	*g*) Caste or ethnic associations	*h*) India's Organization of the Rural Poor	*i*) Trade unions without shop committees
None, by center itself	Generalist	Prefectorial Deconcentration	*j*) Prefects w/village councils	*k*) Chinese commune party secretaries w/party cells	*l*) Kenyan district commissioners w/appointed chiefs

Table 2 (continued)

Intermediate Representative Organizations			Local Participatory Organizations		
(None, by center itself–cont.)		General Type of Decentralization	Inclusive	Exclusive (Alternative)	None
	Specialist	Ministerial Deconcentration	*m*) Rural health agency w/village committees	*n*) Nutrition education w/groups of poor women	*o*) Agricultural extension to individual farmers
	Specialist	Delegation to Autonomous Agencies	*p*) National irrigation board w/watercourse committees	*q*) Kenya Tea Development Authority w/smallholder advisory committees	*r*) Regional development authority hiring for labor-intensive public works projects
None, privatization		Philanthropy	*s*) CARE w/village community development committees	*t*) Ford Foundation w/alternative local organizations	*u*) Catholic Relief direct to individuals
None, privatization		Marketization	*v*) Private wholesalers w/primary co-operative societies	*w*) Commercial loans to groups of poor peasants	*x*) Full privatization, i.e., private wholesalers and retailers

Decentralization of authority to a functionally specialized field agent of the national government can be called *ministerial deconcentration*. When villagers or their organizations are reached by generalist national government machinery, we use the term *prefectorial deconcentration*. A prefectorial system is the most common form of such multi-functional organization. In it a *préfet* or district commissioner heads a team of ministerial field officers and exercises general control and coordination of government operations in his area. A variant of the prefectorial system is found in disciplined one-party states where the party secretary serves as the *de jure* or *de facto* head of government in his jurisdiction.

Parastatals represent a special form of decentralization. These specialized, legally distinct corporations vary in their character depending on the method of constituting their boards of directors. A regional development corporation with a board appointed by autonomous local governments is a form of functional devolution. When the board of a state corporation is centrally appointed, however, the parastatal becomes much like a national government department. It differs from the latter in being free of detailed supervision by the standard, generalist agencies of national control—the Treasury and the Civil Service Commission. Such parastatals are grouped under the heading of *delegation to autonomous agencies* (Rondinelli, 1979; Cohen et al., 1981; United Nations Centre for Regional Development, 1981: 10-12).

Where neither the national government nor intermediate representative bodies extend their reach into the villages, the role may be played by business or voluntary organizations. The resulting coverage provided often is uneven but the results actually achieved frequently are superior to those of governments. The generic name for this form of decentralization is *privatization*. When services are provided directly to villagers by businesses (with their own networks of intermediary supply, wholesale, and service firms), the term *marketization* is used. *Philanthropy* provides the alternate nongovernmental linkage organization for inclusive and alternative local groups—and sometimes villagers themselves. Churches, foundations and secular private voluntary organizations all operate to provide services to the poor.

These many forms of decentralization provide a significant range of alternatives for the program designer. The appropriate choice depends on the program and its context.

THE ARRAY OF LINKAGES

The preceding typology of decentralization provides the framework for specifying the organizations involved in a particular rural development program and for identifying which of those bodies has the lead responsibility for it. It does not tell us what the relationships are between the organizations, however. The character of such linkages has almost as much of an impact on program implementation as does the structural allocation of responsibilities embodied in a form of decentralization.

Center-local linkages can take a number of forms and be conceptualized in various ways. The simplest would be a purely descriptive classification, based on the mechanism used, and might distinguish five types of linkages:

1) Finance: provision of credit, savings bank facilities, direct grants of various types, material transfers, etc.
2) Regulation and Monitoring: audits, administered market prices, required ratios of credit to savings, registration or certification of local organizations, recruitment and program standards, inspections, evaluations, etc.
3) Technical and Personnel Assistance: in-service and entry-level training, temporary and perpetual secondment of staff, technical, management and program advice, etc.
4) Services: provision of inputs, performance of selected tasks, etc.
5) Representation: various forms of formal and informal local participation in planning and implementing programs, community consulting groups, political parties, patron-client networks, etc.

A central government can utilize any of these mechanisms singly or in combination to attempt to influence local units. Representational linkages also may involve influence going "upward" from the local unit toward the central unit.

The descriptive classification just given is helpful in providing a concrete image of the actual linkage mechanisms used. Its utility for the program designer is limited, however, for it has little prescriptive significance. Additional methods of categorizing linkages are needed that will help to identify them according to the purposes they serve and the consequenes they are likely to have. All five descriptive types of linkages can be distinguished as well by their underlying purposes.

Control Linkages. Inter-organizational linkages perform two major functions—control and assistance.[1] The purpose of control linkages is to enable one organization to determine some aspect of another's performance. Their very existence indicates that one organization is concerned that the other may perform in an unacceptable manner. A wide variety of control mechanisms can be used. All regulation and most monitoring devices are control linkages. Technical and personnel assistance, particularly the secondment of staff, may also be designed to gain influence over the aided organization. All of these linkages are used by central organizations to control intermediate and local ones. The latter units may have their links for control of the center too, through various forms of representation. Some of these may be formal, as when a legislature of locally-elected representatives sanctions and regulates the programs of central agencies. Others are informal, as in the wide variety of ways in which localities may seek to influence agency decisions—ranging from patron-client ties to interest groups.

Control linkages need not be simple dyadic relations between two organizations. Frequently different central agencies will regulate different aspects of a local organization's performance. Similarly, a central agency may be subjected to conflicting influence attempts from a variety of local bodies.

Assistance Linkages. The other purpose of linkage is to provide assistance. Finance, service, and most technical and personnel assistance have this facilitative function. It develops when a local or intermediate organization has certain advantages for implementing a program but is lacking in others. A central organization then facilitates the program by filling the gap.

In principle, assistance can be provided without control; in practice, this rarely is the case. Inter-governmental assistance virtually always has some degree of control attached to it—facilitative linkages with regulation. Nonetheless, the mix between them does vary. Furthermore, controls by the center are sometimes counter-balanced

[1]This distinction parallels and is derived from that made by Inayatullah in his study of cooperatives between regulative and facilitative linkages (1972: 253-55).

with representative ones by intermediate and local organizations. The nature of the linkage amalgam is important to performance.

CONCLUSION

Linkages are not a minor theme in development administration; they are one of its most important issues. Linkages can be extremely powerful and can have at least as much effect on implementation as the designation of the formal structures to be involved. In the United States, for example, state and federal "grants" have transformed local school boards from autonomous to dependent organizations without any change in formal structure. Linkages are a central component of all international aid. The expectations for their performance are frequently exceedingly high; they are often expected to turn inegalitarian organizations into progressive ones. Yet the development literature has very little to tell us about how effective various linkage devices are and why. Without this knowledge, effective institutional development and program implementation for the rural poor are impossible. Thus we turn in the following chapters to concrete experiences with different forms of decentralization and with interorganizational linkages. In our concluding chapter we will then draw these experiences together into a number of generalizations and lessons for program design.

REFERENCES

Adams, Richard H. 1981. *Growth without development in rural Egypt: a local-level study of institutional and social change.* Ph.D. dissertation, Department of Political Science, University of California, Berkeley.

Almond, Gabriel, and Verba, Sidney. 1963. *The civic culture.* Princeton: Princeton University Press.

Cohen, S. S.; Dyckman, J. W.; Schoenberger, E.; and Downs, C. R. 1981. *Decentralization: a framework for policy analysis.* Berkeley: Project on Managing Decentralization, Institute of International Studies, University of California.

Garzon, Jose M. 1981. Small-scale public works, decentralization, and linkages. In *Linkages to decentralized units,* ed. D. Leonard and D. Marshall. Berkeley: Project on Managing Decentralization, Institute of International Studies, University of California.

Harik, Iliya F. 1974. *The political mobilization of peasants: a study of an Egyptian community.* Bloomington: Indiana University Press.

Heiby, James R.; Ness, Gayl D.; and Pillsbury, Barbara L. K. 1979. *AID's role in Indonesian family planning: a case study with general lessons for foreign assistance.* Washington, D. C.: U.S. Agency for International Development. Program Evaluation Report No. 2.

Hyden, Goran. 1973. Government and cooperatives. In *Development administration: the Kenyan experience,* ed. R. Jackson, G. Hyden and J. Okumu. Nairobi: Oxford University Press.

Ilchman, Warren, and Uphoff, Norman. 1969. *The political economy of change.* Berkeley: University of California Press.

Inayatullah, ed. 1972. *Cooperatives and development in Asia: a study of cooperatives in fourteen rural communities of Iran, Pakistan and Ceylon,* Vol. VII of *Rural institutions and planned change.* Geneva: United Nations Research Institute for Social Development.

International Confederation of Free Trade Unions. 1977. *Organization of the rural poor: progress report, April 1975-March 1977.* New Delhi: ICFTU Asian Regional Organization.

Johnston, Bruce F., and Clark, William C. 1982. *Redesigning rural development: a strategic perspective.* Baltimore. Johns Hopkins University Press.

Johnston, Bruce F., and Kilby, Peter. 1974. The design and implementation of strategies for agricultural development. *Agricultural Administration* 1, 3 (July): 165-97.

Landau, Martin, and Eagle, Eva. 1981. *On the concept of decentralization.* Berkeley: Project on Managing Decentralization, Institute of International Studies, University of California.

Long, E. C., and Viau, A. D. 1974. Health care extension: using auxiliaries in Guatemala. *Lancet* 7848 (26 January): 127-30.

Migdal, Joel S. 1974. *Peasants, politics and revolution: pressures toward political and social change in the Third World.* Princeton: Princeton University Press.

Ralston, Lenore; Anderson, James; and Colson, Elizabeth. 1981. *Voluntary efforts and decentralized management.* Berkeley: Project on Managing Decentralization, Institute of International Studies, University of California.

Rondinelli, Dennis. 1979. *Administrative decentralization and area development planning in East Africa: implications for United States aid policy.* Madison: Regional Planning and Area Development Project, International Studies and Programs, University of Wisconsin.

Schurmann, Franz. 1966. *Ideology and organization in Communist China.* Berkeley: University of California Press.

Seers, Dudley. 1972. What are we trying to measure? *Journal of Development Studies* 8, 3 (April): 21-36.

Tendler, Judith. 1979. *New directions for rural roads.* Washington, D. C.: Office of Evaluation, U.S. Agency for International Development.

Thoden van Velzen, H. U. E. 1977. Staff, kulaks and peasants: a study of a political field. In *Government and rural development in East Africa: essays on political penetration*, ed. L. Cliffe, J. S. Coleman, and M. R. Doornbos. The Hague: Martinus Nijhoff.

Thompson, James D. 1967. *Organizations in action.* New York: McGraw-Hill.

United Nations Centre for Regional Development. 1981. *Implementing decentralization policies and programmes: report of UNCRD workshop held at Nagoya, Japan from 21 to 27 July, 1981.* Nagoya.

Uphoff, Norman. 1980. Political considerations in human development. In *Implementing programs of human development*, ed. Peter T. Knight. Washington, D. C.: The World Bank. Working Paper No. 403.

__________; Cohen, John M.; and Goldsmith, Arthur A. 1979. *Feasibility and application of rural development participation: a state-of-the-art paper.* Ithaca: Rural Development Committee, Center for International Studies, Cornell University; January.

__________, and Esman, Milton J. 1974. *Local organization for rural development: analysis of Asian experience.* Ithaca: Rural Development Committee, Center for International Studies, Cornell University. Rural Local Government Monograph No. 19; November.

__________, and Ilchman, Warren. 1972. *The political economy of development.* Berkeley: University of California Press.

Chapter II

LESSONS FROM THE IMPLEMENTATION OF POVERTY PROGRAMS IN THE UNITED STATES

Dale Rogers Marshall

In the United States the number of intergovernmental programs has grown enormously in the last two decades. These national government programs involve subnational governments and organizations in implementation.[1] They include a wide variety of programs focusing on the problems of poverty and the development of depressed areas. While it would be misleading to suggest that the literature on these programs has treated organizational linkages (the mechanisms by which one organization interacts with or attempts to influence others) systematically, there is such a vast amount of material that generalizations on linkages can be teased out in ways not always possible in studies of Third World countries.

In this chapter we will examine American poverty programs in order to suggest linkage lessons and stimulate discussion about their relevance to rural development in other countries and situations. We will examine the characteristics of organizational linkages in the U.S. grant system, particularly that segment concerned with poverty and development broadly delineated. Of particular interest are the consequences of these linkages for increasing the flow of benefits to the poor and for enhancing the capacity of local organizations. We argue that organizational linkages have a limited but important impact on program implementation. Both the choice of organizations to implement grant programs (the form of decentralization) and the

[1]The term "subnational governments" refers to state, county, and city governments. It will be used interchangeably with the term "local governments." In this chapter distinctions between the various types of U.S. subnational governments are deemphasized in order to reduce complexity and facilitate cross-national comparisons.

interactions between these organizations (the linkages) seem to be important, though it is difficult to isolate the independent effects from other aspects of the context. The U.S. grant system and its associated linkages have evolved over time, resulting in a new type of decentralization, at least in the poverty and development programs, in which both locality and center are strong and interdependent partners.

The fact that linkages are important should not be interpreted to mean that well-designed and operated linkages can prevent local implementing organizations from distorting central purposes. On the contrary, distortion is increasingly recognized as inevitable in the implementation of large-scale complex programs regardless of the degree or forms of decentralization (Williams, 1980: 13). The U.S. experience suggests, however, that the direction of program implementation can be influenced by the selection of implementing agencies and the nature of linkages between those agencies, and that careful attention to these dimensions can decrease the amount of distortion which will occur. This argument will be presented after first reviewing some of the basic characteristics of the contemporary U.S. grant system.

THE U.S. GRANT SYSTEM

The U.S. federal system is characterized by a high degree of decentralization. The powers of subnational governments are constitutionally established, and the central government typically uses some combination of these governments to deliver national programs at the local level. As the scope of national programs has grown, the central government has developed an increasingly elaborate repertoire of linkage mechanisms to influence the activities of the local units. These units have in turn created their own techniques for influencing national policy and programs. These downward and upward linkage mechanisms are important attributes of the national grant system.

Some features of the grants are strictly delineated in statutes, some are formulated in agency regulations, and some depend simply on agency practice. The grants involve choices about the central and local implementing agencies, the size of the grants, the funding mechanism, the distribution, and the locus of control over programs.

Recent national administrations have been associated with different types of grants. The administrations of Presidents Kennedy and Johnson were characterized by intergovernmental grants with high federal control, namely categoric grants. In these grants the national government chooses the local recipients from among competing governmental and alternative organization applicants. The central government also has total discretion over the size and distribution of the grants and exercises a high degree of control over the operation of the local programs by attaching "strings" to the use of the funds—that is, specific conditions about what is done, who it is done for, and how it is done.

The administrations of Presidents Nixon and Ford designed programs with less federal control, with fewer strings attached to the subsidies. General revenue sharing illustrates this approach. It provides funds automatically to general purpose units of local government. The amount and distribution of the money are determined by formula, and very few conditions are attached to the use of the funds, so most of the decisions about program content are made at the local level.

The current system of grants includes a mix of grants ranged along the spectrum from high federal control to low federal control, from categoric to general revenue sharing grants. Grants which fall in the middle of the spectrum are referred to as block grants. The recipients of block grants are either general purpose or specialized subnational governments. The size and distribution of the grants are usually determined by formula, and there are fewer restrictions on local recipients than in categoric grants but more than in general revenue sharing.

The different types of grants in this tripartite grant system serve different purposes. Categoric grants stimulate local activity to meet national priorities (USACIR, 1978b), while block grants and general revenue sharing enable local governments to design programs which meet their own priorities. Such grants increase local governmental power and discretion and enhance local capacity, but have been less effective than categoric grants at targeting programs to the needy and promoting innovation (USACIR, 1977b: 21, 27; Williams, 1980: 34-43). While all three types of grants are used by recipients to substitute for local funds, categoric grants have been found to be more effective at stimulating new efforts than the other two types (USACIR, 1977c: 38, 41; USACIR, 1978b: 67; Whitman and Cline, 1978).

Continual adjustments are made in each type of grant over time as the federal government responds to political pressure from various interest groups, including subnational governments. Attempts to remedy the deficiencies in one kind of grant move it closer to one of the other types. For example, when categoric grants were criticized by local recipients as being overly restrictive, some of the federal controls were relaxed, permitting more local discretion and coordination of programs. ("Integrated grant administration" and "annual arrangements " were the terms applied to two such innovations.) Block grants and general revenue sharing, on the other hand, have been criticized for not promoting national priorities and for their lack of innovation. Repeated efforts have been made to increase federal control over these grants via the recategorization of the grants—"hardening of the categories," as some like to call it. Distinct cycles emerge in which categoric grants are decategorized and block grants are recategorized by the addition of requirements such as targeting. These adaptations blur the distinctions between the types of grants.

The adaptations in the tripartite mix of grants in the United States have occurred partly in response to upward linkages in which local recipients of grants interact with national legislators and administrators in an attempt to influence them. The growth of an intergovernmental lobby has increased the ability of local governments to modify the design of the grant system and exercise discretion over its administration (Beer, 1976; King, 1978; Farkas, 1971; Haider, 1974). Parallel efforts are made by the nongovernmental alternative organizations involved in the grant system. Various formal and informal consulting mechanisms have emerged to facilitate these interactions. For example, state and local officials lobby national officials through national associations such as the League of Cities and Council of State Governments and through their own Washington lobbyists. Another example of consulting mechanisms is the review and comment procedures whereby proposed federal grant regulations are made public and interested organizations are able to criticize them before they become final.

THE CONTEXT FOR THE POVERTY PROGRAMS

Programs oriented toward combating the problems of poverty and depressed areas have constituted an important segment of the

U.S. grant system. We use this category broadly to refer to social service and community development programs but not to programs of direct payments to individuals, such as Medicaid. Some are categoric programs initiated in the 1960s, and others are block grant programs which started later. They cover a great many functional areas, including education, health, employment, housing, business development, public works, and legal services. Although the programs are typically thought of as urban, they often involve rural components, such as the Rural Loan Program of small-farm and nonfarm operating loans to rural individuals and cooperatives, the Migrant Farm Workers Program (Plotnick and Skidmore, 1975: 7), the Appalachian Regional Commission (USACIR, 1977b: 38-44), the Area Redevelopment Administration and its successor the Economic Development Administration (Pressman and Wildavsky, 1979) and various Rural Development Acts (Brown, 1980; Sokolow, 1981).

These poverty programs were implemented in a distinctive context which shaped their design, evolution, and success.[1] In Chapter I David Leonard proposes four parameters or contextual variables which must be taken into account in designing development programs. These parameters are useful in characterizing the U.S. context and comparing it to Third World contexts. Such comparison reveals important differences as well as similarities between the settings in industrialized and developing countries.

First, program vulnerability to inequality, which varies widely in less developed countries (LDCs), is consistently very high in the United States. Due to the high level of U.S. development, local elites have not typically shared the interest of the poor in securing indivisible benefits. Even in very poor rural areas, elites in the United States have access to the resources necessary to pursue their livelihoods, obtain education, and protect health. Thus the economic incentive to improve a community's access to these resources is not high. So in the United States, unlike developing countries, it is usually not possible to design programs in which elite and poor interests would coincide. It is possible, however, to select central and local

[1]Despite important political shifts, that context remained much the same throughout the 1960s and 1970s. The election of Ronald Reagan to the presidency in 1980 may well significantly alter that context, but it is too early to analyze that shift properly. This chapter reflects the picture at the end of the Carter administration.

administering agencies and design linkages between them to reduce the influence of those who do not share the interests of the poor and increase the influence of those who do.

These selections refer to the second and third variables discussed in Chapter I—commitment of national leaders and local leaders. These commitments have been quite variable in the United States and have been important factors in program design. In the 1960s and 1970s, national officials in the United States tended to be more committed to the interests of low-resource groups than were subnational officials, but the commitment varied over time in different agencies and in different areas of the country (USACIR: 1978b). Sometimes specialist officials were seen as more committed to services for the poor than generalist elected officials, while in other situations the reverse was true. In general, U.S. program designers would have to answer affirmatively if asked about whether the central agency has had a positive commitment to the poor and negatively if asked about whether the interests of intermediate and local elites coincide with the interests of the poor. This pattern is similar to the situation in certain Third World countries, though the subnational officials in the U.S. federal system have more autonomy than those in more centralized Third World countries (Montgomery, 1970: 528). The greater proliferation of alternative groups committed to the poor in the United States may provide opportunities for alternative service delivery systems which are difficult to devise in other contexts.

Administrative capacity—the fourth variable discussed in Chapter I—is dramatically different in the United States from that in most LDCs. The capacities of the U.S. national government, subnational governments, and alternative organizations are undoubtedly greater in general than the capacities of their Third World counterparts. Even weak units in the United States have more political and administrative resources than many weak and some strong units in developing countries. Due both to federalism and the society's level of affluence and education, weak local units in the United States have enough resources to sustain themselves and exercise some discretion even when subjected to high central control. When one compares the relative capacity of various organizations within the United States, however, national organizations have greater administrative capacity than some, but not all, local organizations (Honadle, 1981; Sokolow, 1981: 3; Blakely and Zone, 1976; Bradshaw and Blakely, 1979).

While the more sophisticated local governments and organizations sneer at national bungling and national talk about lack of local capacity, in general the U.S. situation parallels the context in most LDCs in that the center has greater capacity than the localities.

In this chapter, then, we are examining some of the major lessons about linkages suggested by poverty programs which have developed in a context characterized by high program vulnerability to inequality, greater national than local commitment to the poor, and high levels of administrative capacity. Several Third World countries are similar to the United States on at least some of these dimensions. (The parallels in India are quite close.) Even in countries which have very different contextual parameters, the types of interventions by governments and development agencies and the dynamics of organizational responses may have enough similarity that the U.S. experiences can be instructive, suggesting patterns which may occur and lessons which may be adaptable to Third World settings (see National Academy of Public Administration, 1980; Esman et al., 1980: 429). Similarly, lessons from Third World development programs may be transferable to the United States (Montgomery, 1971).

There are, of course, conflicting general assessments of the results of the U.S. poverty programs. Many of the early evaluations were extremely critical (Moynihan, 1969; Levitan and Taggart, 1976). They contributed to the widely held view that the programs failed, that the results fell short of what "we had a right to expect," both in terms of reducing poverty and effective implementation. The implication was that better policy design and implementation could overcome the problems. When the programs were redesigned to correct the apparent deficiencies, however, the problems of implementation and impact did not noticeably diminish. The contribution of the programs to reductions in poverty was not at all clear, and distortions in implementation did not disappear although there were some changes in the types of problems. Analysts and the public were very critical of the programs, contributing to public disillusionment with government's ability to promote desired change (Aaron, 1978: 1-10; Haveman, 1977: ix, 42).

There is, however, a revisionist interpretation of the programs. Looking at a wider range of direct and indirect results over a longer time span, these analysts conclude that the programs were qualified successes because they promoted political change—i.e., the redistribution of political resources (Haveman, 1977; Levitan, 1969). They examine not just the direct effect on poverty levels and poor recipients but also the indirect effects on the political system—on the distribution of power between the center and localities, on the programs and capacities of the local agencies, and on the organization of low-resource groups. These analysts consider programs to be successful if they stimulate local governments to provide new services for the poor and increase the ability of the poor to organize and promote local government responsiveness.

This broader perspective and the willingness to lower expectations about reasonable success criteria for efforts at major social change have led to a more favorable interpretation of poverty programs. That perspective is conveyed in the subtitle of a classic poverty program study, *Implementation: how great expectations in Washington are dashed in Oakland, or why it's amazing that federal programs work at all* (Pressman and Wildavsky, 1979). Pressman and Wildavsky stress that implementation is an evolutionary process in which learning occurs via adaptations to feedback and that distorted programs may be better than no programs at all. The awareness is growing that a long-term perspective is necessary in order to see the beneficial effects of poverty programs (Williams, 1980: 13; USACIR, 1977c: 38, 39), and that it is extremely difficult to anticipate the course of social policy (Haveman, 1977: 1).

The effects of poverty programs on the political system are a central concern of this chapter. We argue that these grants have helped create an intergovernmental system characterized by mutual dependence between the federal grantor and the local grantees (Williams, 1980; Reagan and Sanzone, 1980). In this "uneasy partnership" (Williams, 1980: 14), the center has some control over the localities, but that control is tempered by the center's dependence on the localities for service delivery. The localities likewise have some control over the center but are dependent on the center for resources. Both the localities and the center are strong and interdependent. This mutual dependence and need for mutual adaptation have given rise to a different style and use of resources than occur in systems where either those above or those below have disproportionate power (64).

This mutual dependence has been partly stimulated by two characteristics of the U.S. poverty programs: the choice of organizations to implement programs (form of decentralization) and the types of interactions between the central and local organizations (linkages). These two characteristics will now be examined.

DUAL FORMS OF DECENTRALIZATION: PARALLEL LINKAGES FROM THE CENTER TO LOCAL RECIPIENTS

U. S. poverty programs illustrate the way the form of decentralization influences the implementation of development efforts. The interests and administrative capacities of the central and local agencies being linked together have a major impact on program performance. Thus the selection of these organizations is a key decision.

During the early years of the poverty programs two forms of decentralization were followed simultaneously. In each functional area two parallel sets of links were created. One involved what we call functional devolution from established central specialist agencies to intermediate governmental specialist agencies (see Chapter I). For example, the federal health agency selected subnational governmental health agencies as recipients of health grants for the operation of health programs; similar choices were made in education and agricultural programs. The other involved decentralization to interest organizations in which new, redistribution-oriented central agencies established links to intermediate or local alternative groups selected on the basis of their commitment to targeting programs to low-resource groups. For example, the Office of Economic Opportunity (OEO) chose some community organizations to run health programs and others to run education or agricultural programs.

This dual strategy arose in response to the political realities of the American federal system. The strength of subnational agencies and existing federal departments made it necessary to involve them in development efforts. Given the missions of these agencies and their past record, however, some policymakers felt that efforts to force them to target their programs toward the poor would meet with limited success. Some of the grants were therefore funnelled to alternative groups sharing the interests of the poor and willing to target programs to them. The partial bypassing of established agencies was a strategy to create constructive competition. It was hoped that the infusion of resources to alternative groups would increase their capacity and establish model programs which would stimulate changes in state and local programs in the direction of increased targeting to the poor (Donovan, 1967; Marris and Rein, 1967).

Examples of the dual strategy abound in rural development, education, and health. In rural development, the first strategy was used when existing national government agencies supplied funds to specialist intermediate governmental agencies. For example, in the State Rural Development Demonstration project, the Department of Housing and Urban Development and the Department of Agriculture (USDA) selected state governments as recipients of federal funds to improve state delivery systems for underserved rural residents. The participating state agencies developed different types of delivery systems ranging from direct provision of services by a lead state agency to state support for local agencies and nonprofit organizations which provided the services (Council of State Community Action Agencies, 1980). A similar strategy was followed in the USDA's grants to Cooperative Extension Programs in order to develop services for small poor farmers in the South (Orden and Buccola, 1979).

Other rural development projects followed the second strategy of selecting alternative organizations on the basis of their commitment to redistribution and linking them to foundations or specially created federal agencies, primarily the OEO (which became the Community Services Administration, CSA). The movement to establish poor people's cooperatives is a good example. This effort was not stimulated by existing large-scale cooperatives, but by civil rights and religious organizations. They received funds from the CSA or foundations to support nonprofit technical assistance organizations (e.g., the Southern Cooperative Development Program, which merged with the Federation of Southern Cooperatives) and community development corporations designed to promote local poor people's cooperatives (Marshall and Godwin, 1971: 37). Another example of this strategy is the Rural Community Assistance Program, in which the CSA funds nonprofit regional technical assistance organizations to assist local groups, often community action agencies, to develop adequate water services for rural low-income people (Heath, 1980). The organizations provide training and assist local groups in developing needs assessments and work plans.

In education the Elementary and Secondary Education Act (ESEA) Title I illustrates the first strategy of linking to intermediate specialist organizations. In this grant program federal funds were distributed by the Department of Health, Education and Welfare (HEW) to state education agencies according to a formula based on the number of children from low-income families living in the state. Local districts then applied to the states to obtain funds and decide how the money was to be used (Levin, 1977).

Head Start illustrates the alternative linkage strategy in education. The program was originally administered by OEO. The established education agency, HEW, was not given jurisdiction because it was oriented toward different clientele groups and the professional norms of teachers. OEO usually gave Head Start grants to local alternative groups operating outside the established state and local educational structure (Levin, 1977). Another illustration of this alternative strategy is provided by the numerous experiments with "community control" of the schools, whereby special powers are given to sub-district school boards, circumventing the traditional educational system in which teachers and a central school board are typically dominant (Altshuler, 1970; Gittel et al., 1972, 1973; Zimet, 1973).

Health grants also illustrate the dual strategy. The first strategy was illustrated by the Partnership for Health block grant and the alternative system by neighborhood health centers. The former consisted of grants from HEW to state health agencies which passed the funds through to local health agencies for the provision of health services. The latter involved OEO grants to a variety of local organizations (nonprofit health corporations, agencies, medical schools and societies, and local health departments) to run neighborhood health centers designed specifically to improve health care for the poor, to employ poor residents and train them for new health career roles, and to demonstrate new modes of serving the poor (Hollister, Kramer, and Bellin, 1974; Davis, 1977; Davis and Schoen, 1978).

What lessons can be learned from the U.S. utilization of two forms of decentralization? Evaluations of programs run by established agencies have confirmed the importance of agency commitment in shaping grant implementation. The evidence clearly shows that it is extremely difficult to force established agencies to target their programs to the poor when their leaders oppose this kind of targeting. It has been demonstrated repeatedly that grants can facilitate change in local agencies willing to move in the direction desired by the center but cannot force that change on resistant recipients (Ingram, 1977; Derthick, 1970; Berman and McLaughlin, 1976; Berman, 1978; Browning, Marshall and Tabb, 1980; Williams, 1980; Sabatier and Mazmanian, 1980; Wirt, 1970; Pressman, 1975). Programs run by local authorities tend to be used to serve the more advantaged members of communities (Van Horn, 1977). Money ostensibly directed to the poor is spread to other uses which more directly serve the needs of the local elites (Nathan et al., 1977; Murphy, 1971; Browning, Marshall and Tabb, 1980). For example, the State Rural Development Demonstration project showed that improved state delivery systems for rural areas could not force local officials to target programs when they were opposed to targeting (Council of State Community Action Agencies, 1980: 75). Similarly, Cooperative Extension was a recipient agency which resisted reorientation to serving rural poor residents. The principal factor influencing whether the grant funds are used to stimulate new activities in the desired direction or to substitute for local funds in supporting ongoing activities is "the recipient's taste for the aided activity in preference to other competing uses of funds" (USACIR, 1978b: 41, 67).

Evaluations of programs run by alternative organizations have been much more controversial. This strategy aroused the wrath of the bypassed units, and they strongly criticized the quality of the programs run by the alternative groups, using epithets such as "unprofessional," "second-rate," and "ghettoization" (Hollister, Kramer, and Bellin, 1974: 3). They argued that mainstream professionals could implement the programs better and that the competition was costly and stimulated unproductive conflict (Kramer, 1969; Davis, 1977). Evaluators with less direct stake in the "turf" issues also pointed to shortcomings in the alternative programs, but many positive evaluations have also been made (Kramer, 1969; Levine, 1970; Haveman, 1977; Lamb, 1975; Marshall, 1971: 472). The grants increased the capacity of the organizations to deliver services and thus the quality of programs for low-income people. A study of 269 cases of decentralization in education, health, and economic development examined community school boards, neighborhood health centers, and community development corporations. The study concluded that these programs improved services and increased client control and the flow of information (Yin and Yates, 1975: viii). The efforts of alternative educational organizations, (i.e., community school boards) were particularly effective because there was both political and administrative control by groups of the poor, low levels of professional control, and a relatively open delivery system.

Other studies of neighborhood health centers described them as effective in improving the quality of health care for the poor (Davis and Schoen, 1978: 173). For example, a cooperative health clinic in a Southern rural county contributed to improved health care, inspired many local employees to pursue further education, provided them with financial support, developed the skills of community board members, and stimulated development activities in other functional areas. The clinic also established a "cooperative relationship with the hospital that includes the sharing of resources, joint purchasing, and other mutually desirable arrangements," and contributed to the black community's "sense of strength and participation in the political process" (174).

Studies of alternative programs reinforce the point made in Chapter I about the importance of fitting the task to the administrative capacity of the recipient organization. Alternative organizations with minimal administrative capacity are found to be more effective in cases where there is a focused, flexible, simple task. They are less effective when there is a diffuse, inflexible, complex task requiring formal, neighborhood-wide, large assembly types of groups (Yates, 1973; Gittel, 1980). Overloading an alternative group with a complex task makes the development of capacity much more difficult and often impossible.

Arguments about the administrative capacity demonstrated by alternative programs may miss one of their central contributions, however. Alternative programs serve as a political catalyst for changing the commitments and programs of established agencies at both the national and local levels. Development strategies must not be judged solely on the basis of their immediate influence—in this case, on the quality of alternative programs—but also by their influence on future resources (Gamson, 1968: 98).

In the early years of the poverty programs, there was a great wailing and gnashing of teeth by local jurisdictions about the impossibility of doing more for poor people than was already being done. The local governments seemed to be saying: "If it is worthwhile and possible, we are already doing it; if we are not doing it, you are wrong to ask us to do it." The alternative programs, however, even though strongly criticized, demonstrated new ways of reaching the poor and organizing new constituents. In the face of these pressures, the established agencies had new incentives to search for ways to meet the needs of these constituents more effectively. Some feel this could have been achieved in a less disruptive, more effective fashion without the use of alternative organizations. Others (and we count ourselves among these) suspect that the increased interest in and commitment to programs for the poor were stimulated by the competition from alternative organizations and the pressure they generated for new programs.

For example, neighborhood health centers appear to have stimulated the growth of new community-oriented programs in medical schools and new residency programs in family medicine and to have spurred health agencies to relate to communities in new ways via consumer participation and the employment of local residents (Hollister, Kramer, and Bellin, 1974: 307; contrast with Alford, 1975: 165, 166). Similarly in education, school boards have been changed "irreversibly for the better because they have been challenged by Head Start programs oriented toward innovation, parent participation, and poor kids, none of which many school boards had been particularly interested in before" (Levine, 1970: 144). The alternative education programs have also been credited with increasing parent interest and participation in education and the improved delivery of services (Gittel et al., 1972: 158).

Examples of cases where an alternative program stimulated change in established public agencies include the following. In Portsmouth, Ohio, an alternative program stimulated public schools to initiate job-oriented adult education programs in neighborhood centers in poverty areas. In Fremont, California, an alternative program was responsible for the school board's initiating a child care center using paraprofessionals from poor neighborhoods. In Lowell, Massachusetts, an alternative program induced the welfare department to participate in a surplus food program run at a neighborhood center. An alternative program in Milwaukee, Wisconsin, stimulated the decentralization of welfare services to neighborhood centers (Levine, 1970: 166, 167). In Boston and Newark, health clinics providing free service to entire geographical areas of the poor have changed the traditional ways health departments operate (Washnis, 1974: 15).

If grants to alternative organizations have had these positive effects, the question arises as to whether any of the grants should have gone to established organizations. We think the redundancy made an important contribution to the success of the alternative strategy. The wrath of the established units would have been even greater if they had been totally bypassed. They were kept relatively content by the infusion of additional funds which they could use at least partially according to their tastes. Grants to local governments, then, promoted a favorable political climate by minimizing the opposition from the intergovernmental lobby. The additional resources also enabled local governments to respond to the increased competition from alternative organizations. As the public agencies gradually succeeded in gaining control over alternative programs, the "mainstreamed" programs were actually more oriented to the poor than they would have been in the absence of federal financial incentives (Davis, 1977: 172). If the central government had simply dictated to local governments that they must change in this direction, or had completely bypassed them, their commitment and capacity would probably not have changed as much or been as institutionalized as it was under the competitive dual strategy.

CONTROL LINKAGES

The choice of organizations to implement a development program discussed above is one important characteristic of a linkage strategy. The second major characteristic considered here is the nature of the interactions which take place between the implementing organizations. In Chapter I five descriptive types of linkage mechanisms or forms of interaction are specified: finance, regulation and monitoring, technical and personnel assistance, services, and representation. These mechanisms involve various mixes of two purposes—control and assistance. The purpose of control linkages is to enable one organization to determine some aspect of another's performance. The purpose of assistance linkages is to facilitate program implementation by compensating for gaps in the performance of implementing organizations.

In the United States there has been a great deal of controversy about the mix of control and assistance in the linkage mechanisms of the poverty programs. Most of this controversy has focused on the amount of central control which is desirable. The logic behind the dual forms of decentralization described above suggests that different amounts of control were utilized depending on the commitment and capacity of the recipient. Established agencies lacking commitment but high in capacity might have been subjected to high central control over what was done and whom it was done for, but given more discretion over how it was done. This would allow flexibility in adapting to local variations. Alternative organizations having high commitment but lower capacity might have been subjected to less control but given more assistance in doing the task. Political realities rather than logic, however, guided the national linkages to recipients. Formally the U.S. poverty programs established linkages with high federal control to both types of local organizations because the central policymakers wanted to maintain as much central control as possible in a decentralized system.

The initial poverty programs therefore were designed as categoric grants with high central control linkages. This was true whether the recipient was a governmental or an alternative organization in rural development, education, health, or other fields. Regulations were attached to grants specifying eligibility, geographic distribution, program content, operating procedures, and reporting mechanisms. The purpose was to keep these programs separate from the ongoing routines of the organizations, and to change the behavior of the organizations. For example, OEO attempted to exert high control over the local alternative groups which typically operated Head Start programs, requiring the hiring of poverty area residents, high levels of parent involvement, and intensive monitoring (Levin, 1977). Formally tight linkages also characterized the neighborhood health centers. Specified goals included the following: health care for the poor, employment of poor residents, training for new health career roles, consumer participation in program planning and operation, and the demonstration of new modes of health care delivery. The central government had the tools to monitor the program strictly, including line-item deletions from the budget, the attachment of special conditions to the receipt of funds, and termination of funds if the conditions were not met (Hollister, Kramer, and Bellin, 1974). The Elementary and Secondary Education Act (ESEA) was also an example of formally strong control linkages. Regulations specified that federal funds supplement rather than supplant local funds and that the size of grants was to be a function of state fiscal effort. A variety of local conditions were also specified, such as the creation of advisory committees including representatives of the poor (Levin, 1977: 133).

Political conditions limited the central government's ability to maintain the desired control, however. The actual amount of control and its results have varied greatly across functions and over time according to the national and local political situations. Very often the sanctions and inducements which the federal government was willing to exercise were not as great as their formal controls suggested and were not sufficient to overcome the resistance due to recipient agencies' lack of commitment or capacity or both.

This dilemma is demonstrated in both ESEA and the Partnership for Health Acts, which have been characterized by low control throughout much of their history. There was continuing tension between the federal desire to direct local efforts toward national priorities and the local professionals' desire to use federal funds as general support for ongoing programs. The local refrain was "Don't tell us how to run these programs because you don't know how and we do." The second verse was "Let us run these programs and show you how much better we can do when you leave us alone." The professionals were able to exert enough political pressure both locally and nationally to transform what were formally high control linkages into informally much lower control relationships. In the field of health, given the political power of the medical profession, it is not surprising that categoric grants were merged as early as 1966 into the looser block grant called Partnership for Health (Davis, 1977; USACIR, 1977a). Even though ESEA was not formally redesigned as a block grant, in reality the high controls were not enforced. State and local education agencies were given a great deal of discretion over the use of funds (Levin, 1977: 133). In both cases, the strength of groups supporting strict targeting to the poor was not as great as the strength of those favoring spreading the funds as a general subsidy.

The difficulty of enforcing high control is also demonstrated in the programs implemented by alternative organizations. Even in programs like Head Start and neighborhood health centers, the federal government often did not exercise the strong controls which were formally available. Federal officials recognized the limits in local capacity and the need for time in which to increase capacity via trial and error (Marcus, 1981). Close scrutiny is also difficult and costly. Some alternative organizations had enough political support to make intervention politically costly as well (Hollister, Kramer, and Bellin, 1974). Monitors thus had to face the difficult question with alternative as well as established organizations of whether intervention would do more harm than good.

Thus both types of recipients learned ways of changing high control links into low control links. The credibility of the sanctions declined as the players learned that the likelihood of their being imposed as a result of problems uncovered in the monitoring was not great (Sabatier and Mazmanian, 1980: 548). The possibility never declined to zero, however, and the local governments continued to try to change the formal design of grants toward block grants and away from categoric grants so that both the formal and informal controls would be low rather than high.

What lessons are suggested by these experiences with formally high control but in reality low control linkages? There is a view emerging in the United States that a mix of control and assistance linkages is desirable in order to promote development. The balance of the two types of linkages depends on the commitment and capacity of the particular recipient and is designed to create sufficient inducements and sanctions to move that recipient in the desired direction. In other words, the mix will vary according to the characteristics of the recipient (Berman, 1980).

ASSISTANCE LINKAGES

This view of the desirability of a mix of types of linkages entails a new awareness of the importance of assistance or supportive linkages. The earlier emphasis on regulation and compliance is now recognized as self-defeating when carried too far. Implementors with a regulatory mentality become preoccupied with procedures rather than program substance (Williams, 1980: 38, 109; see also Rondinelli, 1979: 129). Instead, implementors in the United States are now being encouraged to establish linkages designed to facilitate local commitment and capacity. This involves a movement away from control to influence via bargaining (Williams, 1980: 72). As Williams says: "Bargaining becomes the appropriate strategy where the power of hierarchical control. . . ends, where the credible threat of command and control with clear sanctions that apply to discernible boundary points no longer holds" (74). The center attempts to establish "directional influence, not direct command" (74) and a "viable working relationship between the federal and local partners" (111). The intergovernmental grant system is seen as a "two-way street."

Assistance linkages need to be distinguished from low control linkages, which in the United States have been associated with grants like general revenue sharing, where redistribution of benefits to the poor is not a goal. Low control linkages have meant letting the local recipients pursue their own priorities. Supportive linkages, in the sense we use the term here, refer to techniques designed to promote the well-being of the poor by increasing local commitment to and capacity for achieving that goal. They do not mean an abdication of central responsibility. The federal government uses its influence to promote movement in the desired direction but uses it flexibly, with constraint and deference in order to encourage maximum local effort towards the goal (Williams, 1980: 72-73, 111). Monitoring still occurs but less frequently because the local recipients have been given a good deal of responsibility and discretion (Blau and Scott, 1962: 170).

An example of supportive linkages replacing low control linkages is provided by recent trends in the implementation of ESEA Title I. As indicated above, in previous years ESEA's formally high control linkages had been transformed into informally low control linkages. The very existence of new educational programs ostensibly directed to the poor was sufficient, however, to stimulate the formation of new clientele groups with interests different from those of the teachers and school board members. These new groups include the people hired to work in the programs, the parents of children in them, the members of federally mandated advisory boards, and advocacy-oriented community organizations. They have an interest in the national priorities as opposed to general subsidies for education, and they create new pressures in the political system. Pressures from these groups serve to counter somewhat the interests of the professional education lobbies. As the resources and ability of these groups to intervene changed, it was politically feasible for both federal and local implementors to orient the programs more toward the poor (Sabatier and Mazmanian, 1980: 548, 551, 553). The new interest groups stimulated more active use of federal influence, in the form of supportive linkages, to promote local adaptations in the direction of improving education for the poor. These adaptations have improved program implementation in education as the funds have been more effectively targeted to programs for the disadvantaged (Kirst and Jung, 1980). In sum, the ESEA example suggests that flawed programs can set into motion some of the political forces which gradually can create a context in which new, more effective linkages become feasible. This process is possible if, and only if, there is enough stability in the program to allow these kinds of adaptations in linkage strategies to evolve. Another example of the gradual transformation of low control linkages is provided by the Community Development Block Grants, where increased targeting occurred during the Carter administration (Dommel et al., 1980: 179) in response to new political pressures generated partly by earlier programs.

Technical Assistance. A key component of supportive linkages is assistance by the center rather than simply the threat of sanctions. Technical assistance refers to the provision of resources which will serve as an incentive for the increase in local capacity to implement development programs effectively. These resources may include finance, services, and technical and personnel assistance (see Chapter I).

The experience with linkages in U.S. poverty programs and with earlier efforts such as Cooperative Extension suggests that technical assistance is an extremely important contributor to improving the performance of both local governments and alternative organizations. It can reinforce positive local commitments and capacity in the face of competing pressures, and it can decrease negative tendencies by creating new positive pressures. A key variable in explaining current high levels of capability to implement grants is prior experience in the operation of federal grant programs (Nathan et al., 1977; Sokolow, 1981). Recipients learn to administer programs by administering programs. The existence of the programs contributes to capacity, and if those programs include a component designed to facilitate learning, there is reason to think that capacity is enhanced.

A great many studies of U.S. poverty programs call for increases in technical assistance to improve local capacity. For example, studies of poor people's co-ops find that neither direct national technical assistance services for local co-ops nor indirect support via multipurpose agencies is sufficient. Studies stress the fragility of cooperatives and their need for better planning, management, marketing skills, and credit supply (Marshall and Godwin, 1971: 85). Cooperatives have difficulty mobilizing sufficient local resources partly because of problems in establishing relations between local co-op clubs and central co-op boards, the uncertainty of short-term funds, and reduced incentives for productivity because members are not required to invest their own resources and repay loans (Finney, 1975: 45, 48; Rochin, 1980: 6). What is needed is the creation of more "autonomous, representative supra-local structures of integrated support for local co-ops" (Finney, 1975: 58). Finney advocates funneling support indirectly through "multi-level specialized, mediating institutions whose sole business would be provision of the proximate, continuous, specialized and yet integrated supports so desperately needed" (58).

Studies of neighborhood health centers also stress the importance of technical assistance, especially the training of staff and members of the advisory boards (Hollister, Kramer, and Bellin, 1974: 76; Levin, 1977). Similarly the evaluation of the State Development Project for rural services urged that when local people are hired they be trained so they can be more effective in their outreach work.

Some U.S. studies suggest that it may be better to hire local people with a commitment to the poor and train them rather than to hire more educated people who lack that commitment. For example, a study of cooperatives found that managers who are "technically incompetent but dedicated" are more effective than the reverse types (Marshall and Godwin, 1971: 88). Similarly, a study of Cooperative Extension's outreach program for small farmers found that field worker success in working with the farmers on a one-to-one basis diminished with formal education and increased with years of farm experience (Orden and Buccola, 1979: 11). Training of staff was associated with positive results, but at the same time, too close supervision appeared to interfere with the performance of high quality field workers. Decisions about the amount of supervision should be made locally and should be related to the needs of the field worker. These findings are similar to the point made above in connection with the dual strategy. In the United States at least, it appears easier to increase the capacity of committed groups than to change the will of uncommitted ones. Commitment appears harder to reform than administrative capacity.

In spite of the importance of technical assistance in improving local capacity, care must be taken so that support from the center stimulates rather than discourages local effort. Too many attempts at technical assistance have involved ad hoc discontinuous relationships with a narrow problem perspective. More effective technical assistance aimed at institutional capacity-building requires continuing close relationships and a broader community-wide perspective. In this kind of assistance the emphasis is on teaching and educating rather than on short-term problem-solving. There is also a willingness to invest resources in low visibility programs and to plan with, rather than for, the recipients (Brown, 1980). The need to stimulate local effort has led some to favor loans for such purposes as local co-ops, rather than annual grants (Finney, 1975: 49), and to encourage matching requirements whereby local recipients provide contributions to grant programs (USACIR, 1978a: 161). People are motivated to work harder when they have a personal stake in the program, and technical assistance seems to stimulate more effort when the locus of power is left with the local organization rather than assumed by the outside organization.

A study of two rural cooperatives, for example, found that when the support system removed too much of the locus of power from the local cooperative and placed it with the outside technical assistance organization, the incentive for cooperation within the local organization and its performance declined. In one cooperative, the intermediary support agency kept the power to review cooperative decisions including hiring of personnel, management of records, and handling of money. In the second cooperative, the control was left primarily within the cooperative, and the banks imposed a minimum of stipulations over internal operations, simply doing financial auditing and providing advice on business practices as it would for any client. The latter strategy was more successful in strengthening the local organization's capacity (Wells, 1982: 22). In the first case the federal government and a private bank designated a local community development corporation as the monitor of the loans to the cooperative. The community development corporation developed linkages with much higher control than mandated by the federal government or the bank. In the second case, the intermediary agency lost funding shortly after the founding of the co-op. The bank then left most control within the co-op, utilizing only its own usual monitoring system and a special advisory committee of technical advisers familiar with cooperative development. This committee was consulted by the co-op, but the decisions were made by the co-op itself.

Supportive technical assistance, then, should be oriented to increasing the flow of information to organizations and to citizens who can in turn pressure the organizations (Williams, 1980: 92, 94). In order to make that information useful, however, good staff must be in the field and must adapt the information to the needs of the recipients (94-95).

Representation. Another key component of a linkage relationship is representation, or local participation in programs. Just as poverty programs have provided some lessons about technical assistance, they have increased understanding of the strengths and limitations of local representation.

There have been two main approaches to representation or upward linkages. One approach—elite participation—is characterized by an effort to increase the involvement of the leaders of important local institutions, to obtain their support, and to improve the coordination between the program and other activities in the area. The second approach—citizen participation—focuses on organizing poor constituents in order to create new political pressures for redistribution of power and resources.

The experience with these kinds of linkages in poverty programs confirmed Selznick's (1966) earlier finding regarding the Tennessee Valley Authority, namely that neither type of local participation inevitably improves programs or redistributes power. Elite participation may improve programs or subvert them via elite capture of the agency (or what Selznick calls informal co-optation). Similarly, citizen participation may redistribute power; it may formally co-opt potential competitors for power and thus retard the redistribution of power; or it may increase controversy to the point of stalemate. Marris and Rein (1967) provide one of the best analyses of the tension between the two kinds of upward linkages: if in order to promote coordination, the structures involve elites, it is very difficult also to have high levels of citizen participation. If the structures increase participation of the poor, they make coordination among elites difficult due to the larger number of people involved in the process.

U.S. citizen participation efforts have involved wide variations in who participates, how, and why (USACIR, 1979: 8, 9; compare with Uphoff, Cohen, and Goldsmith [1979] and Esman [1980] on citizen participation in Third World countries). In some projects the focus is on low-income citizens, and in others on middle-income citizens. The participation mechanisms range from temporary convenings such as public hearings and task forces to the creation of ongoing committees, boards, or commissions (Benson, Conway, and James, 1978; USACIR, 1979: 8, 9). These mechanisms vary from those which are an exercise in tokenism, informing, consulting, and placating to those which involve some degree of power because the citizens are partners in decision-making and have been delegated power or even control (see Arnstein, 1969).

Some analysts view citizen participation as a valuable end in itself because it is democratic or promotes human development. Others see it as a means toward the redistribution of resources. Those who take the latter view are increasingly aware that it may or may not be conducive to that end. Under certain conditions citizen participation may redistribute benefits to the poor, and under other conditions it may not be an effective means toward development. Thus for those in the United States whose primary commitment is to development, the utility of citizen participation is now more than ever an empirical question.

A recent study of sixteen citizen-participation organizations (Gittel, 1980) suggests that as more federal grants include mandates for citizen participation, citizen-participation organizations have become less oriented to advocacy and more oriented toward service delivery and advice (242). The study concludes that as a result these organizations are less effective at gaining access to the political system for low-income groups (43).

Nevertheless, U.S. poverty programs also suggest that both kinds of representation—elite and citizen—can contribute to program goals (USACIR, 1979). Poverty programs have stimulated elite participation by the formation of a great many new coordinative bodies which cross traditional agency boundaries and expose leaders to new perspectives (USACIR, 1979: 48). These bodies may articulate new demands beneficial to the poor and join in lobbying efforts to strengthen programs. For example, the State Rural Development Program stimulated the formation of coordination committees, including local, state, and federal representation, or at least more frequent consultations among these actors.

Federal requirements for citizen participation in grant implementation can stimulate countervailing pressures against the tendency of such programs to serve the more advantaged members of communities (Van Horn, 1977). For example, the boards of neighborhood health centers select staff; set service priorities, hours of service, and budgets; recruit outreach workers; and settle grievances. They also sometimes become new constituency groups pushing for the orientation of health services to the poor (Hollister, Kramer, and Bellin, 1974; Davis and Schoen, 1978). Similar examples are given in education (Yin and Yates, 1975: viii). Even if citizen-participation boards had only limited impact on the immediate substance of policy (Levin, 1977), they contributed to the upward pressures which helped change low control links into supportive links (see above, p. 56) and to the development of leaders and the political sophistication of the members (Ambrecht, 1976; Marshall, 1971). Citizen participation, then, can contribute indirectly to the organization of the poor by involving them in planning, implementing, and monitoring programs (Greenstone and Peterson, 1976; Peterson and Greenstone, 1977: 269, 270; Piven and Cloward, 1977; Browning, Marshall, and Tabb, 1980). Moreover, the ability of supportive constituencies to intervene may improve program implementation (Sabatier and Mazmanian, 1980). Of course, it is not possible to prove unequivocally that such changes would not have occurred in the absence of poverty programs, but the causal chain is clear enough to indicate that the programs and citizen participation were associated with the emergence of new interest groups committed to and increasingly capable of promoting the interests of poor people.

CONCLUSION

The changes in the political system sketched above—changes in the roles and capacities of the central and local agencies and alternative organizations—have been relatively small. No claims are made here that they are major changes or that they have reduced the continuing problems of poverty and a permanent underclass in the United States (Gershman and Clark, 1980). The changes have been and will surely continue to be fraught with conflict among the participating organizations. The subtle shifts which have occurred, however, underscore the importance of organizational strategy in development programs, both in the choice of central and local implementing agencies and in the nature of the links between them.

It is true that the implementation context in the United States may have been rather unusual because national governments in the 1960s and 1970s were fairly supportive of at least some efforts to redistribute resources to the poor. This kind of commitment at the center is rare and transitory. Where it is lacking, different linkage strategies will surely be necessary to promote redistribution. We believe that the U.S. case illustrates the utility of analyzing linkage problems in terms of the commitment and capacity of national and local organizations and of attempting to select forms of decentralization and linkage appropriate for those specific conditions. The U.S. case suggests the kinds of results associated with specific strategies in a setting where there is high program vulnerability to inequality and a committed and administratively capable center.

We have argued that the U.S. poverty programs have been characterized by a dual strategy of linkages both to local governmental organizations and to alternative organizations and by an increased emphasis on the importance of assistance linkages rather than control linkages. The dual strategy created competition between the two types of local implementing agencies, a competition which served as a catalyst for improving development programs. Supportive linkages also have been beneficial because they have created incentives for increases in local commitment and capacity to implement development programs. In our view these linkages have contributed via a gradual process of organizational learning and adaptation to the emergence of an intergovernmental system in which both the center and the localities are strong and interdependent.

Our interpretation of these various types of linkages has called attention to their political results—to the indirect political ramifications of strategies which were not manifestly political. In closing we want to underscore the difference between approaches to redistribution which nurture these latent political functions of linkages and other approaches which are overtly oriented toward partisan change in the electoral, as opposed to the programmatic, arena of organizational implementation. The changes in U.S. decentralization discussed above took place in the administrative arena. While these were of course influenced by electoral changes, they were also shaped in important ways by bureaucratic or intergovernmental politics, which is less partisan in character. Sometimes when the American experience is analyzed in political terms as we have done here, the analysis is misinterpreted as an argument for overtly political strategies. In the U.S. context, that would stiffen resistance to change by increasing the visibility of conflicts and enlarging the number of competing groups, thus changing the possible outcomes (Schattschneider, 1960). Similarly, the strategy of linking with alternative organizations and thus promoting the organization of the poor was not primarily oriented toward stimulating the poor to take sides in partisan political activity. Instead, the poor were organized to influence particular policies and programs within administrative agencies rather than electoral politics. This approach builds on felt needs and/or existing groups in localities and provides assistance or incentives rather than imposing pre-existing partisan agendas (and thus may avoid some of the dangers pointed out by Ralston, Anderson, and Colson, 1981).

We think that the indirect political shifts associated with the U.S. poverty program, while small, are still suggestive of the way linkages which are not manifestly political can cumulate into institutional changes which may influence the distribution of resources. This experience suggests that those interested in development are well advised to continue in their efforts to be politically sensitive without abandoning their commitment to the administrative implementation of programs. The two dimensions of linkages are closely related and can reinforce each other in the delicate balancing act called rural development.

REFERENCES

Aaron, Henry J. 1978. *Politics and the professors: the great society in perspective*. Washington, D.C.: Brookings Institution.

Alford, Robert. 1975. *Health care politics: ideological and interest group barriers to reform*. Chicago: University of Chicago Press.

Altshuler, Alan A. 1970. *Community control: the black demand for participation in large American cities*. Indianapolis: Bobbs-Merrill.

Ambrecht, Biliana C. S. 1976. *Politicizing the poor: the legacy of the War on Poverty in a Mexican American community*. New York: Praeger.

Arnstein, Sherry. 1969. A ladder of citizen participation. *Journal of the American Institute of Planners* 35, 4 (July): 216-24.

Beer, Samuel. 1976. The adoption of general revenue sharing: a case study in public sector politics. *Public Policy* 24 (Spring): 127-95.

Benson, Jonathon; Conway, Richard; and James, Jr., Thomas. 1978. Citizen participation for urban management. *Quarterly Report* 3, 2 (Winter). Columbus: Mershon Center, Ohio State University.

Berman, Paul. 1978. The study of macro- and micro-implementation. *Public Policy* 26 (Spring): 157-84.

__________. 1980. Thinking about programmed and adaptive implementation: matching strategies to situations. In *Why policies succeed or fail*, ed. Helen Ingram and Dean E. Mann. Beverly Hills: Sage.

__________, and McLaughlin, M. 1976. Implementation of educational innovation. *The Educational Forum* 40, 3 (March): 347-70.

Blakely, Edward J., and Zone, Martin. 1976. *Small cities and the Community Development Act of 1974*. Davis: Institute of Governmental Affairs, University of California.

Blau, Peter M., and Scott, Richard. 1962. *Formal organizations*. San Francisco: Chandler Publishing Co.

Bradshaw, Ted K., and Blakely, Edward J. 1979. *Rural communities in advanced industrial society*. New York: Praeger.

Brown, Anthony. 1980. Technical assistance to rural communities: stopgap or capacity building? *Public Administration Review* 40, 1 (January/February): 18-23.

Browning, Rufus; Marshall, Dale; and Tabb, David. 1980. Implementation and political change: sources of local variations in federal social programs. In *Effective policy implementation*, ed. Daniel Mazmanian and Paul Sabatier. Lexington: Lexington Books.

Council of State Community Action Agencies. 1980. *Housing and community development in five rural areas*. Washington, D.C.

Davis, Karen. 1977. A decade of policy developments in providing health care for low income families. In *A decade of federal antipoverty programs: achievements, failures and lessons*, ed. Robert Haveman. New York: Academic Press.

__________, and Schoen, Cathy. 1978. *Health and the War on Poverty: a ten year appraisal*. Washington, D.C.: Brookings Institution.

Derthick, Martha. 1970. *The influence of federal grants*. Cambridge: Harvard University Press.

Dommel, Paul R.; Bach, Victor E.; Liebschutz, Sarah; Rubinowitz, Leonard S.; and Associates. 1980. *Targeting community development*. Washington, D.C.: U.S. Department of Housing and Urban Development; January.

Donovan, John C. 1967. *The politics of poverty*. New York: Pegasus.

Esman, Milton. 1980. Development assistance in public administration: requiem or renewal? *Public Administration Review* 40, 5 (September/October): 426-31.

__________; Colle, Royal; Uphoff, Norman; and Taylor, Ellen. 1980. *Paraprofessionals in rural development*. Ithaca: Rural Development Committee, Center for International Studies, Cornell University.

Farkas, Suzanne. 1971. *Urban lobbying: mayors in the federal arena*. New York: New York University Press.

Finney, Henry C. 1975. *Problems of local, regional and national support for rural poor-peoples' cooperatives in the United States: some lessons from the War on Poverty*. Ann Arbor: Institute for Research on Poverty, University of Wisconsin. Reprint No. 142.

Gamson, William S. 1968. *Power and discontent*. Homewood: Dorsey Press.

Gershman, Carl, and Clark, Kenneth B. 1980. The black plight: a debate. *The New York Times Magazine*, Sunday, 5 October.

Gittel, Marilyn. 1980. *Limits to citizen participation: the decline of community organizations*. Beverly Hills: Sage Publications.

__________; with Berube, Maurice R.; Gottfried, Frances; Guttentag, Marcia; and Spier, Adele. 1972. *Local control in education: three demonstration school districts in New York City*. New York: Praeger.

__________; with Berube, Maurice R.; Demas, Boulton; Flavin, Daniel; Rosentrau, Mark; Spier, Adele; and Tatge, David. 1973. *School boards and school policy: an evaluation of decentralization in New York City*. New York: Praeger.

Greenstone, J. David, and Peterson, Paul E. 1976. *Race and authority in urban politics*. Chicago: University of Chicago Press.

Haider, Donald. 1974. *When governments come to Washington*. New York: Free Press.

Haveman, Robert H., ed. 1977. *A decade of federal antipoverty programs: achievements, failures and lessons*. New York: Academic Press.

Heath, Billie. 1980. Field research project. Davis: Community Development Program, University of California; June.

Hollister, Robert M.; Kramer, Bernard; and Bellin, Seymour, eds. 1974. *Neighborhood health centers*. Lexington: Lexington Books.

Honadle, Beth Walter. 1981. *Capacity-building (management improvement) for local governments: an annotated bibliography*. Washington, D.C.: Economic Development Division, Economics and Statistics Service, U.S. Department of Agriculture. Rural Development Research Report No. 28; March.

Ingram, Helen. 1977. Policy implementation through bargaining: the case of federal grants-in-aid. *Public Policy* 25, 4 (Fall): 499-526.

King, Anthony, ed. 1978. *The new American political system*. Washington, D.C.: American Enterprise Institute.

Kirst, Michael, and Jung, Richard. 1980. The utility of a longitudinal approach in assessing implementation: a thirteen year view of Title I, ESEA. Paper read at the 1980 Annual Meeting of the Western Political Science Association, 27-29 March, 1980, in San Francisco, California.

Kramer, Ralph M. 1969. *Participation of the poor: comparative community case studies in the War on Poverty*. Englewood Cliffs: Prentice Hall.

Lamb, Curt. 1975. *Power in poor neighborhoods*. New York: Wiley and Sons.

Levin, Henry. 1977. A decade of policy developments in improving education and training for low-income populations. In *A decade of federal antipoverty programs: achievements, failures and lessons*, ed. Robert Haveman. New York: Academic Press.

Levine, Robert. 1970. *The poor ye need not have with you: lessons from the War on Poverty*. Cambridge: MIT Press.

Levitan, Sar. 1969. *The Great Society's poor law*. Baltimore: Johns Hopkins University Press.

__________, and Taggart, Robert. 1976. *The promise of greatness*. Cambridge: Harvard University Press.

Marcus, Isabel. 1981. *Dilemmas of health care reform*. Lexington: Lexington Books.

Marris, Peter, and Rein, Martin. 1967. *Dilemmas of social reform: poverty and community action in the United States*. New York: Atherton Press.

Marshall, Dale Rogers. 1971. Public participation and the politics of poverty. In *Race, change and urban society*, ed. Peter Orleans and William Ellis. Beverly Hills: Sage Publications.

Marshall, Ray, and Godwin, Lamond. 1971. *Cooperatives and rural poverty in the South*. Baltimore: Johns Hopkins Press.

Montgomery, John D. 1970. Programs and poverty. *Public Policy* 18, 4 (Summer): 517-38.

__________. 1971. Transferability of what? The relevance of foreign aid to the domestic poverty program. *Journal of Comparative Administration* 2, 4 (February): 455-70.

Moynihan, Daniel P. 1969. *Maximum feasible misunderstanding.* New York: Free Press.

Murphy, J. T. 1971. Title I of ESEA. *Harvard Education Review* 41: 35-63.

Nathan, Richard; Dommel, Paul R.; Liebschutz, Sarah; Morris, Milton; and Associates. 1977. *Block grants for community development.* Washington, D.C.: U.S. Department of Housing and Urban Development; January.

National Academy of Public Administration. 1980. *Fighting poverty in the Third World.* Washington, D.C.; November.

Orden, David, and Buccola, Steven T. 1979. An evaluation of southern Cooperative Extension programs aimed at small farmers. Unpublished manuscript.

Peterson, Paul E., and Greenstone, J. David. 1977. Racial change and citizen participation: the mobilization of low-income communities through citizen action. In *A decade of federal antipoverty programs: achievements, failures and lessons,* ed. Robert Haveman. New York: Academic Press.

Piven, Frances Fox, and Cloward, Richard. 1977. *Poor people's movements: why they succeed, how they fail.* New York: Vintage Books.

Plotnick, Robert D., and Skidmore, Felicity. 1975. *Progress against poverty: a review of the 1964-1974 decade.* New York: Academic Press.

Pressman, Jeffrey. 1975. *Federal programs and city politics.* Berkeley, University of California Press.

__________, and Wildavsky, Aaron B. 1979. *Implementation.* 2d ed. Berkeley: University of California Press.

Ralston, Lenore; Anderson, James; and Colson, Elizabeth. 1981. *Voluntary efforts and decentralized management.* Berkeley: Project on Managing Decentralization, Institute of International Studies, University of California.

Reagan, Michael, and Sanzone, John G. 1980. *The new federalism.* New York: Oxford University Press.

Rochin, Refugio I. 1980. Historical notes on the emergence of limited resource farm cooperatives in Northern California. Paper read at the National Conference on Agricultural Production Cooperatives, 15 January, 1980, at the University of California, Davis.

Rondinelli, Dennis. 1979. *Administrative decentralization and area development planning in East Africa: implications for United States aid policy.* Madison: Regional Planning and Area Development Project, International Studies and Programs, University of Wisconsin.

Sabatier, Paul, and Mazmanian, Daniel. 1980. The implementation of public policy: a framework of analysis. In *Effective policy implementation*, ed. Daniel Mazmanian and Paul Sabatier. Lexington: Lexington Books.

Schattschneider, E. E. 1960. *The semi-sovereign people*. New York: Holt, Rinehart and Winston.

Selznick, Philip. 1966. *TVA and the grass roots*. New York: Harper Torchbooks.

Sokolow, Alvin D. 1981. Local governments in nonmetropolitan America: capacity and will. In *Understanding nonmetropolitan America*, ed. Amos H. Hawley and Sara M. Mazie. Chapel Hill: University of North Carolina Press.

Uphoff, Norman, T.; Cohen, John M.; and Goldsmith, Arthur A. 1979. *Feasibility and application of rural development participation: a state-of-the-art paper*. Ithaca: Rural Development Committee, Center for International Studies, Cornell University; January.

USACIR [U.S. Advisory Commission on Intergovernmental Relations]. 1977a. *The Partnership for Health Act: lessons from a pioneering block grant*. Washington, D.C. January; A-56.

__________. 1977b. *Improving Federal Grants Management*. Washington, D.C. February; A-53.

__________. 1977c. *Block grants: a comparative analysis*. Washington, D.C. October; A-60.

__________. 1978a. *Categorical grants: their role and design*. Washington, D.C. May; A-52.

__________. 1978b. *Summary and concluding observations: the intergovernmental grant system*. Washington, D.C. June; A-62.

__________. 1979. *Citizen participation in the American federal system*. Washington, D.C. March; A-73.

Van Horn, Carl E. 1977. Decentralized policy delivery: national objectives and local implementors. Paper read at the Workshop on Policy Analysis in State and Local Government, 22-24 May, 1977, at the State University of New York at Stony Brook.

Washnis, George J. 1974. *Community development strategies: case studies of major model cities*. New York: Praeger.

Wells, Miriam. 1982. Political mediation and agricultural cooperation: strawberry farms in California. *Economic Development and Cultural Change* 30, 2 (January): 413-32.

Wirt, Frederick. 1970. *Politics of Southern equality*. Chicago: Aldine Publishing Co.

Whitman, Ray, and Cline, Robert. 1978. *Fiscal impact of revenue sharing in comparison with other federal aid*. Washington, D.C.: Urban Institute.

Williams, Walter. 1980. *The implementation perspective: a guide for managing social service delivery programs*. Berkeley: University of California Press.

Yates, Douglas. 1973. *Neighborhood democracy: the politics and impacts of decentralization*. Lexington: Lexington Books.

Yin, Robert K., and Yates, Douglas. 1975. *Street level governments: a Rand Corporation research study*. Lexington: D. C. Heath.

Zimet, Melvin. 1973. *Decentralization and school effectiveness*. New York: Teachers College Press.

Chapter III

GOVERNMENT, COOPERATIVES, AND THE PRIVATE SECTOR IN PEASANT AGRICULTURE

Stephen B. Peterson

Agriculture is the key to the improvement of the incomes of the poorer half of developing societies. The strategies that best promote agricultural development make very intensive demands on local organizations. In this chapter we analyze the ways in which the state can promote and sustain the community-wide organizational structures that are needed for broad-based agricultural growth.

UNIMODAL DEVELOPMENT AND ITS POLICY IMPLICATIONS

The main productive resource which the disadvantaged possess is their labor. An industrialization-first strategy of development which neglects agriculture typically creates an inappropriately capital-intensive pattern of manufacturing within a modern enclave and contributes little to the growth of employment (Healey, 1972; Morawetz, 1974). The stimulation of small, labor-intensive industry, on the other hand, permits and demands broad-based agricultural growth. Such industry depends on rural development to provide both food for its growing labor force and the mass market for the goods it produces (Mellor, 1976).

Yet not just any form of agrarian development will do if broad-based economic development is to be achieved and the welfare of the poor majority protected. What Bruce Johnston calls a "unimodal" pattern of agricultural growth is essential to the multiple objectives of development. Such a strategy is based on small-scale farm units. As the engine of growth it relies on labor-using, capital-saving technologies and on innovations which can readily be scaled down to suit small farms. An example of the latter is the promotion of high-yielding, fertilizer-responsive hybrid crop varieties.

Such unimodal agriculture is to be contrasted with a "bimodal" growth strategy. Here the focus of development is on the large-farm sector, which comes to adopt labor-saving, capital-using technologies. In the process, the impact of agricultural growth on employment is dampened and the small-farm sector is left to atrophy, together with the incomes of the poor who are dependent on it. Such a pattern of growth is termed bimodal because it has two categories of typical farms—the large, dynamic, capital-intensive farm on the one hand, and the small, stagnant, labor-intensive unit on the other (Johnston and Clark, 1982; Johnston and Kilby, 1975).

The advantages of unimodal over bimodal agriculture both for production and for welfare are well established. In the words of Johnston and Clark,

> There is substantial evidence of an inverse correlation between farm size and output per hectare, and the proposition that technologies adopted by small operational units are labor-intensive is well established (Berry and Cline, 1979; Bardhan, 1973; Lau and Yotopoulos, 1971; Johnston and Kilby, 1975) . . . . The great majority of farm households are inevitably bypassed if a late-developing country pursues a bimodal pattern of agricultural development. This appears to be a "hard conclusion." [Thus] during the last decade a considerable consensus has emerged concerning the importance of fostering a broadly based, unimodal pattern of agricultural development (1982, Chapter 3).

If developing countries are to get the greatest production possible out of their scarce good land and are to use fully the labor which they and the poor possess in abundance, a unimodal strategy is essential.

The choice between unimodal and bimodal strategies applies to socialized as well as mixed economies. Since the 1960s the Chinese have used smaller units and labor-intensive technologies, resulting in production gains which contrast with the disappointing performance of the large-scale, capital-intensive Soviet methodology (Johnston and Clark, 1982, Chapter 3). Of course equity and welfare are accommodated under both strategies in socialized economies. The major gains in the unimodal for them are in use of surplus labor and in agricultural production.

Unimodal agriculture does have a welfare dimension in a mixed economy. It is true that it does not help those poor who are unable to work; no production strategy can address the needs of the aged, handicapped, orphans, etc. Clearly, the strategy benefits most the small landowners and tenants upon whom it focuses; but, as it is labor intensive, it works to the advantage of agricultural laborers as well. The important point is that a unimodal strategy both provides the broadest spread of benefits of any production strategy and seems to be the best base for economic development in general. No choice between welfare and development is necessary over the long term.

Johnston and Clark note a considerable number of policies which promote unimodal agricultural development. We summarize them here in order to draw out those measures which have implications for local organizations. The first and most obvious need is to promote small units of production. The greatest gain for income distribution is provided by land reform, either in individual or very small collective units. Lesser but significant gains also can be made by converting large operational units into smaller tenant farms. The historical restraints against innovations in tenant farming can be overcome by legal or customary conventions that require the sharing of input costs between landlord and tenant (Bardhan and Rudra, 1980).

The second critical need is for the development of technological breakthroughs for productivity that are labor intensive (Gotsch, 1974). The important factors here are the quantity of funds devoted to agricultural research (investments which have a very high rate of return), the structure of the research priorities adopted, and the sensitivity of the research programs to the realities of small-farm production.

The third policy requirement is that pricing policies and foreign exchange rates do not put capital-saving, labor-using technologies at a disadvantage. The economic policies of most developing countries effectively subsidize more capital-intensive investments, with obvious negative effects on employment and small-farm agriculture.

Fourth, it is necessary that the small farmer be provided with the infrastructure needed to adopt and employ profitably the available labor-using technologies for intensifying his productivity. There are a large number of these infrastructural items—agricultural extension, irrigation works, roads and transportation, input supply networks, marketing systems, and credit. Frequently such infrastructure is already available for large farms and its absence is a major constraint on small-scale production. The inadequacies in smallholder oriented economic infrastructure also are often the cause of a fall in production after a major land reform, preventing the usual gains in productivity associated with small units.

Agricultural research and terms-of-trade policies are national issues. Local organizations and their relationships with the center are critical to the execution of land reforms and the provision of economic infrastructure, however. In this chapter we examine the organizations which provide agricultural services to all rural dwellers and ask how they can be made most amenable to the needs of the rural poor. In the next chapter we will turn to those alternative local organizations which are composed of and serve the rural poor alone.

THE DECENTRALIZATION OF RURAL ECONOMIC INFRASTRUCTURE

Small-holder agriculture requires decentralization of its economic infrastructure. The tremendous variation in the social, economic, and ecological conditions under which small producers operate makes flexibility and speed of response essential to organizational efficiency. It is difficult to provide such adaptiveness unless decisions about service delivery are made close to the farmers and their problems.

There are a wide variety of ways in which decentralized economic infrastructure services can be provided. Almost all the types of decentralization outlined in Chapter I (Table 2) can be found in agriculture. Extension services almost always are provided by the state itself, usually a Department of Agriculture, working either with individuals or groups of farmers. Decentralized operations in this area are a form of ministerial deconcentration. A variety of arrangements for marketing can be found. A vertically integrated, parastatal crop board may administer sales all the way from the farmer to export—delegation to an autonomous agency. Alternatively, marketing may be organized through a primary cooperative society (an inclusive local organization) which sells in turn through a district cooperative union (a specialized, inclusive intermediate organization). Here we have functional devolution. Finally, local traders may purchase the produce and market it through wholesalers (which also are intermediate organizations). This is marketization. That the decisions made by traders in response to local variations and changes are private and viewed only in the marketplace does not make them any the less adaptive and decentralized.

It is important to remember this array of decentralized organizational responses. Over the last three decades, cooperatives and parastatals (functional devolution and delegation) have been the favored vehicles for state support of small-holder agriculture. We consider that privatization has been unduly overlooked as an appropriate response in many of the contexts in which development activity must take place. We also believe that philanthropies, interest organizations, and deconcentrated government agencies working with local alternative organizations have become increasingly relevant as the focus of development work has shifted from the promotion of agricultural growth to the generation of income for the rural poor.

In this chapter we analyze two of the important forms of decentralization—cooperatives and private business. We seek to establish the functions in rural development to which each is suited and the contextual conditions in which one would be more appropriate than the other. We also examine the policies and organizational linkages to the center that will improve the effectiveness of these two forms of decentralization in serving the rural poor. We consider the interests of the poor here, however, in the context of organizations that are serving all rural dwellers. In the next chapter we will turn to the special problems of stimulating and sustaining alternative local organizations specifically for the benefit of the poorer members of a community.

We will start with an analysis of cooperatives because, since the Second World War, they and parastatals (delegation) have been the favored method of meeting the needs of farmers for organizational infrastructure in the Third World. Whatever one's doubts about their effectiveness, no analysis of rural development can ignore cooperatives. They dominate the economic structure of many rural areas, and their problems preoccupy most rural development practitioners. Most states in the developing world take the cooperative form as their starting point in dealing with organizational infrastructure for the rural areas.

Our treatment of cooperatives will commence with an analysis of the functions they most frequently are called upon to perform. In the process of this analysis we will delineate the array of circumstances in which privatization would appear to be a more effective response and the kinds of links between the state and private enterprises that then would be appropriate. Interwoven with our examination of the appropriate functions for cooperatives and then more fully following it we will examine the types of links between the state and cooperatives that best promote rural development. Even though we conclude that cooperatives have been overused as a vehicle for decentralized rural organization, we have much to learn from them about organizational linkages. The issue of linkages with the state has been empirically analyzed to a greater degree for cooperatives than for other forms of local organization (Inayatullah, 1972). In the next chapter we then will apply the organizational linkage lessons of the cooperative experience to the question of how the center can support alternative local organizations of the poor.

WHAT IS THE ROLE OF COOPERATIVES IN RURAL DEVELOPMENT?

Cooperatives had very different origins in the developing world than they did in the now industrialized countries. In the latter they usually were independently organized by smaller farmers in order to combat oligopolistic middlemen. In poor countries, on the other hand, they generally were promoted by the state, frequently created (rather than competed with) marketing facilities for their areas, and were designed to service the needs of the wealthier members of the small-farm communities who were emerging from subsistence into export agriculture.

Thus formal cooperatives often have several important characteristics in developing countries which distinguish them sharply from the informal forms of cooperation which preceded them. (1) They tend to be tightly regulated by the state. (2) They frequently have been granted a monopoly for at least one of the services they provide. (3) They are dominated by the wealthier members of the farm communities. (4) They were originally designed to market export crops, the production of which often distinguished their members from the majority of subsistence producers. These characteristics are not necessary attributes of cooperatives nor are they to be found in all developing countries. To the extent that they prevail, however, they pose a potential problem for unimodal agricultural development and for programs designed to reach the poor majority. They signal that the cooperatives concerned may already be tied to an emerging bimodal pattern of production, and that their leaders may be members of a local elite with interests quite different from those of the poor majority. With this general context in mind, let us turn to the specifics of different functions which cooperatives are often called upon to perform and examine what the organizational alternatives might be.

SUPPLIES

Supply cooperatives are often an effective means of introducing the cooperative form into traditional areas because they provide immediate and tangible services, such as consumer goods and agricultural inputs, which are desired locally. Many cooperatives continue to exist because they supply goods and services which would otherwise be unavailable or too exorbitant. The argument for government support, particularly capitalization, is that cooperatives can provide superior service at lower costs. The general tendency for cooperatives to be elite-dominated, however, limits their orientation toward service for the rural poor in societies where rural inequalities are significant. As long as these cooperatives have to contend with either the actuality or imminent threat of competition from private traders, they will have to be efficient to survive and services to all consumers, including the poor, are likely to be improved. There even is a case for direct or indirect subsidies to such cooperatives in settings in which private traders otherwise would not face competition. The grant of a monopoly to a cooperative for a particular commodity is a dangerous form of subsidy, however. Monopoly immediately deprives the poor of their major weapon—exit from use of the cooperative. Where the cooperative is dominated by an elite that is either incompetent or unresponsive to the poor, monopoly vastly expands the danger of exploitation.

The Comilla Cooperative program in Bangladesh demonstrates the threat of cooperatives' becoming a vehicle for elite absorption of subsidized inputs. The Comilla program used a two-tier cooperative organization as a mechanism to distribute credit and subsidize inputs rather than to organize production (Khan, 1979: 398). Comilla was initiated with the belief that large producers could not be excluded from the subsidized inputs and that the rural poor would benefit by the increased demand for labor generated by expanded production. Comilla exemplifies several problems that subsidized supply cooperatives can create for equitable and efficient growth. First, the use of an elite-dominated cooperative to distribute production inputs furthered the differentiation of producers and increased landlessness. The wealthy farmers pre-empted the input subsidies and the credit and used their surplus capital to purchase the land of smaller producers. Second, the oversupply and high subsidies of inputs limited the resource contribution of the local farmers, as the state pre-empted local investment opportunities (401). These resource "gifts" tended to be underutilized, as there were no individual opportunity costs attached to the inputs. Finally, because the cooperative did not have responsibility for organizing production, the increased production due to these inputs was not related to the cooperative form. The inputs rather than the cooperative organization became important. The cooperative was viewed as an instrument for extracting resources from the center and not as a basis of indigenous organization that commanded local commitment.

Comilla is a dramatic case of the danger in an unequal society of pursuing development through extensive assistance with virtually no control linkages. The productivity of the targeted large producers was found actually to be less than that of the small nonmember producers, thus demonstrating the limits to input-induced development. Large infusions of productive inputs attract the larger producers and discourage small producers. Small producers did not join Comilla for several reasons: they did not meet even the modest entry requirements; the poor peasants realized that the benefits would accrue proportionally to landholdings; and they feared an unequal production partnership with large farmers (414). The permissive attitude of the state allowed an elite-dominated cooperative to accelerate rural inequalities.

While Comilla represents a failure of an input cooperative to assist the rural poor, the farmers' associations of Taiwan are effective in promoting more egalitarian development and illustrate the preconditions of success. The farmers' associations have two features which contribute to their success: they are effectively regulated by redundant linkages, and they are self-financed.

Effective control linkages are established at both the sub-association level (village) and at the association level. Redundancy of control at the village level is achieved by the agricultural and irrigation group heads, as they are supervised by each other as well as by the village head and the clerk at the township levels. There are three separate administrative hierarchies which can supervise each other: the township office, the farmers' association, and the Nationalist Party service station. Redundancy of administrative channels limits the potential for communication breakdown and also facilitates state penetration of the rural areas.

The township farmers' associations are essentially local corporations and are self-supporting, as their staff and activities are funded through supply, marketing, and credit functions (Stavis, 1974: 68). The association receives a handling fee for collecting the government's rice tax and it also generates a profit by processing grains. It receives income both by selling fertilizer and by marketing produce, though quantities and profit margins are strictly controlled. The second and perhaps more important source of income is the credit department, which provides both lending and savings facilities. The level of income derived varies, depending on the economic surplus of the community, the extent the association can compete with local banks, and the "general standing of the farmers' association in the community" (69-70). The government does not subsidize association credit departments, thus creating a highly competitive rural financial market which improves services and widens access. Only for special experimental programs does the government provide subsidies, as it never funds regular activities of the associations.

With their local resource base, the farmers' associations are assigned four crucial tasks in rural development: equitable distribution of seeds and fertilizer; introduction of new crops and farming techniques; reinvestment of the economic surplus into rural development; and the provision of a key organizational base for politics (103). By making the associations self-sufficient and providing extensive controls, the government has assured both a mobilization of rural resources and an equitable reinvestment process due to assured access by all producers to the inputs.

Except for a few programs, the government has not tried to counteract regional inequalities and has focused attention on ensuring that within a region (township farmers' association) there is a degree of equity in the access to agricultural inputs. Because of the desire to maintain high productivity in agriculture, the government is unwilling to redistribute resources from the high productivity areas. Therefore, the township associations are mechanisms for mobilizing surplus by the center and for monitoring the access of inputs, but are not a vehicle of government subsidy or regional redistribution.

A major function of the farmers' association is to distribute fertilizer under strict guidelines and supervision from the central government's Provincial Grain Bureau. Given the small scale and labor intensity of production in Taiwan, fertilizer is perhaps the key factor of production which determines variation in output. Because of its importance and potential for providing a basis of corruption, the associations have a complete monopoly over distribution, and violations are strictly punished. There has evolved an ethic in Taiwan of equality of access to this resource (76). Fertilizer is now distributed on a cash basis, but the amounts are carefully determined according to size of holding and type of crop grown. Formerly it was distributed only in exchange for rice. The shift from a rice-fertilizer barter system to cash purchasing has raised the potential for corruption, but close monitoring has virtually eliminated this problem. The rice-fertilizer barter system may be useful to replicate in other developing contexts where the introduction of cash purchases in the absence of controls virtually guarantees corruption. A valued feature of this sytem is that it forces the farmer to produce a staple crop and if cash crops are produced instead, their production is taxed by forcing the farmer to purchase rice at inflated prices to exchange for fertilizer.

> This exchange system has two consequences. First, it encouraged farmers to grow rice, which is synonymous with wealth and security . . . Secondly, because most farmers grew rice, virtually every farmer had access to chemical fertilizer in rough proportion to his production above home needs. This slightly favored the families with larger farm size, but pretty much assured that everyone would get some fertilizer (75-76).

A key implication of the Taiwanese fertilizer program is that the introduction of land reform (redistributing the means of production), without strict assurances of equality of access to the other factors of production, will produce, not reduce, inequities, especially if production is input intensive.

An important feature of these local organizations is their authorization to use their resources to hire staff, which assures a degree of local administrative capacity, makes these officials accountable to the farmers, and ensures a high responsiveness to local service demands. Even the personnel system is regulated, as the province associations set staff size and salary scales. The salary scale is set according to the profitability of the association, which provides incentives to increase production but lessens the ability of less productive associations to attract talented administrators. The provincial level sets the township's overall export quotas and strengthens the association's General Manager by allowing him to distribute the quotas. While these discretionary powers lead to patronage and a degree of corruption, they also infuse the local political process with limited yet tangible stakes which induce participation. The extensive regulation by the government in all other phases of production makes this limited corruption both tolerable and desirable in that it strengthens local leadership. The farmers' associations do have a significant upward political linkage, as they signal approval or disapproval of government policies, which have been changed by association demands. The distinctive feature of the Taiwan cooperatives is that they provide a new basis of local status which is circumscribed by the limited discretionary power of local officials, as well as regulations that ensure equitable *access* to productive inputs. Status, then, cannot have a significant impact on economic differentiation because it is not based on control over access to the means of production.

We note that in neither Comilla nor in Taiwan is it argued that the cooperative network was the most efficient channel for providing inputs to the rural areas. In the case of Comilla the cooperatives were a vehicle for subsidizing farmers; in the case of Taiwan they were a vehicle for preventing the development of inequalities in the rural areas and for strengthening the position of the smallest farmers. In both cases the effect of the governments' intervention was to give the cooperatives an unearned advantage over traders in the inputs which they supplied—in Comilla, by making it the vehicle for subsidies to the largest input consumers, and in Taiwan, by giving the cooperatives a legal monopoly. In Taiwan the monopoly was efficient and beneficial to the poor. The undercutting of private trade in Comilla was disadvantageous to the poor because they lacked the same access to the cooperatives as the wealthy members had.

In other societies where cooperatives are given a monopoly and are not particularly efficient, the real effect may be to raise the price of inputs to the farmer or to limit their geographical distribution. Thus the case for subsidies or for monopolies must be reviewed critically in order to assure that either will in fact benefit the rural poor. In societies in which the political commitment of the state to the poor, the administrative capacity of the state to enforce that commitment, or the administrative capacity of cooperatives to operate efficiently are missing, measures to increase the competitiveness of private traders and/or to lower their costs of doing business in the more remote areas are more likely to benefit the poor.

MARKETING

Most cooperatives are organized for providing marketing service functions, and marketing was the earliest and primary impetus for cooperative development. Group marketing is seen to provide three advantages for the small farmer: economies of scale, vertical integration of services, and bargaining power (Fox, 1979: 305). While this traditional wisdom persists, particularly the potential of gaining leverage in the marketplace by eliminating the middleman, many development theorists recently have been questioning the value of small-farmer marketing groups. An argument made increasingly is that instead the government should "improve the [conditions in the private] markets for agricultural products, inputs and rural consumer goods" (305). Before considering this alternative policy of market improvement, we shall assess the three key arguments for group marketing by cooperatives.

Economies of scale accrue to farmer groups when marketing requires investments in preliminary processing, storage, or transport that large farmers usually provide for themselves but the capacity for which is beyond the needs of individual small farmers. The greater such economies of scale are for a particular crop and the fewer the private middlemen competing to provide for them, the more attractive cooperative marketing will be to small farmers.

A second purpose for group marketing is to capture the advantages of vertically integrated production. Marketing cooperatives are most successful with traditional cash crops (sugar, tobacco, coffee, cotton), for these require further processing, export from the region and centralized marketing (Fox, 1979: 310). Given the export character of these organizations, however, they tend to serve larger producers where there is a lucrative cash crop that underwrites its organizational costs; where an effective collection and processing network can be brought into existence; where the nature of the crop allows small-holders to participate; and where there is commitment and effective monitoring by the government. The achievements of the Indian National Dairy Development Board (NDDB) and the Kenyan Tea Development Authority (KTDA) attest to the value of these "vertical cooperatives."

Marketing cooperatives that are vertically integrated generally are not useful for food crops because there is little processing and the crops are sold locally. These are the primary crops of the farmers who require the most assistance. Small private entrepreneurs can provide the service more effectively without having to bear the costs of organizational management that any cooperative incurs. Even when cooperatives are less efficient as a marketing vehicle than comparable private middlemen, however, they may be attractive as a means of directly subsidizing small farmers.

The third argument for cooperative marketing is that it enhances the bargaining power of the small farmer. Recent research on traditional marketing systems, however, contradicts the accepted wisdom that these traditional markets are disadvantageous to the small farmer:

> Most studies of traditional marketing systems find a high degree of competition with intermarket-price differences usually small and commensurate with the costs of transportation and handling. Where excessive price differences exist, the reasons are usually associated with imperfections in the general marketing system that cooperative action by small farmers is unlikely to resolve. This observation suggests that the solution to monopolistic practices is not to discourage trade through overt or covert means, as is done by many governments, but rather through governmental action to remove the conditions which lead to monopolistic practices (Fox, 1979: 312).

The advantages to cooperatives of scale and vertical integration are in tension with the objective of strengthening the power of the poor farmer. Cooperatives which are vertically integrated or which enjoy substantial economies of scale almost always are managerially more complex. The complexity of marketing stems from its crucial demands for timeliness in the coordination of pricing policies, processing, inputs, transportation, and storage facilities. If these cooperatives are to be efficient, they have to be run either by a managerially competent local elite or with extensive oversight by an administratively strong government. The first alternative is congenial to the interests of the rural poor only in the relatively rare circumstance in which rural equality is achieved at a fairly high level of development (e.g., Costa Rica). The second alternative depends not only upon the administrative competence of the government but a commitment on its part to use it on behalf of the rural poor.

When management is beyond the capacity of the local cooperative, an outside employee is frequently provided, either by the government or a government-sponsored federation. Government assistance does not end with the provision of a manager, as it often has to provide the capital for initiating and sustaining the cooperative enterprise as well. The role of government in direct management expands because the complex record-keeping and continued dependency on government funds require extensive monitoring (King, 1975: 205). In his study of Nigeria, King found that the government required cooperatives to maintain fourteen separate sets of books, a condition which finally forced the government to take over the cooperatives' accounting itself. There have been simplified accounting schemes developed (Gentil's analysis of groundnut marketing in Niger) that allow illiterates to manage the cooperative and retain control over this key function (King, 1975: 205).

While accounting systems that provide the local cooperative members control are potentially desirable, it is doubtful whether such a crucial task should be exclusively the function of the cooperative, as it facilitates elite control and corruption. In most cases it is preferable for the state to audit cooperative accounts closely and sometimes even to manage the accounting. While state accounting would appear to be a negative policy, as it reduces the cooperatives' autonomy, the very process of marketing integrates the cooperative extensively with the state. *If* the state can provide accounting services efficiently, its interference probably represents less of a danger than does elite dominance or incompetence in cooperative financial management.

Cooperatives are expensive for the government to operate; therefore the government seeks to recapture some of these costs by using the cooperative as a marketing monopoly. While this action may be justified on the grounds that the inefficiencies of monopoly marketing are actually the indirect costs of subsidizing the small farmer (assuming that cooperative members do comprise the lower 50 percent of the rural population, which is rare), this policy further distorts rural markets by introducing monopolies of varying strength and overlooks the value of private traders and alternative marketing channels. The private traders and markets have an essential role in providing timely services and credit to small-scale producers in remote areas that is far more cost-efficient than government or cooperative agencies (Lele, 1977: 502). A crucial role for private markets is in the rural consumer goods markets, particularly in perishable food products.

A major criticism of the private market intermediaries is that they charge excessive margins. Uma Lele cites considerable evidence from Africa and Asia, however, to show that, "Unlike in the case of most co-operative organizations and marketing corporations, rural traders have low overhead costs. They work on low margins and earn a meagre income" (1981: 59). Research in Kenya has found that given a realistic assessment of the difficulties of transport and the perishable nature of the product, the intermediaries do not charge excessive margins (Wilson, 1976: 267). The policy question posed by Wilson's research is "Should these 'excessive' margins be counterbalanced by price control or the establishment of a marketing board—or could these perhaps not be better reduced by seeking to remove the underlying constraints which at least in part cause (and justify) them?" (267). Recent development literature shows a shift in perspective that suggests governments should seek to improve the market conditions and not pursue costly and administratively difficult targeting programs. This does not mean that special targeting programs should be abandoned, but rather, in the absence of government improvement of general marketing conditions, special marketing programs will have little impact.

The change in perspective from organizational and administratively intensive government marketing policies towards general market improvement poses a difficult task for governments: how to intervene and improve the market yet also expand resources to appropriate groups in the rural areas. Wilson's study on small-scale marketing systems argues that partial rather than comprehensive approaches are best (268). He found that the creation of a local cooperative monopoly for marketing had proven particularly ineffective in coping with perishable food and that the really effective form of cooperation for these crops was an informal grouping. "It could be claimed that its basic informality and flexibility was its main strength, bearing in mind the perishable nature of the product handled" (268). Wilson suggests that establishment of grades and standards must match local market conditions rather than impose technical criteria based on higher quality products and sophisticated markets. The government needs to improve the environment where market intermediaries function—market *infrastructure* and *communication* (268). In several countries, local authorities do provide wholesale and retail markets and collection centers. These are often viewed as sources of revenue for the local authorities and the funds are rarely reinvested to expand local services. These services and the standards of their maintenance must be established and monitored by the central government and not left to local discretion (268).

Given the new orientation to improvement in general market infrastructure, Fox details a program for governments to pursue. This program entails three stages: market infrastructure; economic policies directed at producers, consumers, and marketing agents; and legal and organizational means for improving the marketing system. Market infrastructure includes:

> (1) The maintenance, improvement and construction of roads, waterways, ports and other transportation facilities that link producers and consumers.
>
> (2) The collection, analysis and dissemination of information on such items as prices, quantities, qualities and crop conditions.
>
> (3) The maintenance, improvement, and construction of storage and marketing facilities in both the rural and urban areas.
>
> (4) Improvements in the decision-making and managerial skills of marketing agents, including farmers (Fox, 1979: 307).

There is considerable agreement in the literature that such infrastructure is a prerequisite to effective marketing of any kind, that it should be the first target of government intervention, and that cooperative organization is appropriate only after it has been provided (Lele, 1981: 63). Lele would accompany the preceding measures with:

(5) The establishment and enforcement of a uniform system of grades, weights, and measures.

(6) The development of regulated commodity (exchange) markets to promote orderly trading and to assist in the formation of price expectations, especially open auctions (63).

Fox would keep these two measures for a later, higher stage of government intervention and would precede them with economic support activities (1979: 307-9), such as buffer stocks and price policies.

Beyond the specific policy prescriptions of Wilson (1976: 268-69), Fox and Lele and the minor differences between them, Fox's suggestions illustrate an important sequence of linkage development in reaching rural areas: *infrastructure* (physical, informational, decisional); *incentives* (price supports and subsidies); *organizations* (cooperatives, marketing boards). This sequence suggests that direct organization of rural producers is difficult and also is the last phase of intervention rather than the first (Fox, 1979: 307-8).

A strategy of improving private local markets for the benefit of the poorer people may, paradoxically enough, involve government support for what is effectively a traders' cooperative. This phenomenon is illustrated in King's (1975) analysis of Nigerian cooperatives. Produce is purchased by buyers who are nominated by their primary societies. These in turn sell either on the private market or to the cooperative marketing board. The relationship between primary society members and the union level (marketing board) is tenuous. The cooperative member's only action is to elect a buyer who buys independently and often sells on the private market to get a higher price, which is illegal but difficult to trace. This approach has several benefits which King points out:

> In reality, the effect of the cooperative marketing policy is to increase the money available in the existing marketing system. The average member sells to the subagents to whom he habitually sells

> and does not know whether his produce is eventually resold to the cooperative buyer or not . . . Thus the financing is a way for some existing traders to increase their scale of operation. There may be some indirect advantage for the cooperative in that the cooperative buyer is highly motivated to support other cooperative activities and to ensure the cooperative's continued existence (204).

Cooperative marketing in this case is a vehicle for the government to funnel funds into the rural areas to purchase farmer's produce and stimulate further production. There are several advantages to such a policy: the use of elected cooperative buyers creates an agent who becomes accountable to *local farmers* rather than a regional administrative authority; it creates competition among these crucial intermediaries for providing marketing services to members as well as nonmembers (thus lessening the intermediate margins); and it provides a flexible (though illegal) marketing intermediary which will use private and administered marketing channels. Restated, the key value of this approach is that the government has intervened and strengthened market intermediaries and at the same time fostered competition and local control of these crucial agents. The poor benefit from this aid to private traders because it increases the efficiency of the latter and enables them to pay better prices more promptly for the products of the poor.

In concluding this section, note should be made of the fact that advocates both of cooperative and private marketing arrangements argue for government regulation and support for improved infrastructure. The issue is not whether government has a linkage role in decentralized marketing systems but rather the medium by which it will have the most effect and progressive impact.

CREDIT

Provision of credit is often viewed as a key service cooperatives provide and a main inducement for people to join. Cooperatively-managed credit has several advantages over credit administered to individuals: reduced costs of supervision and assistance; efficiency in administration by stimulating group control and sanctions for noncompliance; and opportunities for building economic and social infrastructure as well as farm capital on a community-wide basis (Carroll, 1969: 92). Despite all these advantages, the introduction of formal credit into the rural areas through an organization that is elite-dominated or influenced poses serious problems of management. In this section, several issues are analyzed: the general problem of rural credit; linkages between government and credit cooperatives; and alternative government policies (linkages) for the provision of credit.

As with cooperative marketing, the policy of providing formal credit through cooperatives has been critically reconsidered. The debate has broadened, with several economists even questioning the value of formal credit because of its distorting impact on rural financial markets (RFMs), particularly its effect on informal credit sources.

The rationale for providing extensive credit to rural areas is the strategy of "supply led" development, where financial markets force the pace of development. This strategy is based on the assumption that the expansion of small-farmer production is dependent on farmers' access to high profit technology, and that to induce farmers to purchase these materials, credit with concessionary interest rates has to be provided. Several other features of the small farmers and their RFMs are assumed as well: that interest rates (not transaction costs) are the bulk of the borrowing costs; that loan demand is interest-rate elastic; that small farmers have no capacity to save; and that informal credit is inadequate, nonexistent or too expensive (Adams, 1977: 4).

The first issue to assess is the crucial assumption that concessionary interest rates are useful in both expanding rural production and reaching the marginal farmers. Several economists have argued that concessional rates are anti-developmental: "low and fixed interest rates on financial instruments retard savings and capital formation, fragment financial markets, cause inefficient allocation of resources, and also cause distortions in income distribution and asset ownership" (3). At the core of these critiques is a rejection of two government policy assumptions: that governments *can* closely regulate RFMs and that manipulation of RFMs is justified, for it offsets price distortions in other markets (5, 43). That RFMs are usually the most heavily administered and distorted markets in developing countries points to the patent failure of extensive government intervention and the need to reconsider methods of strengthening RFMs that are less aggressive (e.g., use of flexible interest rates tied to price fluctuations) and that will allow a gradual rearticulation of urban-rural markets.

In addition to the dubious value of compensating one distorted market by distorting another, the problem with using concessionary credit for compensation is that the lower interest rates concentrate credit delivery on elites and not small producers. Concessionary interest rates increase the transaction cost component of loans, forcing the lender to limit the number of borrowers and the size of the loans, such that large farmers generally are given preference.

> With higher interest rates, large borrowers would likely reduce the amount of formal loans they use. With excess loanable funds, formal lenders would attempt to expand their lending among current users of small loans as well as among new borrowers. To do so, the lender would be forced to make it more convenient for small or new borrowers to get access to formal loans. This, in turn, would reduce loan transaction costs for this class of borrowers. The drop in transaction costs may more than offset the increase in interest payments made by this group (17).

Concessionary credit may actually lessen the possibility that the targeted small producer will receive credit, and it also depresses the potential for rural savings.

An issue which formal credit programs do not confront is that borrower transaction costs for the small farmer may be quite high. These costs can be monetary or non-monetary. The former might be informal payments (bribes) to those controlling the funds, undesired expenditures on farm improvements to qualify, etc. Non-monetary costs include long periods spent travelling to and waiting for loan officials, time and transport expended as a result of having to obtain inputs at an inconvenient official outlet, productivity lost through the late arrival of credit and thus crucial inputs, and so on. These hidden costs are sometimes higher than the interest charged and often make "usurious" informal credit cheaper and more available than formal credit.

A major assumption of the "supply led" strategy is that concessional formal credit is a precondition for rural innovation. This assumption entails other assumptions about rural development which have been challenged: that small farmers do not innovate without government assistance, and that informal rural markets are inadequate for financing innovation. Analysis of the Comilla project shows that there are effective informal markets, that small farmers do innovate with informal funds, that formal credit rarely reaches these producers, and that, if it does, their position may be worsened by the diffusion of larger amounts of credit to wealthy farmers. The Comilla project accepted the impossibility of reaching the small producer and channelled credit to the medium and large producers. Not only did the larger members control the administration of credit, they directly contributed to its failure by defaulting on the majority of the credit dispersed (Khan, 1979: 412). Also because the large farmers did not have to pay for services, they used their access to cooperative credit to purchase land, thus increasing landlessness in the area (413). The improvements on the land created by subsidized government services also drove up the value of the land, increasing both its purchase price and rents, which further reduced the expansion of benefits to the rural poor. Comilla demonstrates not simply the failure of cooperative capitalism where there are high levels of inequality, but also the danger of excessive introduction of formal credit, which not only goes to the wealthy but raises land prices at a faster rate so that the poor producers cannot afford to own it. The value of credit and saving programs is that rural capital is mobilized and development stays in equilibrium with rural accumulation. There is a danger in providing so much credit so fast that the rural poor cannot absorb it and are then displaced by those who do.

King's analysis of Nigerian cooperative members found that 90 percent of informal credit was used for expenditures that increased agricultural production, while only 67 percent of the formal credit was used productively (King, 1976: 131). Informal credit is preferred because, contrary to assumed wisdom, it is often provided by friends and relatives at no interest, while formal credit entails interest.

King does point out, however, the subtle interplay of formal and informal credit, in that farmers use informal credit more often for innovation, yet the supply of formal credit may ease the access to informal credit. This phenomenon can be seen in terms of Nigerian borrowing rates, as the cooperative members who had access to more formal credit than nonmembers borrowed 82 percent of all funds from friends and relatives, while nonmembers borrowed 64 percent of their credit informally (103). The cooperative members were wealthier and thus had greater access to non-interest credit. King's analysis demonstrates the distortions created by a non-interest informal credit network and the danger of elites' not just monopolizing formal credit, but also progressively altering the informal market by reverting back to anti-usury traditions that prohibit interest (121). These traditions limit the access of the poor to informal credit. The government's provision of formal credit in areas where expanding elites revert to traditional non-interest loans is critical in re-establishing interest rates on credit and counteracting these distortions.

A complementary production relation of formal and informal credit can be derived from King's work. Farmers relied on informal credit because of its timely availability while formal credit was distrusted. Still, there was a value to the farmer in knowing that the cooperative (formal) credit would be available, albeit late and intermittent. Access to formal credit improved the farmer's community credit rating, gave him access to informal credit channels, and allowed the farmer to maximize the use of informal credit—90 percent devoted to increasing agricultural production. King argues that formal credit policymakers who seek to restrict the use of loans to productive purposes are mistaken and should consider the positive indirect impact of formal loans on the productive use of informal credit and its availability.

On the other hand, the argument that the provision of formal credit will either reach targeted small farmers or at least give them access to increased informal credit supplies is questioned by the results of the Brazilian credit program. The program has generated the largest increase in agricultural credit in any country in the world (increasing fifteen times over fifteen years with eight billion U.S. dollars committed in 1975) (Adams, 1977: 34). The ratio of agricultural-loan-to-gross-domestic-output-from-agriculture was 0.6, which is similar to U.S. levels (34). The goal of the policy was to flood the RFMs with concessional formal credit in the belief that this would filter down to the small-farmer target groups. In fact, the large farmers received a disproportionate amount of the credit, and in one area, eleven of the largest farmers received two-thirds of the increased volume of credit given to 338 farmers (34). Further research indicated that large farmers could obtain formal credit in excess of their total farm expenditures. When concessional credit is given, large farmers will demand excessive amounts, and the lender will have incentives to lend to larger producers: lower lender transactions costs; capacity to absorb larger loans; lower risks per unit of money; and secure collateral (35).

This brief discussion about the general problem of credit provision underlines the difficulties and contradictions in credit policies. The mechanisms for providing formal credit usually distort RFMs and benefit the elites. Yet formal credit is seen as positive in situations where it allows the maximization of informal credit use for productive purposes, and where it reintroduces interest rates to RFMs which have become non-interest informal credit markets. The crucial issue for government credit policy is how to strengthen the informal sources of credit and stimulate competition between formal and informal lenders. One particular need is to devise programs that orient formal lenders to direct funds through the informal lenders who service small-scale producers.

Two reasons are often given, however, for trying to eliminate informal sources of credit altogether. First, it is argued that to create a successful rural credit program with high repayment rates, a rural monopoly has to be introduced so the small farmers cannot use the informal network as an alternative. For the formal mechanism to work, the farmers must believe that they are tied into a credit system from which they cannot exit. This argument assumes that governmental credit is sufficiently beneficial and/or essential to the economy to justify monopoly costs in making it work. It is precisely this benefit which we are now doubting.

The second reason given for eliminating informal credit is that it is held to be usurious. Bottomly's studies on credit in Nigeria have indicated, however, that a 50 percent interest rate on small farmer loans was *not* high, and that it truly reflected the components of the interest rate: opportunity costs, administrative premium, risk premium (Bottomly, cited in King, 1976: 115-16). Bottomly doubts the ability of rural lenders to make substantial profits and suggests that government formal credit programs which disarticulate RFMs (separate rural from urban markets) create the preconditions for monopoly profits. He argues for improving the informal market:

> to improve the efficiency of rural financial markets it is not desirable to replace moneylenders, but to encourage institutional changes which reduce their costs . . . [I] t should be made easier for rural moneylenders to obtain finance from urban markets, they should be given stronger legal backing, and it should be made easier for borrowers' assets to be used as collateral (116).

There are two strategies by which countries can alter the RFMs: by creating new specialized financial institutions to assist small producers, or by inducing a major part of the RFM to reorient its lending to small producers (Adams, 1977: 31). The first strategy is needed where financial institutions are scarce (Africa), but not where there are ample facilities (Asia and Latin America). The creation of a new small-farmer credit agency does have the short-term impact of having a new portfolio directed to rural producers. Initial solvency generally is short-lived, however, and within two years refinancing of the small loans tends to force the agency to service larger farmers (Adams, 1977). A problem with many credit institutions is their failure to provide facilities for savings and their discouragement of savings by not demanding deposit ratios for credit. This failure to provide savings facilities in conjunction with credit services stems from the erroneous beliefs that there are no surplus funds in the rural area and that farmers would not use savings institutions.

Howse's (1974) analysis of savings clubs in Rhodesia, Lesotho, Zambia and Malawi demonstrate that they are administratively simple and yet effective. Extension agents can assist in the formation of the clubs and savings can be recorded in a stamp book. Financial control can be exercised by central authorities through the use of stamps to monitor the savings. Corruption can be limited by issuing only a small amount of stamps (e.g., a month's worth) with receipt of the completed financial forms (261-62). Savings clubs have reduced administrative costs, expanded local financial resources, and stimulated demand for high growth agricultural inputs which were in short supply.

If a new institution is to be provided to assist in the distribution of credit, it should be closely and effectively monitored by the state. If this is not possible, then institutional redundancy should be encouraged. The Taiwan cooperatives are both rigidly regulated and encourage competition among credit agencies to improve services, as interest rates are fixed at the national level (Stavis, 1974: 78). The extensive regulations of the farmers' association credit departments have limited the risk of lending, but have also increased the transaction costs to the farmers, which has driven them to commercial banks and individual lenders. There are four obstacles that the association creates for the farmer: high collateral; extensive and embarrassing credit checks; slow processing of applications; and inadequate loan size (79). The regulations governing the credit departments specify an adequate loan-deposit ratio and the deposits are kept in government banks. While the high level of regulation of the associations' credit departments is discouraging to the farmer, it does ensure access to credit; the stringent conditions also ensure that it will be used productively.

A persistent myth of rural credit is that the small farmer has a high default rate and therefore would not be served by commercial lenders. Although studies are often misleading about the actual targeting of credit to "small" producers, research in some locales has shown small producers to have a lower default rate than large producers (Khan, 1979: 412; Tendler, 1976: 27). The default rate of small farmers is largely due to vagaries in production, so that more flexible credit repayment policies and contingency funds for small-farmer credit institutions could improve the default rate.

The major problem in dealing with small borrowers is the development of effective sanctions to assure repayment. This is a particular difficulty when the attachable assets of the borrower are limited, as with tenants or those farming on communal land. One response in this situation has been informal group lending, which enhances repayment levels through joint liability and peer pressure (Adams and Ladman, 1979: 5). When used by formal institutions the results of this program have been mixed, as the lender costs of organizing the groups create relatively high transaction costs, which can restrict the expansion of loans to the rural poor (6). Informal lenders, however, often have much more ready access to social group sanctions and do not incur the same transaction costs as formal institutions. This phenomenon reinforces the desirability of strengthening informal credit markets.

A second strategy which governments can pursue is to induce the financial system to serve the small producer better through: increased supply of formal loans; use of loan size limits; adoption of lending quotas; loan guarantees or crop insurance; differential rediscounting spreads; differential reserve requirements; allocation of government free deposits or government purchases of equity in financial institutions; and differential institutional interest rates for certain ultimate borrowers (Adams, 1977: 31). Two of these mechanisms have widespread use: lending quotas and rediscount spreads.

Lending quotas are designed to aid small producers by forcing a percentage of the portfolio to be devoted to a target group with a specified loan size limit. There are three disadvantages to these quotas: loans may be redefined to meet the quota; quotas may alter the portfolio, forcing lending outside the lenders' area of expertise and raising costs; and fixed loan limits may be either inadequate or excessive (37).

Rediscount spreads are often used by host governments and particularly donors. By giving a wide spread for certain target group loans, the lender can be compensated for providing credit to the small producer. There are problems with this popular method: it may lessen the incentive of lenders to mobilize loans through savings because the discount rate is lower than the savings rate they must pay out—thus depressing rural savings; and a lender may rediscount most of the small-farmer loans and use the additional funds for larger borrowers (39). If existing financial institutions are used, then separate offices should be created for serving small-farmer clients (Tendler, 1976: 32). There is a negative bias in both lending to and interacting with the smaller clients, and this can be partially overcome through separate facilities.

Adams (1977) provides a series of policy conclusions for improving rural financial markets:

1. Flexible, nominal interest rate policy should be adopted which allows RFMs to charge and pay positive real rates of interest on agricultural loans and savings deposits.

2. Interest rate policies plus other incentives should be used to induce a major proportion of the financial market in a country to service rural financial needs.

3. Policies and programs which stress mobilization of voluntary financial savings in rural areas should be initiated. These policies should include strong incentives for households to save in financial forms, as well as providing convenient and inexpensive ways for

households to hold their savings. Initially, savings mobilization and not credit allocations should be the top priority for RFMs.

4. Much less emphasis should be placed on allocating loanable funds among sectors, lenders, and borrowers by administrative fiats. Because of fungibility, the large number of actors involved, and the geographic dispersion of operations, these fiats are largely ineffective, inefficient, and almost impossible to enforce.

5. Much less attention should be focussed on concessional interest rates as a way of inducing small farmers to use formal credit. Rather, attention should focus on reducing borrowers' loan transaction costs. Concessional interest rates have a strong adverse impact on the willingness of lenders to service agriculture in general and small farmers in particular.

6. If monopoly profits exist in informal RFMs, concessional interest rates on formal credit, even with large credit supply increases, will not treat this problem. Higher interest rates on formal credit would induce formal lenders to compete away part or all of these monopoly profits (41-42).

Whether the lack of formal credit is a constraint on improving small-holder production is a continuing debate. In most rural areas there is an informal market that can potentially service credit needs even more efficiently than formal institutions can. The evidence we have examined indicates that in most situations, provision of subsidized formal credit both distorts rural financial markets and limits access by smaller producers. Credit programs also are particularly difficult to manage and therefore strain the capacity of local organizations. Given the inherent difficulties of credit programs, their susceptibility to corruption, and the negative impact mismanagement can have for the small producers, subsidized formal credit should not be provided unless it can be effectively regulated.

PRODUCTION

Production cooperatives are distinct from service cooperatives (which provide inputs, marketing, credit services), because they directly involve the relations of production, whereas service cooperatives mediate the relationship between producers and the outside world. Production cooperatives are much harder to organize than service cooperatives for several reasons: the small scale of operation necessary; the complexity of the production task; the resistance of farmers to communal production; and the political threat posed by peasant organizations based on production relations. It is important to differentiate two categories of production cooperatives: joint production associations, where individual ownership is retained but production and implement-use is coordinated; and collective associations, where land is communally held. The distinguishing features of each cooperative and their linkage problems will be briefly reviewed.

A major constraint to the effective organization and linkage of production cooperatives is the small scale of organization required, which hinders administrative delivery. Unlike service cooperatives, which can have several thousand members and reap economies of scale, production cooperatives are effective when membership in the basic unit is kept to under 100 families (preferably to about fifty families). A major weakness and cause for failure of many production cooperatives is the superimposition of a large-scale service function onto a small-scale production function. This is perhaps the key design fault of the Ujamaa program in Tanzania, where the establishment of Ujamaa villages of several thousand members was conducive to service delivery but not collective production (von Freyhold, 1979: 59). Agricultural administrative systems are frequently designed on this faulty basis despite increasing evidence that the nature of production and, more specifically, the character of the technology and cropping pattern "place limitations on the organizational forms that can be used for production and thus indirectly affect the effectiveness with which cooperative institutions can be established and maintained" (Long, 1970: 344).

Complexity of the production task is a second difficulty which production cooperatives must overcome. To be successful, cooperatives have to employ a technology and crop mix that will effectively utilize the local labor supply and thus overcome a major problem of cooperative production—the intelligent use of communal labor (von Freyhold, 1979: 30). Cooperative production, particularly communal, requires that there be some productivity gains to underwrite the organizational costs of the cooperative. These requirements both to employ labor and yet to provide greater returns to labor through the introduction of technology seem contradictory, especially if mechanization is chosen as the route to higher productivity. The problem of balancing these two demands is best solved through a diversified system of production which includes both cash and subsistence crops and spreads out peak labor demands, in contrast to large firms which specialize in one or two crops. "Also, it seems that smaller working groups are more compatible with a more diversified system of production and can allow for the development of ancillary nonagricultural activities" (Long, 1970: 347). The problems of peak labor demand also can be lessened by the use of perennial crops like sisal, which require high and constant labor levels. Irrigation, too, provides the possibility of staggering crop cycles and thus using labor more evenly. Even when there is an appropriate match between crop types, technology mix and the labor supply, cooperative production demands discipline which is difficult to elicit, much less impose. An additional complicating factor to collective production is the mechanism of payment, which poses accounting problems and raises the potential for corruption.

A third obstacle to cooperative production is the peasant farmers' resistance to collective production because of their perception of risk and their subsistence orientation. Even in socialist communal production, the individual plot remains a crucial economic and symbolic asset for the peasant. In discussing peasant resistance, it is important to distinguish the ownership pattern of the land that is turned into a cooperative. Communal production is most easily formed on state or expropriated foreign lands, where large-scale production has occurred previously (Grissa, 1973: 72). It is most difficult to form communal production cooperatives from existing private holdings, as wage payments for work are not acceptable tradeoffs for the loss of land. The problem of resistance underscores the need for local commitment to make cooperatives function and the inadequacy of imposing cooperatives from above, even where there is a degree of central commitment.

Production Cooperatives with Individual Land Parcels. This is the most common form of production cooperative, and collective management can range from simple pooling of equipment to complex management of production decisions. Irrigation facilities or machinery allocation are typically the basis of these production cooperatives. Because of the instrumental focus of these cooperatives (machinery or irrigation facilities), they are rarely autonomous and often entail committee leadership, which usually includes a member of the local administration. To examine the problem of organization and linkage to production cooperatives composed of individual parcels, the experience of several countries will be assessed: Taiwan, Sri Lanka, and Thailand.

In Taiwan, the irrigation system has proved to be highly efficient due to the close ties between the farmers and the association-employed technical management. The responsiveness of the technical staff is due to several factors: they are employed by the farmers, there are rewards and punishments for management results; managers have a high level of technical training; and the operating budget is dependent on collecting fees that increase with program effectiveness (Bottral, 1977: 247). A major problem with production organizations is the "distance" between the individual producer and the technical assistance personnel and managers of production. There often is little or no incentive to induce these local agents to improve their services, especially to the poorer producers. Taiwan has limited these problems by making the technical assistance agents accountable to local producers and by subdividing the irrigation associations into small working squads (ten to fifteen farmers) which can effectively monitor local irrigation and service delivery. The local associations are also forced to become financially involved in irrigation, as the government has limited its role by providing only 50 percent of the construction budgets and making the associations cover the balance, as well as recurrent costs. These associations are very effective and in consultation with the technical staff achieved a major innovation in crop rotation. This latter system allows programming of production and controls the cropping pattern by the distribution of water (247). In Taiwan, rigid control by the state over the provision of inputs (water and fertilizer) is a key mechanism by which production is controlled and equitable distribution of resources is assured.

The organization of Taiwanese agricultural production is very effective due to the intensity of administration. The sophistication of the local administration, coupled with the commitment of the center to rural development, distinguishes Taiwan from most developing countries. The local organization of production, though, does provide insights into the problems of local production organizations and their relations with the state. The township farmers' association is the organization linking the farmer to government services and is essentially a locally owned corporation (service cooperative) that derives its income from its monopoly in grain processing and storing; marketing of agricultural products and supplies, and consumer goods; and credit (Stavis, 1974: 61). It is through these township associations that the government exercises close control and assistance linkages.

Farmers' associations are divided into sub-components (150-200 members) called "agricultural small groups," which are coterminous with a village and elect their own chairman, who is an unpaid linkman with the township farmers' association (64-65). The agricultural small group, along with the irrigation small group, is the only collective institution at the village level and is highly dependent on the farmers' associations. There are two features of agriculture that pose alternatives to the "level of local organization" question in Taiwan. First, the farms are very small, with a mean size of one hectare, and extremely labor intensive, both of which would facilitate small-scale local producer organizations and cooperatives. The high productivity, though, of these farms is dependent on an effective organization of services that provides access to large quantities of fertilizer, high-yielding seeds, and irrigation networks. The scale of local organization, then, was determined by the efficiency requirements of service delivery, rather than the scale of production. This scale has proved possible in Taiwan because of the quality of the rural infrastructure, which limits the costs of service provision to so many small producers. In other developing countries, the issue of service efficiency, given a weaker infrastructure, may have to be achieved at lower levels of scale.

If Taiwan did not heavily regulate input provision (especially fertilizer), competition for inputs would be fierce and economic differentiation would be heightened, thus enhancing the potential conflict local organizations would have to arbitrate. A crucial reason for the stability of Taiwan's rural production and the viability of its local organizations is the rigid allocation by the state of quotas for lucrative export crops. This limits greatly the conflict that local organizations must arbitrate, ensures adequate food crops and stabilizes export prices.

The government limits indigenous organization by making village-level organizations dependent on the township level. "The common thread running through these different village level organizations is that they have no income, no permanent professional staff, and no power to make any allocations. Their purpose is to provide channels for informing the people of various government, farmers' association, and irrigation association decisions and programs" (113).

The case of Taiwan demonstrates the tendency of governments to pre-empt local farmer organizations and to subordinate production cooperatives by making them dependent on larger service cooperatives which are easier for the government to regulate. The use of close control and assistance linkages at the service cooperative level and the absence of such linkages at the production cooperative level suggest the government's belief in using service organization linkages to control production indirectly rather than attempting to organize production directly.

The cultivation committees (CCs) of Sri Lanka demonstrate another approach to the balancing of central involvement and local leadership in agricultural production. The CCs are well-established functional political units, defined in terms of a *Yaya* (tract of adjoining paddy fields dependent upon the same source of water) (Blackton, 1974: 48). The management of irrigation water and the selection of the variety of crops to be planted give these committees a crucial technical core of a scale that limits both institutional expansion and hierarchical control from the center.

The limited successes which the CCs and land reform have attained are in part due to institutional backing by the committed Department of Agrarian Services, which is separate from the other major ministries servicing the agricultural sector. The success of the CCs is also in part due to their direct linkage with local agricultural agencies and their access to political channels of influence. The CCs are locally controlled, technical organizations whose leadership provides access to the local political arena and thus a mechanism for settling technical problems that have become political issues. The arrangement also provides the CCs with access to an alternative channel of influence if they cannot reach agreements with local technical agencies directly. Thus the CC is a small-scale technical agency that facilitates local control and limits direct control or technical intervention, yet can make demands on the center either directly or through village political institutions.

A major threat to the institutional viability of the CCs is the tendency of the center to overload them with a variety of technical tasks. This burden is coupled with the inherent multiple programmatic focus of a production organization. There is a contradiction between the multiple-function imperative of agricultural production and the virtues of single-function local organizations. The simplicity of the latter facilitates local control and provides institutional cohesion based on the provision of a single desired service. This contradiction cannot be resolved, but can be managed by reducing the organization's territorial scale so that there is a uniformity of production that generates a consensus on cropping patterns and other management issues.

The CCs also demonstrate the conditions under which effective local leadership and organization of production are likely to be supported by farmers. "[T]he success of cultivation committees in levying taxes on farmers is related less to the potential level of farmer demand for reciprocal services . . . than to the numerical importance of farmers compared to other elements in the rural population" (Moore, 1979: 247). There are two implications of this hypothesis for the success of locally controlled production organizations. First, a high level of social interaction is related to a high proportion of households engaged in cultivation. The prevalence of cultivation leads to a more intense involvement in village affairs and commitment to organizations that are village controlled. The second implication involves the character of successful local organization leadership, which has two attributes: involvement in agriculture (promoting their own self-interest), yet subject to the moral pressures of local producers; and proximity to local cultivators (247-48). Committees that succeeded had leaders that were involved in agriculture, perceived their self-interest as dependent on the improvement of local production, and were willing to assume the tasks that entailed little reward. The leadership of committees that failed had little interest in cultivation, were partially outside the moral community of production, and had an economic base in trading or landownership. These findings demonstrate two styles of leadership that may be essential for expanding community development, but are contradictory in terms of local control and organizational coherence. The basis of authority (local economic and social attachments) that can successfully exercise control over production does not provide the means for linking the community to a wider environment to attract external resources.

The case of Sri Lanka is important not simply for these propositions about local organization and leadership, but as an example of the implications of rural transformation for local organizations. The homogeneity of function achieved by the involvement in cultivation of a high proportion of the population strengthens local leadership, while the introduction of nonagricultural employment reduces this leadership capacity. To the extent that a progressive government seeks to expand rural employment in nonagricultural activities or even in complementary activities, the basis of local leadership is undermined, which in turn undermines the administrative basis of the strategy—mobilization of the rural resources through strengthened local organizations. With the erosion of local leadership, the state must intervene to limit elite domination of the rural areas.

Despite the limitations and difficulty of creating production cooperatives, in Sri Lanka they are perceived as essential to solving problems of local resource use and application of sanctions to local cultivators (Stavis, 1974: 60). Thus the management of local irrigation systems produced an effective basis of local authority because the issue of *resource access* could be locally rather than externally determined. The cooperatives were not perceived as instruments of changes that required external resources.

A crucial factor determining whether a collective production activity is a success is the incentive structure that is created. Incentives are especially important where success is dependent on changing traditional behavior. The experience of production cooperatives indicates the difficulty of external agents' directly "organizing" the rural population at this crucial primordial level. The failure of the imposed cooperative form in the production function is particularly striking, as it attests to the difficulty of such base-level intervention for purposes of imposing or providing an institutional format. Such low-level intervention requires *incentives*, not just institutional forms. The Phimai Self-Help Settlement District in Thailand was introduced to a silk production project designed to supplement and improve local incomes.

> The project (1) aimed to transform a traditional system that appeared inefficient at the individual farm level, (2) required

(or seemed to require) official collaboration and guidance, (3) depended on a mix of individual, group, and bureaucratic efforts, and (4) promised significant increases in yield and income if farmers would invest greater time, care, and effort in sericulture (Cunningham, 1980: 2).

The project failed partly because of insufficient technical assistance in the operation of machines, but primarily because there were inadequate incentives. The following is a list of problems with the incentive structure of the project:

1. Farmer participants had no personal investments in the scheme, other than time. All important inputs (funds, technical expertise, etc.) came from outside.

2. Silk production was a supplemental source of household income, a way to spread risk and supplement their incomes.

3. The project management staff had no real stake in the success of the scheme. Their salaries, status, and prospects were not much affected by the outcome of this project. Success actually could have had some adverse effects—improving the relative status . . . of peasant farmers in comparison with the civil servants (2).

This project clearly failed to create sufficient incentives to induce either producer or bureaucratic interest.

Production Cooperatives with Joint Land Management. Collective cooperatives are the most difficult to manage, much less provide linkages to. This approach is used for four principal reasons: to promote socialist collective agriculture; to deal with traditional areas where there is communal or semi-communal management (i.e., pasture and forest land); to provide for land pooling as a solution to the problem of production units that are too small; and to facilitate land reform by communally farming large expropriated estates (Carroll, 1969: 38-39). Communal production cooperatives are important to analyze because, unlike production cooperation based on individual parcels, they have a higher potential for autonomy and indicate the difficulties of indigenous organizing by the rural poor.

Latin America's experience with collective production is best seen in the *ejidos* of Mexico, which were initially supported by the government as part of a revolutionary land reform in the 1930s.

The ejidos were formed primarily on large, well-developed expropriated estates which were intensively farmed, and commercially oriented. The peasant unions that created the ejidos were effective local organizations. Despite the coherence and indigenous base of the ejidos, communal production posed two serious problems. First, there was a difficulty in achieving effective leadership and discipline (40). Effective leadership was stifled by the cultural beliefs in the dishonesty of leaders, which was compounded by the lack of visible accounts and simple accounting procedures. A second difficulty which plagues most communal production systems is the difficulty of rewarding effort in proportion to members' contributions. "The system of 'anticipos' [advanced sales proceeds] which the Ejido Bank paid to the beneficiaries frequently degenerated into simple wage payments . . . and . . . often fostered a negative attitude toward hard work and initiative" (41). These internal problems, coupled with the government's shift in policy and withdrawal of assistance, particularly credit, caused most of the ejidos to collapse. Some ejidos still exist and a few of these are prosperous. These successful organizations had the following attributes: access to consumption goods, relatively large landholdings, youthful membership, strong yet open leadership, financial independence, cohesion created by the ejidos' external conflicts, production of a cash crop, effective independent management of accounts, and consensus on job remuneration (42-50). The defining features of the successful ejidos were both their autonomy and the separation of leadership (political) functions from management (technical) functions. A crucial technical task which has been separated from the leadership is accounting, which mitigates the traditional distrust of leaders.

The lack of any reliable system of financial control is considered by some the most serious internal problem of the Tanzanian Ujamaa villages (von Freyhold, 1979: 87). Unlike the ejidos, leaders were trusted by the members and the accounting requisite of institutionalized doubt was absent. This led to extensive corruption by the village leadership. Further, effective accounting required training both for the cooperative bookkeepers and the members so that they could monitor the bookkeepers. In the absence of such training, the state should have provided independent accounting. The inability or unwillingness of the state to supply this service is one reason for Ujamaa's failure (88).

Tunisia's cooperative program demonstrates several difficulties of communal production. Like the ejidos, production cooperatives were created from large, well developed and mechanized expropriated estates (Grissa, 1973: 72). They were kept intact as collective production units because the government feared both loss of productivity if small-holder agriculture took root, and elite dominance if the large farmers purchased the land. The cooperative program was rapidly expanded, which disrupted agriculture, lowered productivity, and forced the state into debt. There were several defects in the Tunisian program. First, the use of such large-scale production units (averaging 1000 hectares) taxed the limited managerial and technical skills that were available. Production units should have been divided into manageable units at first, even though economies of scale were lost. Second, rapid expansion of the movement virtually eliminated possible experimentation with different institutional approaches, as well as the preparation of local producers. Third, the cooperatives were imposed on the peasantry, and as members, they were not consulted, as management was responsible only to government authorities. Fourth, what initiative management might have exercised was limited by extensive external interference which often determined cropping patterns and employment levels that were unsuited to local conditions.

The key failure of communal cooperatives, though, was the government's complete reliance on this institutional form as the means of transforming agriculture. The priority of cooperatives and their lack of liquid assets forced the government to go deeply into debt both to initiate and to sustain these organizations, which were very inefficient (84). The willingness of the government to disregard costs was demonstrated by its denial of losses, as well as the mounting debt due to the cooperatives. Tight state control of the cooperative management, coupled with the cooperatives' access to extensive government financial support, led the managers to view the cooperatives as state enterprises entitled to bailouts. There were few if any incentives or sanctions to increase productivity by the managers, particularly since the state protected them and publicly denied losses. The cooperatives monopolized the access to productive inputs, particularly credit, which deprived the more productive small farmers of credit. Private investment was depressed further because small farmers refused to invest for fear that their farms would be incorporated into the cooperative movement.

The case of Tunisia demonstrates the danger of an agricultural strategy that rejected institutional redundancy. The state became dependent upon the cooperatives for production and employment, and thus could use only assistance linkages as mechanisms of influence. The extensive facilitative linkages promoted agricultural stagnation, as they excluded small producers and overly supported inefficent production cooperatives. The lack of institutional redundancy removed the credibility of the center's terminating support, further weakening the control linkages. Control linkages interfered with the details of cooperative operations, thereby stifling initiative instead of setting production parameters with an incentive structure to achieve output goals. The case of Tunisia clearly underscores the need for the center to promote institutional redundancy which allows inefficient organizations to fail, thereby strengthening both facilitative and regulative linkages.

The cases we have reviewed on the different types of production cooperatives suggest several lessons. The first is the necessity of keeping the effective production units small, certainly under 100 families and preferably much less. Where the attempt has been made to use larger units, as in Tanzania and Tunisia, it has resulted in failure. In the People's Republic of China, where large units were constructed in the Great Leap Forward, the effective unit of production was returned to groups of about thirty families in the 1960s.

The second lesson is the importance of granting substantial autonomy, control, and responsibility to the basic cooperative units. Even in Taiwan, where the state generally exercises extremely tight control over local organizations, the local irrigation associations enjoy substantial operational discretion and themselves employ their staff, who are dependent on the effectiveness of the organization's operations for their benefits. In Tunisia, where the state closely controlled the operations of production cooperatives and the management was responsible to the government, the experiment completely failed. Agricultural production requires prompt and continuous adaptive decision-making and "unreasonable" spurts of effort. These are likely only if operations are controlled by those who will be directly hurt by failure.

The third conclusion is that the state control of production cooperatives that is exercised should be indirect. Taiwan effectively regulates several aspects of its irrigation associations through its tight control of the farmers' associations from which they draw many services. Production cooperatives are best influenced by policies which create incentives for desired types of behavior and parameters within which action is permissible, rather than by detailed regulation.

Fourth, the importance of good and independent accounting is emphasized by both the Mexican and Tanzanian experiences. Action by the state to assure its provision should be seen more as a form of assistance than as external regulation, for it is needed by the membership to control their own leadership.

Fifth, production cooperatives seem to benefit from the existence of separate, parallel, general function institutions of representation. Such institutions provide a second channel for communicating problems to the center and thus often can circumvent blockages in the feedback system directly concerned with agriculture. Equally important, where cooperatives become the primary vehicle for political mobility, their leadership takes on functions and attributes which are not particularly conducive to production. Alternative representative institutions draw off some of the politicization that otherwise infects cooperatives and permit members to concentrate more upon managerial competence in selecting the leaders of their cooperatives.

Finally, those production cooperatives that have been successful have benefitted from relatively egalitarian rural social structures. Taiwan is notable for its strong unimodal system of agriculture. In Sri Lanka the successful irrigation cultivation committees were led by farmers who shared the production interests of the rest of the membership.

CONCLUSIONS ON THE CHOICE BETWEEN THE COOPERATIVE AND PRIVATE SECTORS

The preceding analysis of the supply, marketing, credit and production functions in small-holder agriculture suggests some guidelines for the choice of organizations to provide rural economic infrastructure. Our policy objectives are that small producers have access to the services which they need for high productivity agriculture and that they receive these services with the greatest efficiency and lowest price possible. In principle most of these services can be provided to small producers either cooperatively or by private enterprises. Only in the case of inherently bulky factors of production, such as irrigation, is private ownership incompatible with small-holder agriculture. For the other aspects of economic infrastructure—the provision of supplies, markets and credit—it is an open question as to whether cooperatives or private entrepreneurs are the better vehicle of service. Since private middlemen are in business for profit, it is tempting to assume that cooperatives would provide a better income to farmers by distributing those profits among them.

In effect, the formation of a cooperative socializes some aspect of the economic structure of an area. Cooperatives are a more complex managerial form than small businesses, however. Collective income-generating activities also always carry a high risk that a public benefit will be illegitimately transformed into private good. Leaders may use their position in the organization to shift income from the members to themselves. One of the lessons of the cooperative movement is that exploitation and corruption are as important problems as inefficiency and, indeed, often are the hidden causes of the latter.

From the point of view of the poor the choice between private and cooperative service organizations depends on the availability of managerial skills and controls. If both are supplied, the cooperative form offers a very attractive way for poor producers to overcome deficiencies in economic services without contributing to the further differentiation of rural wealth. When either is absent, however, private enterprises, despite their shortcomings as vehicles of equity, are likely to outperform cooperatives.

Both management skills and controls can be provided either by the membership or the state but they must be ample if the cooperative is to benefit the poor. Internal controls require (a) that information on managerial performance be available to the members in understandable form and (b) that the membership be relatively homogeneous economically and socially. In poor communities managerial skills are usually very limited. Either the cooperative has to be kept small and simple or extensive external management assistance has to be provided if performance information is to be kept before the members. If the second precondition for internal control—relative homogeneity—is not fulfilled, the poor will have difficulty protecting their interests, as those who control an area's resources usually are able to dominate its community organizations as well. The problem is not simply one of economic equality, for in socially divided communities one geographic or lineage faction of the cooperative may take advantage of another (Hyden, 1973). Thus the internal control of democratic "voice" must be supplemented with that of either "exit" (Hirschman, 1970) or state supervision. The combination of effective monopoly and weak controls is the most deadly of all.

When a cooperative enjoys a monopoly or is providing an externally subsidized service, some degree of central control is essential if inequalities are not going to develop in the distribution of benefits. These external controls need to become progressively tighter as differences among the members become more severe. External controls require administrative competence on the part of the state and the political commitment to resist manipulation by local elites. The latter is particularly difficult to sustain when rural inequalities are great, for local elites then often have a good deal of political influence.

When cooperatives have the privileged position of being either a monopoly or a vehicle for providing state subsidized services, one of the following four rigorous sets of conditions must be fulfilled if the poorer producers are to benefit fairly:

(1) The cooperative is small and simple and the members are relatively homogeneous economically and socially.

(2) Good management skills are widely available among a membership which is fairly homogeneous.

(3) A central organization has the administrative capacity to provide management assistance and some supervision to cooperatives with relative homogeneity among the members.

(4) The state has the administrative capacity and the strength of political will to provide detailed managerial assistance for cooperatives and to control attempts by some members to gain advantage at the expense of others.

The first of the preceding sets of conditions would preclude the more complex infrastructural services needed for agricultural production and the latter three alternatives are regrettably uncommon in the developing world. In most circumstances it is imperative that the market remain competitive and that production subsidies for individual farmers not be provided through community-wide (inclusive) organizations.

In most agricultural systems, then, we see a very large role for private enterprise and a quite limited one for formal, protected cooperatives. This means that even those states that are most concerned with rural equity must give more attention to measures that promote the efficiency and competitiveness of private rural middlemen.

A role for cooperatives does remain, however, even when the rural population is not homogeneous and the state is neither progressive nor administratively strong. First, they may be organized by communities to restore competitiveness to markets over which traders have an oligopoly. This was the original and very effective function of cooperatives in East Africa (Hyden, 1976). To survive, such cooperatives often need moderate subsidies to overcome the disadvantages of late entry in the market and the costs of collective organization. These are subsidies to the organization and not to the individuals, however, and they are designed to restore competitiveness to a market, not to undercut it.

A second function of cooperative-like organizations in uncongenial settings is as relatively small groupings limited to the rural poor. As such, these alternative local organizations can tackle a few of the problems that specially concern the poor, although they will be unable to deal with all of their needs for economic infrastructure. Alternative local organizations also often can be vehicles for individual subsidies if the state protects them from community sanction, for they frequently meet our condition number one above. We will return to a fuller analysis of the problems of supporting alternative local organizations in the next chapter.

THE LINKAGE LESSONS OF THE COOPERATIVE EXPERIENCE

Our discussion of the involvement of cooperatives in agricultural supplies, marketing, credit and production has revealed many problems but it also has uncovered a number of lessons about the appropriate links between cooperatives and the center. Some of these were specific to a particular function but more general conclusions can be drawn as well.

The extensive study of cooperatives by the United Nations Research Institute for Social Development (UNRISD) differentiated linkages into two types: facilitative and regulative, which broadly coincide with our assistance and control ones (UNRISD, 1975; and Inayatullah, 1972: 254-55). Assistance (or facilitative) linkages consist of providing local organizations with material inputs, organizational and managerial services, technical knowledge, and facilities for storage, transportation and marketing. Regulative linkages are a subset of control ones and provide registration of cooperatives (definition of membership); auditing control; price structures, laws governing operations; and legal provisions governing savings and lending levels.

The importance of linkages to cooperative success was affirmed by the UNRISD studies, which found that the two central factors affecting cooperatives were the character of the local community and the existence of external linkages. Cooperatives functioned best in communities having the following high solidarity characteristics: homogeneity of belief; uniformity of status; flexible social structure; developmental solidarity (predisposition to community action); extensive external exposure; and an activist orientation to nature (Inayatullah, 1972: 268). Such communities are relatively well developed and only marginally stratified. Uphoff and Esman's summary analysis of local organizations in Asian rural development also affirms the importance of ". . . relative equity in the ownership of assets, particularly land, [as] a precondition for successful organization. . ." (1974: xvii-xviii).

The UNRISD studies found that the cooperatives in high solidarity communities that achieved high impact had a combination of low control and high assistance linkages, while the low impact cooperatives experienced either a high control linkage only or high control and low assistance linkages (Inayatullah, 1972: 254-55). High impact was measured by four factors: extent to which the cooperative increased solidarity in the community and improved its living conditions; ability of cooperatives to innovate; ability to redistribute income; and extent the cooperative had established effective democratic authority (268).

No cooperative was found by UNRISD to be completely autonomous of the center. High impact cooperatives did not have much potential for becoming independent of their linkages to the state, especially the assistance ones (269). Uphoff and Esman found that "local institutions which are separated and isolated from other levels are likely to be impotent developmentally [and that] *linkage* [is] a more significant variable than *autonomy* when it comes to promoting rural development" (1974: xii). Their research indicates that support from the center is important, even if it carries controls with it. The Uphoff and Esman study, unlike those of UNRISD, included a case where both control and assistance were high, and found cooperative performance to be good there.

It seems to us that the issue of linkages between the state and cooperatives is more complex than a simple dichotomy between facilitative and regulative ties. All the major cooperative systems experience a mixture of both assistance and control. What is more important is the purpose for which both types are employed. Either form of linkage can be used to strengthen or destroy the vigor of the cooperative movement.

Control linkages can be broken down into those that are coercive, limiting, supportive and equalizing. Assistance linkages can be categorized as enfeebling, supportive, equalizing and redistributive.

Coercive controls are designed to weaken if not destroy the local organization. Examples of techniques used are: excessively high credit rates; refusals to register or recognize the organization; and withdrawal of supportive control linkages (e.g., accounting). An example of coercive linkages is the Mexican administration's policy toward the ejidos. Most cooperatives cannot withstand the condition of autonomy, much less coercive relations with the state, although the Mexican ejidos that survived were much strengthened by their independence.

Limiting controls are intended not to weaken but rather to freeze organizational development at a particular level. These regulations impose restrictions on the scale and range of functions an organization can undertake, such as exclusion from certain cash crops. Most often limiting controls are designed solely to enable the state to retain dominance over the organization, particularly to keep it from becoming too powerful politically. As such these controls generally are intentionally negative.

On occasion, however, limiting controls are imposed to help the poor. They create a predefined procedural framework to provide legal protection for innocent members and permit only a restricted range of functions so as to reduce complexity and simplify the management task. The problem with such well-intentioned limiting controls is that they often are counter-productive. The members cannot understand their legal rights and thus are subject to domination by those who do. Furthermore, the restrictions tend to stifle the very innovations and initiatives that are necessary to the survival of new organizations.

The Taiwan and Tunisia experiences suggest that the state should not "reach down" and organize local task-specific organizations but rather assist and control such "indigenous" forms through service delivery by intermediate organizations (i.e., cooperative unions). Top-down control is established through the regulation of services and not through imposing a structural blueprint on local organizations. This observation is in accord with that of Uphoff and Esman, who contend that "Local institutions should have more than one level of organization, probably a two-tier pattern, in which the lower tier performs functions at the neighborhood or small group level while the other undertakes more complex business and governmental activities that require relatively large-scale operations" (1974: xviii).

Supportive controls improve the administrative strength of the local organization. Techniques include bookkeeping, management principles, and regulations that assist the members to bring sanctions against the organization.

A crucial supportive linkage that the state can provide is financial auditing. The function performed should be that of an accountant and not that of a comptroller (determining where funds should go). Local organizations need to be able to decide on their own investments and be allowed to fail, but failure need not be facilitated by poor accounting, which is often the case. There is a need for this function to be insulated from the direct control of the elected leadership, for poor and/or corrupt bookkeeping is a primary cause for cooperative failure. An example of such a linkage is the state's provision of bookkeeping services to the Nigerian cooperatives.

Another supportive control is the regulation of salary scales and recruitment standards. These parameters of the personnel system often need to be regulated externally to put limits on the extent of patronage.

Some states control cooperatives very tightly and where central administrative competence is strong, this restriction does not appear to hurt their performance. Nonetheless, it is important that the local leadership always control at least some resources. Central control over all of a cooperative's resources removes any incentive for talented people to seek leadership positions and limits the motivation for members to exert themselves in the organization.

Equalizing controls directly assist the rural poor by imposing limits on access, thus limiting monoplization of benefits by elites. They usually entail limitations on the scale of productive assets that members use. Techniques used are ceilings on credit, fertilizer quotas, and acreage limits. Examples of equity control links are the Ethiopian Peasant Associations' ten hectare land limits and the Taiwan fertilizer quotas.

Controls can ensure that equitable access to cooperative resources is maintained but they cannot generate actual redistribution (Uphoff and Esman, 1974: xvii). Equalizing controls in Taiwan which regulate the distribution of productive inputs are highly effective in *limiting* further rural differentiation, but it took land reform to *change* the distribution of wealth. Equalizing regulations require close monitoring for there is a high potential for corruption. The type of input distribution system also affects the potential for diversion of benefits and the mix of crops produced. A crop-input bartering system appears to be less susceptible to corruption than an input system based on cash transactions. The farmers' associations in Taiwan bartered fertilizer for rice and have only recently switched to a cash system (which has been effective because of the extensive monitoring of the local organizations). The crop-bartering system also allows the center to force the farmer to produce a staple crop as the exchange crop for inputs, thereby taxing the farmer for producing export crops.

Enfeebling assistance so overwhelms an organization with resources that it becomes dependent on the center. This smothering of a local organization's independence and initiative may or may not be intentional. In the former case the state may make irresistibly attractive resources available to cooperatives so as to co-opt them and prevent their becoming politically independent.

As often, generous assistance is unintentionally enfeebling. Excessive assistance linkages often weaken organizations by stifling local contributions and by providing resources which do not correspond to locally felt needs (von Freyhold, 1979: 183). Assistance linkages must stimulate, not replace, local efforts (Uphoff and Esman, 1974: xii). Taiwan has dealt with this problem by limiting the center's contribution for local construction projects to a maximum of 50 percent of construction costs, thereby leaving the balance of construction and all of the recurrent costs to the local organization. A potentially enfeebling aspect of assistance linkages is that they rarely entail clear schedules of termination, which impedes the efficiency of their use. Linkage sequences will be discussed in the next chapter in more detail. Here it is important to stress the need for clear termination schedules to improve use and minimize the dependency attitude of local recipients.

Supportive assistance includes the provision of material inputs, training programs, managerial services, and facilities for storage, transportation and marketing. Supportive linkages are distinguished from enfeebling ones not by their character but by their stimulation, rather than stifling, of local commitment and initiative. Thus, for example, central funding for local projects should be designed so as to draw out community resources and test local commitment. This can be done without necessarily rewarding the areas which already are better off and thus have resources to contribute. Tanzania, for example, requires the village cooperative to contribute labor only, a commodity that is probably more readily supplied in the poor areas than the wealthy ones.

Another form of much-needed supportive assistance is managerial. We mentioned earlier that accounting and other administrative tasks often need to be insulated from the leadership (i.e., political) tasks of mobilizing member support for the cooperative. Where local managerial capability is weak and the state is administratively strong, central managerial assistance is appropriate, especially when marketing is vertically integrated. Such assistance can take the form of advisors or a central cadre of technical personnel whose members are seconded to cooperative societies on subsidized terms. Nonetheless, our research shows the value of the local cooperative's being responsible for the payment of its staff. When the cooperative staff is paid locally it becomes more accountable to the local producers and has a self-interest in making the organization a success.

The wide and inexpensive distribution of inputs needed by small farmers may depend on the removal of market imperfections. In situations in which private traders are making monopoly profits or providing poor service, it often is appropriate to provide cooperatives with a subsidy for entering these markets and restoring competition.

Equalizing assistance is designed to limit but not exclude elite use. Examples include: seeds for crops that elites prefer not to produce; rudimentary implements that best service small producers; extension of advice or non-mechanized small production techniques; and pump wells that provide wide access to irrigation.

Unimodal agricultural production is encouraged by anything which makes inputs that are appropriate for labor-intensive users widely available. This may include subsidies, since even if more advantaged farmers use the inputs they will make greater use of labor. Because equalizing assistance is available to all producers it tends to have lower unit costs of distribution and to attract less elite hostility than would subsidies targeted to the poor.

Redistributive assistance excludes elites and directly reaches the small producer. Examples are highly subsidized credit with asset limitations; extension advice solely for the small farmer; fertilizer quotas based on land holdings; and direct grants to small producers.

Redistributive linkages are targeted and are more costly to provide, as they require extensive monitoring and smaller scale in distribution. They are preferable to equalizing assistance when the program involves direct relief or the local elites would absorb most of the benefits. An example of a targeted redistributive linkage is the Ethiopian extension service (EPID), which is supposed to provide assistance only to members of the peasant associations. We will examine targeted, redistributive linkages in more detail in the next chapter.

The general conclusion from the foregoing analysis of control and assistance linkages is that both can have positive or negative effects on cooperative development for the poor. Enfeebling assistance and coercive and limiting controls have undesirable effects. Supportive controls and supportive and equalizing assistance are most helpful, assuming a moderately committed and administratively competent state. Equalizing controls and redistributive assistance, though positive in their impact, are politically and administratively very demanding. When the state is at all lacking in these attributes the attempt to use them may well be counter-productive, with local elites actually capturing for themselves the benefits that were intended for the poor.

A general linkage prescription that emerges from our research is the value of redundancy for both control and assistance linkages.

Given the weakness of most administrative systems in developing countries, it is desirable to enhance reliability of communication and service delivery by fostering redundancy both of linkages and local organizations. Only where the central administration has both a high administrative capacity and a strong commitment to the small producer should a non-redundant approach be used.

The literature on cooperatives tends to stress the downward-looking aspects of control and assistance linkages. Yet upward channels of representation are vital as well if the needs of the rural poor are to be heard and met. A linkage lesson that was found important in several cooperative experiences (Sri Lanka, Taiwan) was the provision of political channels of mobility outside the cooperatives, which limited their politicization. In Sri Lanka, the access to political channels by local technical organizations (irrigation associations) allowed external arbitration of disputes that threatened to destroy the organization. This access also provided a means to demand services from technical agencies above the local organization. When cooperatives are the central local political arena, their capacity to perform technical functions quickly deteriorates (Uphoff and Esman, 1974: xix).

REFERENCES

Adams, Dale W. 1977. Policy issues in rural finance and development. Columbus: Studies in Rural Finance, Agricultural Finance Program, Department of Agricultural Economics and Rural Sociology, Ohio State University. Paper No. 1; June 15.

__________, and Ladman, Jerry R. 1979. Lending to rural poor through informal groups: a promising financial market innovation. Columbus: Studies in Rural Finance and Economics and Sociology, Ohio State University. Occasional Paper No. 587; March 13.

Bardhan, P. K. 1973. Size, productivity, and returns to scale: an analysis of farm-level data on Indian agriculture. *Journal of Political Economy* 81, 6.

__________, and Rudra, A. 1980. Terms and conditions of sharecropping contracts: an analysis of village survey data in India. *Journal of Development Studies* 16, 3: 287-302.

Berry, R. A., and Cline, W. R. 1979. *Agrarian structure and productivity in developing countries*. Baltimore: Johns Hopkins University Press.

Blackton, John. 1974. *Local government and rural development in Sri Lanka*. Ithaca: Rural Development Committee, Center for International Studies, Cornell University. Rural Local Government Monograph No. 14; November.

Bottral, A. F. 1977. Evolution of irrigation associations in Taiwan. *Agricultural Administration* 4, 4 (October): 245-50.

Carroll, Thomas F. 1969. Peasant cooperation in Latin America. In *A review of rural cooperation in developing areas*, Vol. I of *Rural institutions and planned change*. Geneva: United Nations Research Institute for Social Development.

Cunningham, Paul. 1980. Fail-safe projects: the importance of incentives. Bloomington: Program of Advanced Studies in Institution Building and Technical Assistance Methodology, International Development Institute, Indiana University. Design Note No. 20.

Fox, Roger. 1979. Potentials and pitfalls of product marketing through group action by small scale farmers. *Agricultural Administration* 6, 4 (October): 305-16.

Gotsch, C. H. 1974. Economics, institutions and employment generation in rural areas. In *Employment in developing nations*, ed. E. O. Edwards. New York: Columbia University Press.

Grissa, Abdessatar. 1973. *Agricultural policies and employment: case study of Tunisia*. Paris: Development Centre Studies, Development Centre of the Organization for Economic Cooperation and Development. Employment Series No. 9.

Healey, D. T. 1972. Development policy: new thinking about an interpretation. *Journal of Economic Literature* 10, 3: 757-97.

Hirschman, Albert O. 1970. *Exit, voice and loyalty: responses to decline in firms, organizations and states.* Cambridge: Harvard University Press.

Howse, C. J. 1974. Agricultural development without credit. *Agricultural Administration* 1, 4 (October): 259-62.

Hyden, Goran. 1973. *Efficiency versus distribution in East African cooperatives: a study in organizational conflicts.* Nairobi: East African Literature Bureau.

__________, ed. 1976. *Cooperatives in Tanzania: problems of organization building.* Dar es Salaam: Tanzania Publishing House.

Inayatullah, ed. 1972. *Cooperatives and development in Asia: a study of cooperatives in fourteen rural communities of Iran, Pakistan and Ceylon*, Vol. VII of *Rural institutions and planned change.* Geneva: United Nations Research Institute for Social Development.

Johnston, Bruce F., and Clark, William C. 1982. *On designing strategies for rural development: a policy analysis perspective.* Baltimore: John Hopkins University Press.

Johnston, Bruce F., and Kilby, Peter. 1975. *Agriculture and structural transformation: economic strategies in late-developing countries.* New York: Oxford University Press.

Khan, Azizur Rahman. 1979. The Comilla model and the integrated rural development programme of Bangladesh: an experiment in "cooperative capitalism." *World Development* 7, 4/5 (April): 397-422.

King, Roger. 1975. Experience in administration of cooperative credit and marketing societies in northern Nigeria. *Agricultural Administration* 2, 3 (July): 195-207.

__________. 1976. *Farmers' cooperatives in northern Nigeria: a case study used to illustrate the relationship between economic development and institutional change.* Ph.D. dissertation, Department of Agricultural Economics, Ahmadu Bello University, Nigeria, and Department of Agricultural Economics, University of Reading, U. K.

Lau, L. J., and Yotopoulos, P. A. 1971. A test for relative efficiency and application to Indian agriculture. *American Economic Review* 61, 1.

Lele, Uma. 1977. Considerations related to optimum pricing and marketing strategies in rural development. In *Decision-making and agriculture*, eds. T. Dams and K. E. Hunt. Lincoln: University of Nebraska Press.

__________. 1981. Cooperatives and the poor: a comparative perspective. *World Development* 9: 55-72.

Long, Norman. 1970. Cooperative enterprises and rural development in Tanzania. In *Rural cooperatives and planned change in Africa*, ed. Raymond J. Apthorpe,

Vol. IV of *Rural institutions and planned change*. Geneva: United Nations Research Institute for Social Development.

Mellor, J. W. 1976. *The new economics of growth: a strategy for India and the developing world*. Ithaca: Cornell University Press.

Moore, M. P. 1979. Social structure and institutional performance: local farmers' organizations in Sri Lanka. *Journal of Administration Overseas* 18, 4 (October): 240-49.

Morawetz, D. 1974. Employment implications of industrialisation in developing countries: a survey. *The Economic Journal* 84 (September): 491-542.

Stavis, Benedict. 1974. *Rural local governance and agricultural development in Taiwan*. Ithaca: Rural Development Committee, Center for International Studies, Cornell University. Rural Local Government Monograph No. 15; November.

Tendler, Judith. 1976. *Inter-country evaluation of small farmer organizations–Ecuador, Honduras: final report*. Washington, D.C.: Program evaluation study for the Office of Development Programs of the Latin American Bureau of the Agency for International Development. November.

United Nations Research Institute for Social Development (UNRISD). 1975. *Rural cooperatives as agents of change: a research report and a debate*, Vol. VIII of *Rural institutions and planned change*. Geneva.

Uphoff, Norman T., and Esman, Milton J. 1974. *Local organization for rural development: analysis of Asian experience*. Ithaca: Rural Development Committee, Center for International Studies, Cornell University. Rural Local Government Monograph No. 19; November.

von Freyhold, Michaela. 1979. *Ujamaa villages in Tanzania: analysis of a social experiment*. London: Heinemann Education Books, Ltd.

Wilson, Frank A. 1976. The development of small scale marketing systems: some observations on intermediary activities in the perishable trade. *Agricultural Administration* 3, 4 (October): 263-69.

Chapter IV

ALTERNATIVE LOCAL ORGANIZATIONS SUPPORTING THE AGRICULTURAL DEVELOPMENT OF THE POOR

Stephen B. Peterson

Unhappily for the rural poor, community-wide, inclusive local organizations usually do not protect their economic interests.[1] In most countries rural inequality is such that rural elite and poor interests are in conflict on matters concerned with agricultural production and the state is unable to control community organizations enough to prevent their being vehicles of exploitation. Improvements in the private market thus often serve the interests of the poor better than formal cooperatives do. Yet traders and money-lenders have never been noted for actively promoting equality. The poor should not be left to the market alone.

It is in such inhospitable circumstances as these that central agencies committed to the rural poor will promote alternative local organizations. These organizations are distinguished from formal cooperatives by their restriction of membership to a group of the poor and by their explicit commitment to the interests of a portion of the community only.

Whereas the success stories for the cooperative movement are to be found in relatively egalitarian rural settings, the literature on alternative local organizations draws on the hard cases—Central America, India, the Philippines, etc. (Tendler, 1976; Korten, 1980). We turn now to the linkage problems of working with the poor in settings where governments are ambivalent toward them and the interests of the rural elite are inimical to theirs. In doing so, we will draw

[1] I would like to express my appreciation to David Korten and Judith Tendler, who commented on an earlier draft of this chapter. They are not, of course, responsible for the use I have made of their views, however.

extensively on the linkage lessons of cooperatives developed in the preceding chapter and adapt them to alternative local organizations.

SMALL-FARMER GROUPS: ORGANIZING THE RURAL POOR

To place the issue of linkage to alternative local organizations in perspective, we begin with the generic features of the rural groups which will be assisted. Tendler's studies of Ecuador and Honduras and Korten's work on community organization provide an extensive empirical basis for depicting the characteristics of successful small-farmer alternative organizations. The following is a list of criteria found by Tendler to be associated with effective small-farmer groups and which is consistent with Korten's work as well:

> 1. They organize around a concrete goal, which can be achieved in a limited time period and would not necessarily require the organization thereafter. . . . Though the organization may continue and expand into other activities, once the concrete goal is achieved, the farmers perceive themselves as organizing to achieve this one goal, and not to create an organization.
>
> 2. They start with one task and not several.
>
> 3. That task can be carried out with an organizational form that minimizes the need for non-farmer skills, such as bookkeeping. Examples are the building of infrastructure projects, the application for credit as a group, the distribution of water on a small scale.
>
> 4. Cooperation is required around a task that cannot be done on an individual level—i.e., certain kinds of irrigation, construction of an access road, obtaining credit available only to groups. Examples of tasks that are problematic because they can be done on *both* a group level and an individual level are marketing . . . and communal farming.
>
> 5. They produce goods or services for which there is a *proven* desire on the part of small farmers involved.
>
> 6. The groups are small and unconnected to other groups. Group success has often gone along with the smallness and isolation from other groups because (1) rivalry with outsiders is important in getting some groups to form and in keeping them together; (2) smallness allows for peer pressure to induce group cohesion and

loyalty; and (3) when groups are successful, they tend to become exclusive.

7. The task can be carried out by relatively informal, unsophisticated and familiar organizational forms (Tendler, 1976: 7, 9).

Effective local organizations are characterized as small-scale, single-functioned, differentiated from other small groups, and homogeneous in their membership. The key feature of these organizations is their simplicity, which ensures local control and allows them to evolve and terminate if necessary.

A major weakness of development administration theory as applied to institutional design is the tendency to impose complex institutional blueprints such as cooperatives on rural areas and to neglect existing institutions. There has been the tendency both in theory and practice to impose institutional development strategies that stress the value of institutional differentiation and expansion as critical if not determinative factors in forcing the pace of rural development.

There are two features of the "accepted wisdom" of institutional design which are in tension with the character of alternative local organizations—institutional complexity and continuity. Complexity limits the ability of the rural majority to control the organization and obscures the benefits they will derive, thereby inhibiting their contribution of resources. "The challenge of organization design is to balance the benefits which can be obtained through larger, more complicated organizations against the costs of calculation and control which such complexity tends to impose" (Johnston and Clark, 1982, Chapter 5).

Institutional continuity has also been overstressed as an end itself, which diverts attention from the organization's tasks to a fixation with "certain organizational forms" (Tendler, 1976: 9). Too much emphasis and too many resources are concentrated on constructing an organizational infrastructure, rather than on carrying out the task itself, which creates a relatively high investment in the organization and thus an incentive to sustain it. This tendency to focus on form not function raises several issues about the compatibility of institutional designs and local organizing needs. Organizing at the local level is costly to the individual and thus will most likely occur under short-term conditions where benefits are tangible and quickly realized: high organizational start-up costs will not be tolerated. It is difficult to specify the organizational design that is best for each task; and even if an organization evolves in the performance of a task, it is questionable whether that organization is compatible with pursuing a new task when its original one is terminated. Organizational failure should not be viewed negatively, but rather as an aspect of a learning model of institutional development (Korten, 1980: 499).

Examples of tasks that seem to fit the interests and limited administrative capacities of local groups are the following: organizing to obtain land; building of infrastructure projects; the application for credit as a group; and the distribution of water on a small scale (Tendler, 1976: 7-8). None of these tasks can be carried out by a single individual; their execution facilitates the group's development.

Organizing to acquire land can mobilize strong local support, willing to press demands even to the extent of challenging the central administration (Hollinsteiner, 1979: 398-403). This task is not stressed by donors or host countries both because of its politically sensitive nature and the fact that such organizations will terminate once their goal is achieved. This function is important to rural groups and they are willing to pay for the services of land and land brokerage (Tendler, 1976: 15). Providing local groups with credit for land acquisition and the assistance which allows them legitimately to press their claims provides for partial land reform. Access to credit facilities that provide for both land and production loans prior to land titling legitimizes the group and "this strengthening of a group's initial claims to possession, and provision for immediate income, are important in determining whether such groups will survive" (14). Tendler has also argued that such programs for assisting in land purchase do not have to be comprehensive in scope and that considerable progress can be achieved by strengthening local groups and credit unions (14). Comprehensive land transfer programs, on the other hand, have high visibility, directly threaten elite interests, and increase the potential for confrontation.

Local physical infrastructure projects also are effective for strengthening alternative local groups, as they are not feasible for individual farmers, they are task-specific, and they clearly complement the individual's production. The construction and maintenance of roads and markets can be crucial in improving the competitiveness of marketing, lowering transaction costs, increasing the farmers' sale prices and lowering the cost of their supplies. Using local groups will make infrastructure projects more oriented to local community needs; it also will "counteract the bias of infrastructure projects toward over-design, capital intensity, and unsuitability to local conditions" (11). Locally organized efforts are more likely to be labor intensive, a characteristic which generally favors the poor by expanding the demand for their services.

The local operation of small-scale irrigation facilities and of watercourses often is encouraged by administrative agencies as well. The effectiveness of irrigation depends on local management and supervision at the gate level. Perhaps more than other functions, irrigation imposes the outlines of structure and procedure on the group because of the "role of the physical-environmental factors in shaping, limiting, or determining various forms of group-shared behavior and the regularities that lie behind them" (Coward, 1979, Chapter 1). Irrigation associations are successful because they are formed by an ecological imperative; corruption is extremely visible; few, if any, financial exchanges occur (thus limiting the use of non-farmer skills); access is perceived as crucial and takes on a moral right; and support from the center is strong as it is highly dependent on local organizations for implementation of the program.

The creation of local credit groups is a means to offset individual financial liabilities by offering lending agencies the lower risk of joint liability. The smaller size of these organizations also lowers the transaction costs for individual loans and expedites the application-disbursement process. Small farmers have a better repayment record than large farmers in many countries.

There are several conditions, though, which have to be satisfied for these group credit programs to be a success. First, the loans need to be targeted to smaller producers through loan ceilings and high interest rates which discourage large producers.

Second, Tendler believes that the tendency to include agricultural extension in a program of supervised credit should be avoided and that technical advice should be provided by a separate program. There are several weaknesses in providing extension with credit: technical assistance complicates the credit task; extension imposes a task that requires extensive coordination with other agencies; extension services tend to be diverted to larger producers; extension technical assistance is often diverted to organizational tasks of bookkeeping and auditing; and small farmers do not want extension as much as credit (25).

Third, meeting the technical assistance needs of these small credit organizations in the area of bookkeeping is crucial for their success. Auditing functions are best provided externally by some administratively strong agency.

Fourth, the delinquency problems of small-farm credit programs are often due to agricultural disasters. Contingency funds need to be created which allow lending institutions to delay collection.

Fifth, the success of group credit depends on the social sanctions of the collectivity. Since alternative local organizations are characterized by socio-economic homogeneity, no member will have enough power or status to withstand group pressure. Still, it is important that the group be small enough to have real cohesion and that members have a stake in the credit-worthiness of the others in the group. The latter is automatic if all are dependent on continued access to this source of credit. Generally this is not the case with the poor, however. Alternatively, a requirement that all members contribute to a portion of the loan capital and that members' funds are forfeit first in the case of loan defaults probably provides adequate incentive to the group to monitor its members. It is a general rule for local organizational efforts that centrally provided finances should be matched with local resources to ensure commitment (e.g., Korten, 1980: 487).

Small producer credit groups illustrate a key limiting feature of such informal local groups—the need to keep financial transactions simple and accounting to a minimum. This is a crucial constraint on the capacity of local organizations to be "autonomous." Formal accounting entails bureaucratization of organizations and this limits, if not contradicts, the flexible features of these local organizations. Financial administration probably should be kept separate from the actual implementation of the group's function if it becomes complex. It is generally accepted that an external agency is needed at least to provide auditing assistance (485).

There is a hesitancy to prescribe state intervention in alternative local organizations because of the belief that their autonomy is both a feasible and necessary means of counterbalancing the state. Also, if the state intervenes in one aspect of the organization (e.g., auditing), it is difficult to prevent it from expanding its role. The attributes of effective alternative local organizations listed above, however, do not suggest autonomy via self-contained regulatory capacity, but rather through small-scale ad hoc tasks that induce group participation and pose demands (including regulatory requests) on the center.

THE FUNDACION DEL CENTAVO: AN EXAMPLE OF PREFERRED DESIGN

We now consider in more depth the problems of organizing and linking marginal producers by examining Guatemala's private Fundacion del Centavo. The Fundacion illustrates two issues: the manner in which an incentive program can be conducted, and the attributes of a "brokerage" intermediate organization for linking local alternative organizations. The Fundacion has been successful in providing credit facilities to small farmers and assisting in the institutional and economic development of small-farmer groups in the pre-cooperative stage. The Fundacion is also of interest because, unlike the two public sector programs in Guatemalan agriculture—FENACOAC (credit unions) and FECOAR (regional agricultural cooperatives)—it has successfully reached the marginal producer.

The Fundacion was designed to stimulate private sector participation in development for the rural poor and has become a respectable organization composed of prominent citizens. This provides the organization a crucial interest group at the national center which will press for services for the rural poor and supply a vital consciousness-raising role. The second attribute of the Fundacion is its commitment to the marginal farmer and its diligence in separating out these individuals and targeting assistance to them. The organization stresses its non-sectarian and apolitical position, but the leadership and staff understand the necessity of local organizations' having a political as well as an economic base. They are aware that their efforts to create local organizations has a political content and they fully support this consciousness-raising process, while refraining from providing any doctrinal content (Rusch, Mann, and Braun, 1976: 63).

Four services are provided by the Fundacion which are exclusively oriented to agriculture: group credit, assistance in small group organizing, supply of inputs (fertilizer) and the purchase of land

(63-67). The Fundacion stipulates that all services must be requested through groups of marginal producers, thereby excluding the individual large producers. The agency does not form all of the local groups, as many emerge from the Government's Rural Development Agency program for potable water. These groups have been encouraged to continue as agricultural groups with support from the Fundacion. The Fundacion has provided a catalyst role, stimulating a variety of groups which seek the Fundacion more for its organizing services than its limited development resources.

The Fundacion provides only minimum services to local groups, both to ensure local contributions and to allow broader coverage. In providing credit, the agency carefully determines through local inspection the viability of the groups and the technical feasibility of the projects selected. The provision of credit is used to strengthen local organizing abilities, as "responsibility is left with the group to form its own structure and be prepared to assume joint responsibility for the loan if it is approved" (63). The Fundacion treats the credit program not simply as an exercise in transferring inputs, but as a means of creating institutions that are more self-reliant in providing their own productive services. Credit is a vehicle to initiate organizational learning.

> The basic services provided are informational, regarding the Foundation and the credit arrangement, and motivational, assuring adequate group functioning to facilitate repayment. Some secondary services may also be provided, according to needs of the groups and the ability of the supervisor, on community matters and technical agriculture. It is important to note that a highly valuable service is that of convincing previously isolated farmers to group themselves to meet their needs, and to guide them through the process of using group structures (64).

The Fundacion recognizes that group formation even for a single task is not an easy achievement for marginal producers who previously have been bypassed by government agencies and cooperative programs. There is a crucial need for federation-type structures to provide linkages which stimulate the very process of group formation in rural development. Public agencies that provide linkages only to existing groups are ill-suited to this task.

The success of the Fundacion's credit program suggests that marginal producers should be introduced to formal credit systems as groups rather than as individuals. The group credit approach of this organization has facilitated access to credit which marginal producers could not have received from cooperative institutions. Credit risks are reduced because the group approach creates greater pressure for repayment, and access to production loans does not require that the individual first contribute capital, as in the cooperatives (70).

A key program of the Fundacion is the provision of credit for land purchases. This credit is accompanied by a short-term technical assistance package which raises the potential productivity of the land and thus the ability of the farmers to repay their loans. The Fundacion has often acted as a broker in this program by arranging for the Ministry of Agriculture to provide technical assistance. Both production and land purchase loans are closely monitored and there has been an extremely low default rate.

The local organizations stimulated by the Fundacion's programs quickly gain credibility as intermediaries between farmers and the Fundacion. The following services are provided by the farmer associations:

1. Consolidation of individual needs into one request to the Fundacion.
2. Establishment of credibility before the Fundacion and a local authority.
3. Management of the documentation and arrangements necessary to secure the loan and deliver the commodity to the community.
4. Protection of individual interests by the exercise of an acceptable form of group pressure (64).

Unlike cooperative networks, the Fundacion does not seek to ensure the institutional continuity of its primary societies. About one-third of the groups do not request further assistance: some groups affiliate with cooperatives; others find alternative funding sources; and some disband. The Fundacion does not have the resources to encourage dependency and thus allows the dissolution of weak local organizations.

A major constraint on the Fundacion is its restricted financial capacities, due to its dependence on donations. It has limited its self-sufficiency by charging concessional interest rates on its credit, which undercuts cooperative credit programs (74). Low-cost credit, though, limits its ability to expand technical assistance and it does a disservice to the marginal producers "to accustom them to a lower rate of interest than a cooperative can economically charge" (74).

The primary critique of the Fundacion made by Rusch, Mann, and Braun is that it fails to ensure the transition from pre-cooperative to cooperative organization. This is a classic institutional perspective, which assumes that local organizations are capable of additional collaboration, and further, that they desire or see benefit in it. The low number of farmer groups joining existing cooperatives is indicative of the desire of local groups to retain their autonomy. However, the movement of many of the Fundacion's groups to create "informal federations akin to cooperatives" also shows the need to create federative structures to become both institutionally credible and intelligible. The Fundacion is assisting the creation of these local group federations, which provide an alternative to the cooperative network. Though Guatemalan cooperatives are composed of lower income groups, they are seen as appendages of the state and supportive of its middle class ideology (78).

The transition of small groups to cooperative federations raises the question of whether evolution defined as integration with a cooperative network is desirable for the marginal producer. Rusch, Mann, and Braun frame the question as a problem of creating administration mechanisms for transition. The key problem is that the marginal producer must abandon the local organization and confront the membership of the cooperative as an individual rather than as a group member. Such integration places the marginal producers at a disadvantage, as they are the least qualified and the last to receive cooperative benefits. Only when organized with similar producers can the individual make effective demands for services. The cooperative in this case, while seemingly providing the basis of modernization (i.e., individuation), is in fact an instrument of control that strips away the marginal producers' organizational support.

The experience of the Fundacion carries several implications for linkage to informal groups of marginal producers.

1. Local organization often requires both the stimulus of focus on a specific task and assistance in learning organizing techniques.

2. A central support agency, to be effective in delivering services to the rural poor, must cultivate national elite support.

3. Local organizations need not, and perhaps should not, be

forced into more complex organizational networks. There is no certain benefit in transforming informal groups into formal cooperatives. Organizations at a pre-cooperative stage may provide marginal farmers with greater support than complex cooperative networks would.

4. Local group development and the formation of a federation structure should be evolutionary and not determined by an administrative blueprint.

5. Federations for assisting pre-cooperative group formation need not be the instrument of transition to formal organizational networks. Rather, organizing capacity must be instilled at the local level, which then provides the basis for constructing federative structures if these are perceived as necessary.

6. An institution which seeks to organize marginal producers should concentrate on a few key tasks (e.g., land purchase and production credit). Success at these programs does not signal the need for task expansion (e.g., into rural commerce and infrastructure), as this may spread management too thin.

7. There is a value in combining land purchase credit with technical assistance in programs for the marginal producer. These functions need not be provided by the same organization, but the services are complementary.

8. External assistance is needed initially to capitalize small-farmer organizations. If initial capitalization must come from the individual producers, then the organizations will not form, or if such organizations do form, they will be comprised exclusively of larger producers. Initial capitalization requirements should not be solely supplied externally, however. There must be local contribution of resources, particularly labor.

SINGLE-FUNCTION VERSUS MULTI-FUNCTION LOCAL ORGANIZATIONS

We have suggested that local alternative organizations will function better if they are single-functioned and task-oriented. This conclusion appears to be contradicted by other studies in development administration which argue for multi-function local organizations. It is important to analyze these differences. The Uphoff and Esman study found that local organizations should have three structural attributes: multi-level organization; multiple channels; and multiple functions (Uphoff and Esman, 1974: 67-75). These findings are supported by the U.N. Research Institute for Social Development (UNRISD) studies, which concluded that cooperatives that had the greatest impact on the community were multi-purpose (1975: 41). These prescriptions appear to be contradicted by the work of Korten and Tendler.

The resolution to this conflict within the literature lies in a recognition of the very different contexts to which the prescriptions are being applied. Both UNRISD and Uphoff and Esman state that relative homogeneity in the community is a prerequisite to cooperative success. Their recommendation of multi-functionality thus applies to a setting in which local elites have similar interests to those of the poor and in which their managerial skills can then be used in inclusive organizations. Tendler's and Korten's research is focused on societies where inequality is a very serious problem, however. UNRISD and Uphoff and Esman conclude that cooperatives do not do well in these societies. Tendler and Korten are writing about local organizations that succeed in helping the poor despite an uncongenial environment. Thus they are discussing alternative local organizations for the poor, not inclusive cooperatives with congenial elite leadership. The more difficult setting within which alternative local organizations operate is part of the reason that Tendler and Korten prefer single-function groups.

Another factor affecting the single vs. multiple function debate is the stage of organizational development. In its initial years an organization is likely to strain severely its new managerial capacities if it attempts a wide variety of tasks. When it is well-established, however, it may well benefit from the complementarities among diverse tasks.

We believe that Uphoff and Esman and UNRISD are correct about the value of multiple functions to established, inclusive organizations. Our work suggests, however, that their argument is not applicable to alternative local organizations of the poor, especially at the early stages of their development.

The primary critique of single-function local organizations is their inability to integrate functions and achieve organizational economies of scale. Uphoff and Esman are aware of the tradeoffs posed by these institutional designs.

> There are serious risks in attempting to encompass too many interests or functions in a single organization. It is then vulnerable to immobilization through factional strife, corruption or leadership inertia. To have a great many functions committed to a single local organization may overload its limited capacities, concentrate excessive power in a few hands, or lead to the neglect of some activities. Opportunities for developing membership participation and local managerial capabilities and leadership may be limited. Yet the risks inherent in having a large number of small, specialized single-purpose organizations are more severe. They are likely to be too small in scale for efficient operation and unable to integrate with other specialized activities, thus imposing an unnecessary and unwelcome burden on farmers (1974: 73).

This analysis stresses form not function—"multifunctional organizations, then, have definite advantages in scale and in capacity to integrate services"—which presupposes that such integration is a necessary feature and is in the interest of the local producers, thus stimulating local participation (74). While both postulates are true in homogeneous settings, they are doubtful in inegalitarian ones.

Uphoff and Esman's analysis is based on two related organizational requirements which they contend should exist at all levels of local organization: redundancy of function, and multiple linkages achieved by maintaining multiple functions. This design perspective contradicts the alternative local organizational attributes suggested by Korten and Tendler by stressing organizational form, complexity, and multiple functions from the very start. Our research indicates that single-function production units can provide redundancy and that multi-function production units (i.e., cooperatives) can limit, if not negate, redundancy. Redundancy is critical within the *sector* and *function* rather than within the organization. In an environment which is congenial to cooperative success, local organizations can be trusted to handle several functions. In a more threatening setting, however, putting all the functional eggs in one basket dangerously reduces the poor's exit option and increases their vulnerability to exploitation by organizational leaders.

While single-function ad hoc organizations logically will induce more local participation, they do pose an organizational problem that Uphoff and Esman recognize—the need to integrate a multitude of local organizations. Even if single-function organizations are appropriate at the primary level of local organization, are they appropriate at the secondary, intermediate level? Tendler's study, which treats the topic of federations and other group-assisting organizations in an inegalitarian setting, suggests that these secondary institutions also will have problems if they are given multiple tasks to start with.

> AID [U.S. Agency for International Development] has usually conceived of federations as multipurpose organizations. This usually involves too complex and sophisticated an operation for a new organization in a difficult environment. . . . AID should finance only with great caution those organizations that are set up to be multipurpose from the start—or even locked in by their programming to be so at some future date. A single task should be chosen. Decisions about how the organization will grow should be made only at a later stage, since information on the appropriate design of successive stages will be available only after the organization's initial experience. Even tentative plans for future stages tend to get adopted by default, in lieu of careful midstream evaluation of projects (Tendler, 1976: 18, 20).

Not only do Tendler's studies suggest the effectiveness of single-function credit unions, they also demonstrate that effective federations tended to play a brokerage role. Instead of just providing a service themselves, these federations operated as intermediaries, combining the demands of single-function primary organizations and directing them to government agencies.

An important distinction to be made in discussing the features of secondary organizations is whether these intermediaries are designed to facilitate bottom-up or top-down organization. Intermediate organizations that stem from the center are multi-purpose and distribution-oriented. The complexity and scale of these organizations ensure central control and local dependence. Intermediate organizations that represent local interests of the poor are single-function, production-oriented and facilitate local control if the structure is kept simple.

A crucial point in this debate about multi-function versus single-function intermediaries is that alternative intermediate organizations should be mechanisms by which local groups can place demands on the center. In developing countries, politicized intermediaries are needed to "reach up" to the administrative agencies and place demands. At some point inclusive integration does have to occur to coordinate local demands, central directives, and local administrative programs, so that development proceeds in a coherent fashion. This integration should occur at the district government level, but it should not preclude or usurp local intermediate organization. Integration lowers the potential for participation (Cohen, 1980: 66). It also inevitably leads to the imposition of the unifying vision of whatever elite prevails in the institution of integration. Thus integration should not be required of interest organizations whose special purpose is to service the poor.

The image of a federation or secondary hierarchy in an inegalitarian society, then, is one of an intermediary or "switchboard" organization that channels the demands of primary single-function organizations to the appropriate public and private agencies rather than itself coordinating and supplying multiple services. Implicit in this approach is the assumption that horizontal integration of service delivery at the local level (federation level) is both costly and detrimental to the process of local group formation. The secondary institutional level emerges out of the attributes of the primary level through the vertical expansion of single tasks and the minimization of complexity through limiting horizontal task expansion. The early linkages from the primary organizations should remain single-function and vertical, and this is best achieved if the intermediate organizations are also single-function, especially if they are simply brokers, because then they lack a substantive capacity to coerce primary organizations.

There is a tendency to link primary organizations with multi-function secondary organizations, which not only reverses the appropriate direction of institutional development (bottom-up), but also makes the linkages more complex and thus tenuous. The institutional blueprint for intermediate organizations in inegalitarian settings, then, should entail the vertical extension of single functions and the establishment of brokerage roles that facilitate vertical cooperation. This institutional prescription is quite different from the current emphasis on rural integrated development (horizontal integration) at local levels. The approach preferred here stresses the retaining of single-function, non-integrated, local alternative groups and single-function vertical linkages. Thus integration is achieved vertically—above the secondary interest organizations at least until the poor's ability to manage them is well institutionalized.

> The design feature which makes possible organization with limited communal obligation was spelled out long ago by Chayanov (1966) in his concept of "vertical" cooperation: local outputs and needs are handled by major commercial (exchange) or administrative (hierarchical) organizations at a regional or higher level, without requiring any "horizontal" grouping of the poor with each other (Johnston and Clark, 1982, Chapter 5).

INCENTIVES FOR ORGANIZATIONS VERSUS ORGANIZING THE RURAL POOR

Perhaps the key lesson of cooperatives is that organization cannot be imposed on the rural areas. Effective local organization must stem from local impetus and indigenous forms. Even the intervention of suggesting a structural form is counterproductive, as such assistance will give the organization an alien stigma. The issue of organization is crucial for reaching the poor, as the poor are weak both because they have no resources, and more importantly, because they have no mechanisms by which to demand and pool resources.

Organizations for the rural poor are weak and they often raise elite hostility. Also, organizing in developing societies is a political act that poses a threat and creates the potential for conflict. In such settings the task then becomes one of how to assist the poor's organizations without appearing to have a conscious organizing strategy. Cooperatives often fail or are closely restrained by both the center and local elites, precisely because they are a manifest rather than a latent organizing strategy.

The alternative to organizing is the provision of incentives which will induce the rural poor to create their own organizations. An incentive approach to reaching the rural poor has several advantages over the formation of organizations which have a structural imperative for extensive and continuous linkages. Incentives can be discontinuous; they focus attention on the development task rather than the development organization; and they are less tangible than organizations, thus eliciting less of a threat. Incentives facilitate an institutional redundancy strategy by encouraging multiple organizations and allowing organizational failure. Redundancy is not stressed and is often impeded by strategies that impose blueprints. Redundancy is a crucial strategy for assisting the poor, as it preserves the only option they possess—exit. The poor must be given choices between service organizations, which will foster organizational competition to improve service delivery.

The incentives versus organization debate suggests that there are two very different tasks for linkages: the stimulation of local organizations and the sustenance of existing organizations. Stimulation is a much harder task for an external agency to achieve because resource incentives must be of both appropriate quality and quantity to induce local resource contribution, yet prevent overload. Perhaps the most difficult part of an incentive strategy is to allow incipient organizations to fail and not to support an overly dependent local organization. Korten has suggested that perhaps no more than 10-20 percent of local organizations will survive initial development, deomonstrate their viability, and be worthy of continued, expanded support (1980: 502).

Deciding to bypass existing cooperative organizations and to organize directly alternative local organizations in most countries would require a major social transformation.

> There are several structural factors that may limit the development of new organizational approaches in developing countries. One is the weight of vested interests in present patterns of land exploitation and trade practices. Another concerns features of caste and class systems that prevent full participation of subordinate groups. A third factor is the control exercised by central political and religious authorities or other external agents (UNRISD, 1975: 20).

Incentives pose less of a threat than externally organized structures of the poor and are more feasible when central political support for social transformation is weaker.

The incentives versus organizing debate is more complex with respect to productive activities because the rural poor prefer amenities and do not perceive production as a high priority for group activity. They also seek to reduce the communal content of production in order to lower the threat to their subsistence. Organizations of the poor that engage directly in production not only add uncertainty to the production process, they often attract elite hostility, which requires that production organizations be tightly protected by the center. Given the rural poor's greater interest in amenities, it may be more appropriate initially to encourage institution-building around physical infrastructure projects which support agriculture, such as irrigation, storage facilities, and roads. These allow an incentive approach and the gradual development of local organizing skills. Organizing more directly for production could then be attempted after there have been some experience and success in local self-help. Cooperatives, for example, were generally found to be more effective and have more participation in areas that had experienced community development programs.

Examples of incentives that could be used to stimulate local organizations are the provision of: material inputs for small infrastructure projects; government land and water resources which can be collectively developed; tax breaks for cooperative efforts; legal guarantees which limit both elite and government expropriation of collective resources; and credit available only to groups. The most common incentive is the provision of materials for constructing an infrastructure project which requires the contribution of local labor. An incentive approach requires that resources be provided which complement but do not exceed the management capacity of rural dwellers and which induce participation.

LINKAGE SEQUENCES

We now consider the sequences of linkage development, which can be analyzed in terms of the development process of alternative local organizations. Korten's study concludes that successful rural development requires effective institutional development through a learning process approach rather than an imposed institutional blueprint. While Korten's study is written primarily from the standpoint of international donors and how to improve the donor's performance, it illustrates fundamental development stages for alternative local organizations and thus the stages of linkage development. Linkage "design," then, should facilitate this learning process. Korten contends that institutional development proceeds through three phases: effectiveness; efficiency; and expansion (1980: 499).

The first phase, learning to be effective, requires that the organization be unconstrained by standard administrative procedures, much less an institutional blueprint that sanctions only certain directions of evolution. This period requires assistance linkages—primarily personnel—which help local groups to understand the processes of organizing.

> It is a time of investment in knowledge and capacity building—learning what is required to achieve fit for a given time and setting. Not only does it involve basic learning about community dynamics—even learning what are the relevant questions to be asked—but it also involves learning how to learn through an action research process. As in the beginning of any learning process, it should be considered normal for error rates to be high, though on a downward trend, and efficiency low (500).

The characteristics of this first phase imply linkages of modest financial amounts, a willingness to experiment and fail, and a commitment of adequate personnel to assist in the organizing process. These program features sharply contradict the features of capital-intensive infrastructure programs which impose an institutional blueprint and a large financial "carrot" to implement the designs. Korten argues that providing sizable initial funding destroys the learning process and the incentive for local groups to improve their performance to justify further resource allotments. Further, the traditional emphasis on extensive institutional design criteria conflicts with an important attribute of successful projects—"They were not 'designed and implemented' . . . they and the organizations that sustained them 'evolved and grew'" (501).

The second phase of organizational learning, efficiency, entails a withdrawal of external personnel resources and perhaps the provision of modest material resources. The key attribute of this stage is allowing the organization to function with its own resources and to determine the fit between form and function.

> In Stage 2—learning to be efficient—the major concern shifts to reducing the input requirements per unit of output. Through careful analysis of stage 1 experience, extraneous activities not essential to effectiveness are gradually eliminated and the important activities routinized. . . . In Stage 2, there should also be serious attention

> paid to the problem of achieving fit between program requirements and realistically attainable organizational capacities, recognizing the organizational constraints that will have to be accepted in the course of program expansion (500).

Stage two is a consolidation phase which should not be impeded either by providing new resources to the organization or by adding new functions. Control linkages become more important at this stage, particularly supportive ones that establish administrative standards and provide crucial management services such as accounting. Successful completion of stage two indicates that the organization is capable of surviving. Control and assistance linkages should not substitute for, but facilitate the organization's capacity to survive this phase.

Stage three of organizational learning is the program expansion phase. Given the effective incorporation of control linkages that characterizes stage two, stage three entails an increase in facilitative linkages that channel resources to promote the program's expansion. The organizational routines will already be established and, coupled with the control linkages, will determine the pace at which the organization expands. "The rate of expansion will be governed largely by how fast the necessary organizational capabilities can be developed to support it" (500). Only after stage three is completed should an organization be considered capable of task diversification. Even at this mature stage, the addition of a new task may require the repetition of the learning cycle unless the task is compatible with the existing organization.

Korten's analysis implies a sequence of linkages for assisting indigenous organizations: at the effectiveness stage, the provision of redistributive assistance linkages (primarily personnel); at the efficiency stage the provision of supportive control linkages; and at the expansion stage, the provision of equalizing assistance and supportive controls (added management staff). Korten's work also suggests the danger of governments' and donor agencies' overloading local organizations by compressing the stages. This is particularly true of organizations in the stage two phase, as there is the tendency both to expand the task and to add new tasks.

The types of projects that embody the learning sequence which Korten details violate two imperatives of donor assistance, as well as the administrative styles of many developing countries: high control and quick disbursement of large amounts of funding. While the first phase (effectiveness) of a project may be able to absorb only 5 percent of its projected budget for services, large numbers of agency support personnel are required for this stage (502). Recognizing the incompatibilities between donor policies and the learning model of development, Korten suggests that a division of labor be devised for agencies according to their relative capacity to intervene at a particular stage. A crucial question is whether any governmental agency at present is capable and willing to accept the demands of stage one assistance—"a highly qualified staff, substantial programming flexibility, and no qualms about taking on high risk, staff-intensive activities" (502). Personnel assistance for group organizing is also politically difficult. Hence the need for governments to concentrate only on incentives to self-organization. One possible approach is to accept the inability of governments to intervene directly at stage one and to use *private* organizations such as the Fundacion del Centavo to channel initial support.

Tendler's work makes a valuable addition to Korten's by detailing the role of termination in a linkage sequence. Thus four stages of linkage development can be discerned: efficiency, effectiveness, expansion, and termination. The latter means the cessation of resource support to an organization, not organizational termination. Organizational termination is not necessarily an outcome of resource termination, though a crisis of institution building is created which may either weaken and destroy the organization or strengthen it further. Korten also discusses termination with respect to the attrition of programs, moving through the three stages of learning, particularly the first stage. The high failure rate (perhaps 80 percent) of first-stage projects is a major reason why Korten aruges for the need to limit initial financial resources and to expand personnel—so that fixed resources do not force the continuance of an ineffective program and because failure provides rewards in terms of personnel learning.

Tendler's discussion of termination focuses on international donor linkages to local projects but her findings apply to all central agencies that hope eventually to withdraw their support from an alternative local organization. This is especially true of non-governmental organizations. For example, termination is a central feature of the Fundacion and it demonstrates the value of forcing alternative local organizations to develop institutionally, not just to sustain programs themselves. Termination also improves the bargaining position of the local organization with the assisting agency, as demands do not have to be moderated due to a belief that assistance might be continued.

> The crisis of AID termination is an important part of an organization's growth, however, which is aborted when AID rushes in to alleviate it. . . . Those relationships between AID and recipients that were amicable over a longer period of time, and involved continued renewals of assistance, also made considerably less progress in self-sufficiency. . . . [T]he AID-created programs that survive AID's departure have typically become fed up with AID, and vice versa. This can be seen as a sign of (1) the healthiness of a new organization which has its own ideas about how to do things; and (2) the need of politically significant programs with small farmers to show their constituencies that they are considerably separate from AID (1976: 35-36).

Termination has implications for the type of channels used to link small-farmer organizations, particularly whether a public or private sector approach is used. Private sector approaches to linking small producers have been particularly effective (e.g., the Fundacion del Centavo) and donors tend to use them "because the public-sector approach was considered paternalistic and 'top-down'" (17). While a private sector approach may be more effective in organizing small producers, the exclusion of public sector sources of support may create dependence and a strain on the agency, as well as program failure with the advent of termination.

Our research indicates that termination is a crucial feature for an effective strategy of local institution building, but is not necessarily essential or compatible with task achievement. Restated, while termination and organizational conflict are important processes in the establishment of viable local organizations, such "autonomy" is not always compatible with task achievement, which entails continued support.

At this point it is useful to review Tendler's policy recommendations for linkages to local organizations which enhance their self-sufficiency:

> 1. Penalties for not meeting self-sufficiency targets should be built into programs, as well as rewards for doing so.
>
> 2. Hard-and-fast termination dates for assistance in institution-building should be drawn.
>
> 3. Services should be financed that will generate income for the organization, rather than financing the organization's budget.
>
> 4. The service to be financed should be chosen on the grounds of (1) its easiness and workability as a task for a new organization; and (2) the extent to which peasant groups have shown themselves interested in and willing to pay for this kind of service in the past (e.g., land acquisition).
>
> 5. Programs of budget support to institutions or parts of them should plan from the start to alter the form of assistance at a later date to one that involves considerably greater distance. This will allow the organization to have its own ideas without being punished by withdrawal of its support. Interest income from credit is one such way of providing support with distance; credit provided through intermediate financial institutions . . . is another (1976: 38).

Termination is a key sequence of linkage development that has not been adequately assessed in the development literature. Termination is a logical sequence if one's institutional prescription for organizing the rural poor is the creation of small, ad hoc, single-function, task-oriented organizations. Termination not only limits the complexity and duration of tasks, it ensures that the redundancy of multiple local organizations is retained. A precondition of a termination policy by either the state or an international donor is that the local organizations are expendable—that they can fail. Cooperatives and their networks of federations provide only a single organizational channel, thereby forcing the administration to maintain that channel despite inefficiencies and increasingly dependent local organizations. Cooperative networks negate redundancy and prevent the administration from selectively intervening and disciplining local organizations by threatening and actively terminating assistance.

The UNRISD study prescriptions for high impact cooperatives which suggest the value of high assistance and low control linkages should not be applied to small, alternative local organizations. Continuity of high assistance linkages is a feature of cooperative institution building in homogeneous settings. Assistance linkages that are of moderate levels and are discontinuous are perhaps more suitable for institutionalizing alternative organizations. These assistance demands are more compatible with the resource capabilities of developing countries.

The termination sequence also has implications for the role of control linkages. Termination illustrates how the withdrawal of assistance has a regulatory consequence in that the local organization can be punished effectively by withdrawing resources. Termination is a recognition of the limit of central administrative control over local organizations and the difficulty of reforming corrupt local institutions and strengthening them through control linkages. The pervasive existence of control linkages that UNRISD found among cooperatives is indicative of the weakness and corruptible character of cooperatives and the desperation of governments to sustain these organizations. Given the limits of central control, local organizations should be allowed to fail with the recognition of *local* responsibility for failure enhanced by a termination policy. To make local organizations viable, there must be pressure placed on local leadership by both the state and the members themselves. Entanglement of the state with a faltering local organization through control linkages prevents the creation of this balanced pressure on the local leadership and deflects the blame for failure onto the state. A policy of termination allows both the successes and failures of local organizations to strengthen the indigenous institution-building process.

In terms of implementing a termination policy, it is important to consider that a variety of sequences is possible. Termination can be done in the initial stages of project development through a large grant of resources accompanied by a clear understanding that further resources will not be provided. This strategy presumes that the recipient organization is administratively strong from the start. Termination also can be conducted through a gradual withdrawal of resource levels. Whatever sequence is adopted, though, a clear timetable must be communicated and the *perception* of termination made apparent to the recipients.

Termination of support is dependent, of course, on the function of the organization and the character of financial support received. While "one-shot" financing may be compatible with infrastructure projects with definable objectives, ongoing agricultural projects do not have this characteristic. They also often have a tax base which furthers the autonomy of the organization and limits the extent to which termination of assistance can be credibly imposed. Thus while termination might create an organizational crisis that would strengthen the institution-building process, continued support is needed for task achievement.

CONCLUSION

A discussion of termination policies is an appropriate topic to end a chapter on agricultural linkages. In concluding, though, a few points made earlier should be reinforced. First, productivity projects are highly susceptible to elite domination and corruption. Unlike infrastructure projects in public health or public works, agriculture in developing countries has persistently defied attempts by administrative centers and international donors to direct development. The fact that the poor are dispersed in rural areas inherently weakens their capacity to organize and press demands to improve rural production. Inextricably related to the issue of linkage is the issue of organization, which has been difficult to affect, given the individual character of agricultural production. Perhaps more important than the establishment of linkages is the structure of local organization created by linkages. The discussion of incentives versus direct organizing underscores both the difficulty and undesirability of imposing organizational forms that threaten local elites and require continuous linkages which weak administrations have difficulty sustaining. While the crisis in developing areas would suggest a maximum organization-linkage strategy, this research indicates the value of a mini-max solution—support of only those local organizations which can be protected. A strategy of politicizing local organizations, therefore, must be cautiously used and is dependent on whether extensive control linkages can be sustained by a committed center. Finally, our research indicates that without major social change, the shift from bimodal to unimodal agricultural development must be incremental. Even incremental improvement of the productive position of the rural poor, however, will be an accomplishment and a major step in achieving broad-based development.

REFERENCES

Chayanov, A. V. 1966. *The theory of peasant economy.* Homewood, Ill.: R. D. Irwin.

Cohen, John M. 1980. *Integrating services for rural development.* Cambridge, Mass.: The Administration of Economic Development Programs Baselines for Discussion, The Lincoln Institute of Land Policy and the John F. Kennedy School of Government, Harvard University. No. 6.

Coward, Walter E. 1979. *Irrigation development: institutional and organizational issues.*

Hollinsteiner, Mary Racelis. 1979. Mobilizing the rural poor through community organization. *Philippine Studies* 27: 387-416.

Johnston, Bruce F., and Clark, William C. 1982. *Redesigning rural development: a strategic perspective.* Baltimore: Johns Hopkins University Press.

Korten, David C. 1980. Community organization and rural development: a learning process approach. *Public Administration Review* 40, 5 (September/October): 480-511.

Rusch, William H.; Mann, Fred L.; and Braun, Eugene. 1976. *Rural cooperatives in Guatemala: a study of their development and evaluation of AID programs in their support.* Vol. I: *Summary and General Evaluation by the American Technical Assistance Corporation.* Washington, D.C.: A report prepared for the Agency for International Development.

Tendler, Judith. 1976. *Inter-country evaluation of small farmer organizations–Ecuador, Honduras: final report.* Washington, D.C.: Program evaluation study for the Office of Development Programs of the Latin American Bureau of the Agency for International Development; November.

United Nations Research Institute for Social Development (UNRISD). 1975. *Rural cooperatives as agents of change: a research report and a debate,* Vol. VIII of *Rural institutions and planned change.* Geneva.

Uphoff, Norman T., and Esman, Milton J. 1974. *Local organization for rural development: analysis of Asian experience.* Ithaca: Rural Development Committee, Center for International Studies, Cornell University. Rural Local Government Monograph No. 19; November.

Chapter V

LINKING THE VILLAGE TO MODERN HEALTH SYSTEMS

Sven Steinmo

The delivery of health care to the Third World's rural poor is often inadequate, inappropriate or nonexistent. No more than 30 percent of the population of most less-developed countries (LDCs) use any part of their countries' health delivery systems (Clinton, 1978: 257; McGilvray, 1974: 6). Fendall has written: "Medicine throughout the twentieth century has been brilliant in its discoveries, superb in its technological breakthroughs, but woefully inept in its application to those most in need . . . the implementation gap must be closed" (cited in Smith, 1978b: xiii).

This "implementation gap" all too often characterizes the delivery of health care in the Third World. One frequently observes high-cost and high-quality medical care provided in the major cities for the national elites, while the rural communities receive little or no medical attention. More importantly, the type of medical care we of the industrialized world have come to expect may be wholly inappropriate for less-developed societies. "Long-held maxims about providing rural health care are being proven invalid. All those involved in planning, funding and delivering services have learned that health services designed and implemented from the 'top' and 'handed down' have often failed to attract villagers' participation or to affect their lives" (Clinton, 1978: 259).

Thus we see a broader problem than simply the extension of modern medical facilities into the rural periphery. Even if it were feasible to accomplish such a task (and in many, if not most, cases it is not), the advisability of such a strategy is in doubt. "Health" itself is a problematic concept. Our modern technological orientation has led us to see the medical profession as "producers" and the unhealthy as "consumers" of health. A more appropriate definition of "health" for our purposes is "well-being" or the absence of sickness. "Health care" becomes those activities which maintain or promote well-being, rather than simply curative medicine. Our technological orientation has allowed us to forget that the major advances made in well-being in the past century have had as much to do with standards of living as with medicine. These advances have been products of changes in sanitation, housing, clothing, and nutrition (Berliner, 1980). It is a sad and obvious fact that no amount of medical help can save a child dying of malnutrition. It is equally true that though you can rehydrate a child suffering from amoebic dysentery, you cannot save all his kin until you remove the amoebic contaminant from their living environment.

Well-being or health is a product of the socio-economic environment in which the individual lives (Blum, 1976; Illiach, 1976). It cannot be purchased from an M.D. at any price. Those who are truly interested in improving the health of the rural poor need to look for those structures which point towards avenues of social change. Gunnar Myrdal puts the issue quite well: "The standard of health depends on the whole social milieu, especially the prevailing attitudes of its institutions. Some of the most important reforms in the field of health and education are of necessity social reforms" (cited in Kroeger, 1974: 105).

It is precisely the inability or unwillingness of health planners to see well-being as a concomitant of social change which has undercut so many well-intentioned attempts to deliver health care to the rural poor. Ignoring the connection between well-being and social change, LDC health planners all too often have supported programs emphasizing high-cost curative care which prove to be dismal failures in terms of promoting the rural poor's well-being.

It is the combination of the inability of curative medicine to reach the rural poor and the immense scale of the rural poor's health problems which has encouraged many international donor agencies such as the U.S. Agency for International Development (USAID), the World Health Organization (WHO) and UNICEF, as well as some national governments, to re-evaluate the medical-technical orientation towards health. Faced with the reality of painfully small budgets and the staggeringly high cost of training Western-style M.D.'s, these donors are increasingly interested in new approaches to improving health in rural areas. These programs tend to focus on preventive rather than simply curative medicine and utilize paramedical personnel and/or village health workers (see, for example, Flahault, 1972; Gish, 1975; Storms, 1979; Djukanovic and Mach, 1975; and Newell, 1975).

We shall describe these various alternatives in greater detail below. We must stress here, however, that while modern medical education is oriented towards delivering curative care, it is unquestionable that the most pressing health needs of the Third World lie in the arena of preventive medicine. Though there is a high degree of national variation, it can still be said that the greatest killers in the Third World are preventable. Malnutrition, malaria, gastrointestinal parasites, tetanus, whooping cough, tuberculosis, trachoma, cholera and typhus are not always "curable" in the medical sense; but as the experience of the Western world demonstrates, these diseases are largely preventable. To prevent these diseases, however, requires social change at the village level. It is not simply a matter of prescribing pills or giving immunizations. Prevention of the great Third World killers requires a change in the very way of life of the villager. Culture, custom and religion have upheld many unsanitary or otherwise unhealthy practices in rural villages. Many of these practices must be changed in order to get at the root of ill health in village communities. The traditional Western approach to health fails in the Third World setting both because of its orientation to "cure" rather than "prevention," and because M.D.'s are not trained or generally inclined to promote the basic social changes needed at the village level.

The promotion of new priorities for rural health is especially difficult, however, because one mechanism for promoting redistribution is not available—namely, local pressure. In other program areas, the poor can be organized to challenge the dominance of elites, and these upward pressures can stimulate the creation of supportive national linkages from sympathetic agencies. Whereas poor rural dwellers want water for crops and access to credit and markets, they often prefer curative to preventive health. They accept the medical-technical orientation and do not create pressures which would promote preventive medicine or the social changes which would improve their standard of living and thus their health (see Elliot, 1975: 3).

In this chapter we shall analyze four health care delivery models extant in the world today: those based on hospitals, task-forces, clinics, and villages. We shall focus primarily on the latter two models, both because we see them as far superior in terms of helping the rural poor and because they have received a great deal of attention in the literature in the last few years. The first two models are highly centralized. In treating them we shall highlight linkage issues which pertain to the power and influence of national elites, issues which obviously are important in the development of any national health program. In our third, more decentralized, model we shall focus on the linkages between structural units which the clinic system usually attempts to implement, but rarely succeeds in accomplishing. In the final, most decentralized system, the village-based model, we shall focus on what we see as the most important linkages in this area: those between the modern medical profession and village organizations capable of providing health services. Here we shall attempt to describe the problems of establishing working relationships due to the social and cultural barriers between traditional society and modern medicine. Finally, we shall examine a recently developed proposal for medical services—the Medex system—which falls between the clinic and village-based models and attempts to incorporate the best features of both.

The central administrative issue which has emerged from our review of the health literature is the difficulty of establishing links between the medical profession and local organizations capable of providing health services. Discussions about which levels of government and what types of government agencies should administer the programs are largely absent. This lack of concern in health circles with questions of governmental structure contrasts with the attention given to those issues in agriculture and public works.

CENTRALIZED HEALTH DELIVERY SYSTEMS

Hospital Systems. In the hospital system most, if not all, of the nation's health care budget is spent on large-scale modern hospitals which are usually confined to the major cities. Almost all countries (developed as well as developing) can be said to fit this model to some degree, for most nations spend a very high percentage of their health care budgets on high quality/high technology care. We wish to include in this category, however, only those Third World countries which do not at the same time make significant investments in the delivery of health care to the vast majority of their populations—the rural poor. Though we mention only a few specific countries here, it is an unfortunate fact that a grossly unequal distribution of health care resources is the norm rather than the exception in most of the Third World.

Political power tends to be highly centralized in LDCs and for this reason alone it is not surprising that their health care delivery systems are also centralized. Clearly, those who have political power will demand the best health care their power can buy. The result more often than not is large university-type hospitals. While most nations have these hospitals, in many countries there is either a lack of concern for the politically impotent rural population or a lack of funds once the large hospitals have had their share. Charles Elliot writes:

> I think it is important to emphasize that the urban bias of health services had a logic (if perverted logic) of its own. It did not result only from a wicked oligarchic plot to hog the largest share of the medical cake (which is a picture some more incautious left-wing critics tend to imply), but from an uncritical application of (basically Western) economizing algorithms to a situation of extreme resource scarcity. If medical facilities of all sorts are in desperately short supply, it is neither wicked nor foolish to deploy them where they are most likely to be used (1975: 3).

Though their intent may be neither wicked nor foolish, these hospital-based systems are, according to the Christian Medical Commission (CMC), "both ineffective and inefficient" (1973: 3).

One example of the hospital-based model is Bolivia. The people of this small Latin country have, according to USAID (1975), the worst health status of any American nation. Bolivia is also (and this is surely no small coincidence) the poorest nation in the hemisphere. The bulk of the nation's health budget is spent on the University of Medicine and the large hospitals in the major cities. Though the Ministry of Health (MOH) is charged with delivery of health care to the 80 percent of the populace living in the rural communities, USAID estimates that only 2 to 10 percent of the rural health care needs are being met. Though the University of Medicine produces 220 doctors a year, virtually all of these doctors stay in the big cities or move to the United States.

The problem does not stem from a lack of governmental attention to health. In all, there are thirty-seven public agencies dealing with health care delivery in Bolivia, contributing to what USAID has called "a cumbersome and fragmented centralized bureaucracy" (1975). The most important agencies are the MOH, the University, the Social Security System, the National Social Development Council, railroads, the National Institute of Colonization, the National Road Service and the Public Works and Development Corps. Through these groups Bolivia channelled its $52 million health budget in 1971. Despite this large number of agencies, there are apparently few linkages between them. Rather, each is concerned with its own constituency and uses its resources to maintain its political support.

There are few, if any, ties between the center and rural poor, while at the same time (and maybe for the same reasons) the bonds between urban elites, the medical profession, and government decision-makers are very strong. The central problem in this example is not administrative weakness (though this certainly is *a* problem); rather, there is a lack of will on the part of political decision-makers to deliver health care to the rural communities. Though the MOH is charged with delivering rural health care, its major institutional linkages are with the University of Medicine. The MOH budget, which is small (a single large-sized American hospital can have a budget larger than $50 million), is apportioned according to the strength of the MOH-University linkage. Thus the MOH spends 75 percent of its budget on urban hospitals and 25 percent on rural health care. The orientation of the MOH in Bolivia is to provide high-quality care to the upper and middle classes of society, rather than to reduce that quality and spread out delivery. Virtually all medical students are members of the upper class and hence start their education with an orientation towards quality rather than quantity care. Moreover, it has been noted that "no amount of money could induce these people to move into the primitive bush."[1] The social relationship as well as the institutional power of these doctors prevent the development of a rural system in Bolivia.

Brazil is another case which fits this model. What is most remarkable about Brazil is the oversupply of M.D.'s in most large

[1]Dr. Raul Caetano, personal communication, 30 May 1980. See also Rogahny and Solter, 1973.

cities. In cities such as Rio de Janeiro and Sao Paolo the doctor-to-patient ratio is so low that many M.D.'s join the army simply to survive.[1] Yet Brazil suffers from a drastic undersupply of doctors in the vast majority of the country (Penido, 1965: 38-40). Despite this fact, the Brazilian Ministry of Health continues to allocate most of its budget to the large city hospitals and not to rural health care.

Unfortunately, while some Third World nations are decentralizing their health care delivery systems, others are turning towards this hospital-based system and away from the use of auxiliaries for the delivery of health care. This trend is evident in most of Francophone Africa, with the exception of Algeria (Laib, 1972). Pene (1973) tells us that this move is part of a growing sense of nationalistic pride. While the nations were colonies, the French established a two-tiered system with qualified doctors and registered nurses serving the elite and auxiliaries (*medicine Africains*) serving the black population. (For an historical analysis of the development of medical auxiliaries throughout the Third World, see Fendall, 1972.) Since independence, however, there has been a growing tendency to spend scarce national resources on "qualified" doctors and nurses and to eliminate the former "racist" institution. This is both a poor utilization of scarce funds and of limited utility in terms of sorely needed preventive medicine. Moreover, this tendency is by no means reserved to Francophone Africa (see Gish, 1973: 1251).

The most important ties in the hospital-based model are between medical elites and national political elites. In some cases the medical elites dominate or control the MOH; in others they have de facto, but not necessarily institutional, power over it. In the Third World there is usually, if not always, a meeting of interests between elite providers of health care and other national elites. Doctors in all nations are oriented towards providing high-quality care. This kind of care is almost always technologically oriented, hospital-based and very expensive. Other elites in these nations, for obvious reasons, want high-quality care available for themselves and their families and they have the political power to make sure they get it (Navarro, 1974: 20). While this phenomenon is true for all countries, not simply the few mentioned above, those using the hospital-based

[1]Dr. Raul Caetano, personal communication, 30 May 1980.

model have financed only these urban hospital systems, while many other countries also finance rural auxiliary systems.

Task-Force Interventions. The second model of health care delivery can be called "task-force" interventions. Most Third World countries have engaged in large-scale, highly centralized mass immunization programs and rural campaigns to raise the health status of the rural poor. WHO, UNICEF, and USAID have often promoted these programs, with widely varying degrees of success. Smallpox, formerly one of the world's greatest health problems, has virtually been eliminated through these mass immunization programs. Other similar interventions have proved less useful.

These military-style methods of medical care are somewhat controversial today, for though they often are concerned with the well-being of the poor, they change neither people's health consciousness nor the way they live. It is a relatively expensive mode which does not get at the cause of ill health in rural villages.

Banerji (1975) presents a most convincing critique of this model. He states that while these programs (e.g., malaria eradication in India) are initially very successful, their very nature prevents the development of a health infrastructure which can achieve the final eradication.

> This failure has been responsible for a series of setbacks to the National Malaria Eradication Program, resulting in the costly reversion of large segments of the maintenance phase population back to the consolidation or attack phases. Instead of getting rid of malaria once and for all by 1966, as it was envisaged in the late 1950's, 40 percent of the population have yet to reach the maintenance phase (75).

From their experience in Niger, Fournier and Djermakoye add that "the few rare and rapid tours to the bush made by the more zealous doctors and nurses are often ineffective, so difficult, if not impossible, is contact between an urban official who arrives unrequested and a peasant who merely sees him come and go" (1975: 130). These transitory interventions can be ineffective even when they are tied to relatively local community hospital centers. (See the case in Sierra Leone described in Ross, 1979: 2.)

Another example which points to the problems of this "hit and run" approach is offered by a USAID evaluation team which studied a sanitation project in Guatemala. The original project's goal was to "improve the quality of life of rural Guatemalans by creating sanitary and hygienic living conditions, and by having communities involve themselves in self-improvement projects" (Hill, 1978). This goal was to be achieved by building latrines and water systems in various rural communities. It was assumed that the project would improve health by providing potable water and eliminating the breeding material for disease-carrying flies. Two years later the USAID team said:

> Unfortunately, communities are not benefiting to the extent they should from this project. Systems installed have never been revisited . . . Many faucets leak, creating muddy and unsanitary conditions. Failure to provide community *pilas* [basins] for washing clothes also creates unsanitary situations since women must either wash in tubs near their homes with no drainage or walk long distances to traditional but contaminated water sources. Indications are that once USAID ceases, programs will deteriorate since [the Government of Guatemala] will appoint *less* qualified personnel and not maintain present wage levels forcing local experts to seek employment elsewhere.
>
> The weakest part of the program, however, has been a deficient educational system. Community members need to be more extensively taught the benefits of using latrines. Most Guatemalans prefer defecating in their fields believing this benefits crops. Until proper sanitation is understood, the use of latrines will continually meet with resistance (Hill, 1978).

These interventions fail when they do not establish and maintain linkages to the village community. While immunization and sanitation programs are obviously important, the means chosen to deliver these services is fundamental. The village-based approach is a significantly more effective means of attaining this project-community linkage.

MODELS UTILIZING AUXILIARIES

The clinic and village-based models are patently "better" approaches to the delivery of health care in the Third World. The clinic system is an attempt to improve upon the traditional hospital-based system by decentralizing the delivery of health care. This model is usually characterized by a network of regional hospitals and village clinics staffed by a wide variety of health personnel, including doctors, nurses, midwives and an assortment of auxiliaries. The village-based model, on the other hand, questions the notion of "delivering" health care. The village-based model attempts to mobilize the community itself to attack its own health problems. By creating new community organizations or motivating existing organizations, the village-based model is involved in promoting social change at the village level rather than in delivering curative or even preventive medicine.

There are, however, similarities in these two decentralized models. Both attempt to combat the inappropriate technology and high cost of traditional medical care by utilizing auxiliary or village health workers (VHWs; sometimes referred to as community health workers, CHWs). These health workers have several advantages over doctors. The first is economic; while the education of an M.D. cost over $84,000 in Dakar in 1969 (Bryant, 1969: 260), it cost less than $25 to train *two* village health workers in nearby Niger in 1975 (Fournier and Djermakoye, 1975: 131). Moreover, with a minimal amount of competency-based training, it is highly unlikely that the illiterate VHW will move to the United States or London, as is the case all too often with LDC doctors. In 1965, for example, 50 percent of the graduating class of the Thailand University of Medicine moved to the United States immediately upon graduation (Bryant, 1969: 75). Iran had an annual 30 percent loss to the United States (Rogahny and Solter, 1973: 428), and India loses over a quarter of its M.D.'s to England or the United States each year (McGilvray, 1974: 16). Furthermore, as we saw in Brazil, doctors who do stay in the country often refuse to work in the rural areas.

This new type of health worker has several other advantages, which in the long run may prove to be even more important than the economic ones just cited. To begin with, their training, precisely because it is new, is highly manipulable. The education these workers receive can be made to fit the needs of the local communities. Western medical education, whose standards are understandably high, is often impervious to the needs (medically as well as economically) of the rural poor. The story is often told of the ambitious and well-meaning doctor who in going from his medical school to the bush finds himself incapable of delivering the care he was trained to provide. Without adequate supplies, equipment or facilities and unable to communicate to the rural villagers—who are often socially, culturally, and linguistically completely separated from the M.D.—he goes back to the city to start up a curative care practice. The auxiliary, on the other hand, is often chosen from the village itself and is not trained in the use of high-technology medicine. This worker has fewer linkage problems with the community, allowing the open communication which is often necessary for patient education as well as diagnosis. Dr. Sheldon Margen has noted that auxiliary health workers are sometimes better at early detection of diseases such as leprosy than are M.D.'s.[1]

Though both models utilize these auxiliary health workers, the way in which the VHW is used is fundamentally different. In the clinic model the VHW is an extension of the clinic. His or her job is to assist "qualified" professionals or to make "interventions" into the village. These interventions are supposed to draw villagers to the clinic or facilitate care for those who will not or cannot come to the clinic. In a village-based system, on the other hand, the VHW is based in the village and can be seen as an employee of the village and not of the clinic.

> The major breakthrough normally comes when the community rather than the clinic becomes the actual focal point of program concerns and activities. Field workers consider their communities rather than their clinics as their primary bases of operation, and the clinic moves to the role of a technical back-up system. Field workers no longer simply promote and deliver on a one-to-one basis, but rather concentrate on building a network of community members who take on the promotional and delivery roles (Korten, 1976: 4).

Thus though these two models look quite similar on an organizational chart, they are different because of the nature of their linkages. The clinic system stresses the linkages between structural units in the system. The clinic and/or regional hospital is the basic focus of attention. The village system stresses the linkage between the VHW or team and the village. Though clinics are important to this model,

[1]Personal communication, 3 June 1980.

the focus of attention is at the village level. The village system tends to be primarily oriented towards "well-being"; the clinic system tends to be inclined towards "medical care." We must remember, however, that these are not mutually exclusive concepts.

It is important to realize that balanced analyses of these systems are rare in the literature for the obvious reason that both systems are such significant improvements over the conventional hospital system described above. Also, "the experiences of the newer systems involved are more diverse and it's something of a problem to distinguish between plans and accomplished reality" (Korten, 1976: 19). We shall attempt to highlight the problems as well as the successes of these systems in order to indicate the areas for improvement.

Clinic-Based Systems. Independent India's history in the health sector has been much influenced by its colonial past. In India, as in French Africa, there was a two-tier system of medicine at the time of independence. In 1947 there were 30,000 medical "bachelors" and 18,000 medical doctors (i.e., with postgraduate education). One of the first major health decisions of the new government was to abolish the three-year bachelor's degree in medicine. During the independence struggle, however, the new government had committed itself to the provision of health services to the rural areas, and so it was forced to expand rapidly its output of medical doctors (Banerji, 1975: 73). Since that time India has opened 103 medical colleges with an annual admission capacity of 13,000 and has increased the number of doctors in the country to over 138,000. The MOH has also established an extensive system of national modern hospitals, 5,200 Primary Health Centers (PHCs) staffed by qualified doctors, and 32,000 subcenters staffed by auxiliaries.

The system ideally operates on a referral basis in which a patient who has an illness beyond the capacity of the auxiliary will go to the PHC; if the illness requires it, the patient will then go to a full-scale hospital. Additionally, the government has begun to finance 9,000 ayurvedic (traditional Indian medicine) dispensaries and 195 ayurvedic hospitals with the roughly 150,000 registered ayurvedic practitioners. On an organization chart the Indian health system is a model to be emulated by the rest of the Third World. With multiple, redundant structures, highly trained staff and a genuine national political will to get health care to the rural poor, success would seem to be a foregone conclusion; but it is not. Unfortunately organization charts do not deliver health care.

According to Dr. Margen, who has worked with the health care system in India, "The Indian system is a failure."[1] Another analyst, J. A. McGilvray, tells us, "Each of the five-year development plans has been modelled on this approach and it has failed" (1974: 8). Though the Indians have developed a strong institutional infrastructure, the participation of individual doctors and auxiliaries and hence the villagers' faith in the system are extremely tenuous. Moreover, the means of communication and referral of patients between tiers in the system are very poorly worked out. From the perspective of the ill villagers who are referred from a rural health post (subcenter) to the PHC, "Why bother? They may walk for days to get there, only to find that the doctor has gone to New Delhi."[2] The linkages between structural units are weak at best.

In addition, because the Indian clinic system relies on doctors to head the staff of the PHCs, the entire structure is subject to some of the problems of the hospital-based model of health care.

> One of the saddest ironies of the medical education system of India is that community resources are utilized to train doctors who are not suitable for providing services in rural areas where the vast majority of the people live and where the need is so desperate. By identifying itself with the highly expensive, urban-and curative-oriented Western style medicine, the Indian system actively encourages doctors to look down on existing facilities within the country, particularly in rural areas (Banerji, 1975: 73).

Eric Ram makes much the same point: "Even today the training of young doctors does not take the realities of the Indian situation into full consideration, and what is taught has little relevance to the social, cultural and economic needs of the majority of the people among whom doctors work" (1978: 2).

The results of the inadequate communication between the M.D. and the patient and between the doctor and his staff are not only the alienation of the patient from modern medicine, but also

[1]Personal communication, 3 June 1980.

[2]Judith Justice, M.P.H., personal communication, 6 June 1980.

the alienation of the M.D. from the rural village. There is a powerful tendency for doctors to move to the cities or abroad. The urban population of India, which is 20 percent of the nation, has access to 80 percent of the doctors. McGilvray elaborates on the problem in India:

> In a recent conversation with the director of Health Services of the state of Mysore in South India, with a population of 39,000,000, I was informed that there were at least 1,000 doctors in the state who consider themselves unemployed simply because they are unable to secure employment in the two larger cities of the state but refuse to go elsewhere because the locations did not match their expectations of what a doctor should do and should earn. In spite of this, I was assured that several of the primary health centers in the state, which should have a complement of two doctors each, still had no doctors at all (1974: 8).

There has been much discussion in India as to how to solve these problems. The solution fought for by the elites of the medical establishment has been to upgrade Indian medical services.

> These foreign-trained doctors have been pressuring the community to spend even more resources to attract some of them back to the country by offering them high-salaried prestigious positions and very expensive super-sophisticated medical gadgets. These foreign-trained Indian specialists, in turn, actively promote the creation of new doctors who also aspire to "go to the States" to earn a lot of money and to specialize. Emphasis on specialization, incidentally, causes considerable distortion of the country's health priorities, thus creating further polarization betwen the "haves" and "have nots" (Banerji, 1975: 73-74).

The result of this tension between the professional's desire for prestige and "quality medicine" and the politically dictated need for rural care and "social medicine" defines the character of the Indian health service. The institutional infrastructure is firmly in place (though clearly still sparse), but the practitioner's lack of commitment to providing care in this structure seriously undermines its utility. The goal of preventive medicine is all but forgotten. Those doctors who are out in the field are seriously overburdened with pressing, if not life-saving, demands for curative care. Clearly, when the demand for immediate care is as overwhelming as it is in these clinics, even those doctors who are preventive-conscious are unable to spend the necessary time for patient education, much less for social mobilization.

Thailand is another example of a clinic-based system of health care delivery. Again we see a carefully worked out plan for medical infrastructure but poor linkages between providers, the rural clinics, and the population. These rural clinics are the main channel for providing health care to the rural 80 percent of the population. Ideally the average clinic would serve a population of approximately 50,000 people and cover an area of nearly 600 square miles. The staff of each clinic should number thirty-seven, including those serving the various satellite centers. The health team consists of a physician, two nurses, a senior sanitarian, a number of auxiliary midwives, sanitarians and nurses (Bryant, 1969: 75).

As in India, however, plans are poor predictors of reality. Of the nation's 600 districts, only 216 have the clinics and of these, only 135 have physicians. While the doctor-to-patient ratio in Bangkok is 1 to 940, in many rural areas it is as low as 1 to 200,000. Despite the fact that Thailand was never colonized, the medical system's orientation towards scientific, hospital-based medicine is unmistakable. This in turn encourages the all-too-familiar "brain drain." As we noted above, in 1965, 50 percent of the graduating class of medical students moved to the United States upon finishing their internship (Bryant, 1969: 79).

There are also important problems in the ties between the community and modern medicine.

> The difference between the inundated use of health services in middle Africa and the light use in Thailand is extraordinary. For example, the difference in per capita outpatient visits is nearly tenfold. (A physician serving a population of 100,000 usually sees only five to ten patients a day.) The reasons for this light usage in Thailand are not clear. Clark E. Cunningham has observed that there is often considerable social distance between the government physicians and the people, a distance the people may be unwilling to cross. Or, possibly, the people do not see that effective health care is available at the health centers. They have alternatives—the traditional herbal physicians, the priest, the spirit

> doctor, the pharmacist, the "quack" doctor or injectionists, traditional midwives, friends, and relatives—and they are willing to pay liberally for their help (78).

This social distance is especially important when we see that doctors are unwilling to go into the village even though they have no work in the clinic.

Finally, these clinics have problems of communication in their internal organization. Bryant attributes this gap to the nature of the Buddhist culture. Even though the Thai health plan includes information feedback, there seems to be little use of the feedback structure. Because of the patron-client (superior-inferior) relationships in this cultural system, "the flow of information is almost exclusively from patron to client" (78). The notion of challenge or even suggestion coming from the bottom is quite alien to this culture. Thus the learning aspect of the implementation process is seriously undermined. (For another elaboration on the problem of patient-doctor communication in Thailand, see Boesch, 1974: 108-22.)

Kroeger provides us with one of the most penetrating yet simple critiques of what we have called the clinic-based model in his study of plantations in Sri Lanka. In this analysis Kroeger gives us a description of the "comparatively good health services" available to the poor plantation workers.

> At almost every plantation there was a dispensary with a qualified midwife in charge . . . Besides dispensaries and maternity clinics, a number of plantations had their own small hospital which was usually run by experienced medical assistants. The hospitals were not of a very high standard, which anyway was not necessary, as serious cases and emergencies could always be brought to the next governmental hospital where general doctors and specialists were available. Transportation was then provided in this case by the plantation (1974: 99).

Additionally, the government and the plantation owners attempted to upgrade sanitation for these workers. They built piped water facilities reaching 80 percent of the households and latrines for 67 percent.

Yet despite all these efforts, studies show that disease patterns (morbidity rates for a wide variety of diseases are examined in this study) and infant mortality rates are extremely high—significantly higher than for the general Ceylonese population. According to Kroeger, "These poor health conditions of the plantation populace are obviously not due to a lack of health services. More important is the whole socio-economic situation, the poor living conditions, the traditional behavior of the people, and the extremely low standard of education of the labour population" (100). Clearly social change is needed more than health services.

In this discussion of clinic-based delivery systems, we have tried to highlight two basic linkage problems—those between the clinic and the community and those between the larger medical system and the clinic. As with the hospital systems of Latin America, much of the problem stems from the professional orientation of Western medical education. Even with serious national attempts to establish a rural health infrastructure, the social, cultural, and professional orientations undermine its effectiveness.

Village-Based Systems. The village-based system stresses planning and policymaking at the village level rather than (but not to the exclusion of) organizational structures. The first nation to engage in this form of health organization was China. Today there are over one million "barefoot doctors" (BMDs) in China. This is an especially remarkable accomplishment given the fact that 1965 was the first year such a program was discussed. These BMDs are members of their respective communes and work part-time in the field with their "comrades" and part-time as deliverers of health services.

The most significant aspect of the Chinese system for our purposes is that these BMDs are explicitly intended to provide an institutional link between the center and the periphery. Moreover, due to the strength and administrative capacity of the Party and the social organization of the "New China," these medical cadres are able to provide a charismatic leadership function in the provision of health services. These BMDs are both centers for community health mobilization and subtle tools of the national government in the exercise of health policy decisions.

Due to the strength of the Communist Party, the linkages from the center to the BMD and from the BMD to the village are not necessarily reproducible in other Third World settings. Rogahny and Solter (1974) point out in their study on Iran that even the selection process for BMDs or VHWs must be different due to the differences in Iranian culture. Collective decision making, a central element in the Chinese system, was apparently not easily applied to the Iranian context. "One cannot easily generalize from this limited experience. Iranians are highly individualistic people with a limited history of cooperative enterprise, whereas the Chinese have a long history of close cooperation" (1332). Thus, they conclude, "On the basis of our limited experience in Iran, we believe that the Chinese barefoot doctor is not easily transplantable to Iranian soil and that auxiliary training in Iran must take into account the realities of the Iranian situation" (1333).

We shall focus on attempts made in the direction of village-based health care in more typical LDC settings. The first and probably most successful example is the Comprehensive Rural Health Project of Jamkhed, India. This project was started by Maybelle and Rajanikant Arole, a young Indian couple who, in addition to their medical degrees, had received degrees in public health (M.P.H.'s) from Johns Hopkins University. When they returned to a rural hospital in India they realized that 70 percent of the diseases they were treating were preventable and that once cured the patient almost always returned to the unhealthy environment which caused the illness in the first place.

These two doctors first obtained funding from the Christian Medical Commission to set up their total health care system. They started with four basic assumptions:

> (1) Local communities should be motivated and involved in decision making and must participate in the health program so that they ultimately "own" the program in their respective communities and villages.
>
> (2) The program should be planned at the grassroots and develop a referral system to suit the local conditions.
>
> (3) Local resources such as buildings, manpower, and agriculture should be used to solve local health problems.
>
> (4) The community needs total health care and not fragmented care [as is the case in the rest of India, see above]; promotional, preventative, and curative care need to be completely integrated, without undue emphasis on one particular aspect (Arole and Arole, 1975: 71).

Their second task was to gain entry into the community. When first approached, the villagers were hostile, assuming that the Aroles were simply Westernized doctors who would exploit the community. The Aroles saw this initial entry as especially important because they wanted to gain the villagers' commitment to, not just acceptance of, the project. Thus they went to several communities with their plan and chose the one whose leadership seemed most committed to the project goals. Their experiences in other communities varied widely. In one village the community leader tried to sell the "foreign-returned, wealthy" doctors land at very high prices. In another village the practitioner of indigenous medicine successfully prevented any dialogue between them and the people.

Once a village with a sympathetic leadership was selected, these elites were used as the initial entry into the community. An advisory committee was formed which consisted of elites from all castes and political parties. "Their function is to guide us in health care programs and provide a liaison between the villagers and the project" (74). The Aroles then hired nurses, auxiliary nurse midwives and paramedical workers totalling about twenty people. The community provided the land and built the facilities for the clinic. This contribution was considered very important for it reinforced the commitment between the villagers and the project. Surrounding villages also got into the initial process by providing volunteers and rebuilding roads between Jamkhed and their communities.

In October 1970 they opened the clinic and were immediately inundated with chronic patients. Initially 200-250 patients visited the clinic daily. This number decreased after the backlog had been seen. Still the clinic was swamped, a situation unsatisfactory to the Aroles. Here were those enlightened Johns Hopkins M.D.'s and M.P.H.'s providing nothing but curative care. With a good deal of effort, however, they were eventually able to make it out of the clinic and into the village.

> Popularity and reputation gained in clinical service had to be used as a springboard for launching community health programs. Acquaintances made at the center were useful as points of entry to the villages. A child cured of whooping-cough or tetanus was used as a demonstration case for health teaching in his own

> village, and the community was motivated to organize a mass immunization program (5).

This point cannot be overstressed. The Aroles used their proven curative powers to gain the confidence of the villagers. They then expanded this relationship to other areas which the villagers would normally be less likely to accept, i.e., preventive care.

Having established the initial relationship with the villagers, they expanded to other functions. Most importantly, they used their informal contacts to gain information as to the "felt needs" of the community.

> When the project began, the area was facing a drought. We would visit a village in the late evening over a cup of tea just to talk to the village council members and other leaders. These intimate contacts soon made us realize that their priorities were not health but food and water (75).

Taking seriously their stated goals of grassroots decision-making, the Aroles decided to switch the focus of their project temporarily to the attainment of food and water. Their success in organizing in these areas became a foundation upon which they could expand into preventive health campaigns. The community organization and leadership which solidified around getting food and water later was used to achieve goals which were not originally high priorities for the villagers.

As this project began to grow, the Aroles came to realize that there was a need to link up with the practitioners of traditional medicine in the village. They contacted these people and invited them to the center. The Aroles then carefully explained that they did not want to compete with them but wanted to help them by providing them with simple drugs, enhancing their skills and providing facilities for their patients. "In return they were to help us with regard to nutrition programs, immunizations, and the care of patients referred to them" (77).

The project then attempted to establish two additional linkages to the surrounding villages: the mobile health team and the VHW. The health team, consisting of a doctor, a nurse supervisor, a social worker, auxiliary nurse midwife, driver, paramedical worker and VHW, were to visit villages roughly once a week. It quickly became obvious to these teams that the villagers related far better to the drivers and VHWs than they did to the professionals who were not of the same cultural or class background. These lower-rung workers were then given special training in health promotion.

The team's basic function is to seek out the ill in the periphery. It was apparent to the project leaders that the costs and inconvenience of transportation prevent villagers from coming to the clinic unless they are very seriously ill, when it might be too late, or impossible, to travel. The team provides transport for the ill, seeks out health information and gives preventive education.

The need for continuous care in the periphery quickly became obvious. As open as the health team might be, villagers could still resist these weekly intrusions by outsiders. Though the Aroles originally intended to send some of their auxiliary nurse midwives and/or paramedics into the periphery villages, they soon found that these people were unwilling to go. (Note that even the bottom rung of health professionals resists being sent to the very remote areas.) Therefore the project decided to get volunteers from the villages to come in for VHW training. This was an unintended, yet major, success. Each village submits four candidates, usually women beyond childbearing age, and the project leaders select among them. Most of the VHWs are illiterate and receive their basic training two days a week at the center using flash cards, flannel-graphs, and other audio-visual aids. The VHW also gets on-the-spot training during the weekly health team visits.

> A person chosen from the community and trained is readily accepted, and health promotion can be easily achieved through her. The village health worker feels important because of the new role she plays in the village. *Having once convinced herself of the various health needs she is able to bring about change much faster than a professional.* The volunteer being part of the community does not need a separate house, protection, or special allowances. Since her incentive is not money but job satisfaction her services are not expensive and are within reach of the community (80).

In the village her duties consist of gathering health information (births, deaths, causes of illness when possible, etc.), health promotion in preventive health education and distribution of contraceptives. The VHW has a health kit containing contraceptives, simple drugs, dressing materials, eye ointments, etc. She is paid an honorarium of RS 30.00 a month. Food, transportation, and training cost approximately RS 50.00 a month (RS 1.00 buys a cup of tea in India).

There is little doubt that the Jamkhed project has been a great success. It is, however, difficult to determine how much of this success is due to the unique personalities of the project's leaders and how much is due to the project infrastructure itself. An independent team of WHO and UNICEF representatives concluded:

> Several factors are relevant to success. One of the most important is that the project is based on the recognition, particularly by the project leaders, of the priorities determined by the community. To the community, health is not a number one priority; agriculture, water supplies, and housing are more important. The project has therefore identified itself firmly with agricultural improvement, acquiring a tractor to be hired out to farmers and providing assistance in dairy and poultry farming and irrigation schemes. In effect, it appears that in such communities, which have a low economic status and per capita income, doctors and health services will need to identify themselves with the community's priorities in order to fulfill health objectives (Djukanovic and Mach, 1975: 77).

The second case we examine in the category of village-based systems, the national "simplified medicine" program in Venezuela, illustrates the differences between programs which are instituted nationally and grass-roots projects like Jamkhed. The Venezuelan case is especially important because it is one of the relatively few where the national government has attempted to establish a comprehensive health care system for the rural poor. Although the bureaucratic nature of the program undermines its claim to be truly village-based, the Venezuelan example does illustrate several important points.

The "simplified medicine" program emerged in Venezuela as a result of the leadership of a nucleus of high-level professionals in the Ministry of Health. The initial experiment was conducted in a remote region to overcome the objections of regional medical groups. The results of this experiment and other similar efforts in LDCs were presented to the medical profession and stress was given to the need to extend health services to rural populations which had not been previously covered. Support from the national group was obtained.

The program, which is linked to ongoing regional health center networks, aims to deliver basic health care "through a cadre of auxiliaries working with a system that ensures continuous training, supervision, and referral" (Gonzalez, 1975: 178). The auxiliaries attend a four-month training course held in district health centers. The program has gradually been institutionalized as a regular activity of the Venezuelan health services. Supervision by doctors was not found to be sufficient because of a lack of interest on the part of some of the doctors, infrequent visits, and an excess of consultations. So a regular system of supervision by one or more regional supervisors of simplified medicine has been instituted. They "are based in the regional health office and devote their whole time to the supervision of a number of dispensaries . . . The supervisor's approach is of the in-service training type; he observes the auxiliary on the spot, corrects his errors, and completes his instruction" (185-86).

Gonzalez concludes his excellent analysis of the development and growth of the Venezuelan system with several important points. In addition to stressing the success of the VHWs in terms of integration into the community and the medical system he repeatedly stresses the importance of "support, supervision and referral" (189). The most telling argument he makes, however, has more to do with the community than it does with medicine.

> It is axiomatic that the goal is to encourage local communities to play the most active role possible—in other words, to obtain community involvement. Experience has shown that this ideal cannot be achieved within a short time. On the contrary, it demands a great deal of perseverance and patient educational and promotional efforts, which will, however, achieve little if at the same time other elements of equal or greater importance than health care for the improvement of the overall status of those communities are lacking. These include changes in land tenure systems, improved housing, increased agricultural output, and tax reforms. In other words, no community involvement for health can be expected from communities in which the economic substratum is very small or even negligible (190).[1]

[1] Behrhorst makes a very similar argument in her description of the Chimaltenango development project in Guatemala (1974b).

A particularly significant aspect of the simplified medicine plan is that it received the blessing of the Venezuelan Medical Federation. We must remember that despite the apparent logic of a system which extends the reach of modern medicine, no other Latin American nation has implemented such a plan. Even though Guatemala developed a similar approach, its medical association vetoed it. Why was Venezuela different? Obviously the historical structure of rural care in Venezuela was important, but it was far from unique in the Third World. The critical factor seems to have been the existence of a School of Public Health. Most countries have no such institution because its function is supposedly carried out by the medical schools. If our earlier argument about the orientation of the medical profession and its impact on national policy is correct, then clearly the existence of other professional elites with different perspectives (i.e., *public* health) should affect national policy. Moreover, since a high percentage of public health officials are M.D.'s, it is reasonable to expect that some of this orientation could filter back into the "medical" establishment. This informal linkage may have been the single most important factor determining the successful development of "simplified medicine."

Clearly there is a need for closer examination of these points. A better understanding of why Venezuelan elites chose this route would shed light on how other nations might be encouraged in this direction. Newell (1975), Djukanovic and Mach (1975), Blum (1979) and many others argue that innovative *national* systems are eminently more cost-efficient and effective than specific donor-sponsored projects. If this is true, then we need to understand better what kinds of elite linkages will encourage the development of innovative health programs at the national level. Even if donors step in and set up a program, a commitment from national elites is essential to the program's continued success. Still we must be aware that this elite role in itself may present problems. The major criticism of the Venezuelan system up to this point has been that it is becoming overly "structured," rigid and removed from community decision-making. The balance between too little supervision and too much outside control is a very difficult one to strike.

This difficulty is illustrated exceptionally well in an article by Hendrata (1976) describing the Klampock community health project in Central Java. After two years of efforts to bring the community into the decision-making process the project director said: "The community only participates when we ask it to. This type of participation has no firm roots in the community and will last only as long as we are there to maintain it" (3).

In the director's view the principal problem in Klampock was too much input from the outside. Still, for a modern intervention into traditional society to sustain itself it must have support (linkages) from the modern world. It simply does not work to give basic training to a villager, send him or her back into the village and expect him to hold onto what he has learned—unless you provide continuous support for this "boundary spanner." Without continuous linkages to the center, the external unit will establish such strong linkages with the environment that it loses its original purpose (see Selznick, 1949). On the other hand, as we pointed out earlier, too strong a linkage to the center tends to stifle the essential ingredient of community participation in decision-making.

We can understand the importance of this point only if we remember that these interventions involve social change. It would be the height of Western chauvinism to assume that these traditional peoples will drastically alter their lifestyle simply because some Western professionals tell them it is "unhealthy." This social change process must take place slowly and developmentally. As we have seen with the Jamkhed project, the initial intervention must be one which proves its worth via curative powers, and only then can the more difficult tasks of health promotion and prevention be tackled. Thus the village health worker must establish his/her worth in the community and receive continued support and education in order to promote the social change cycle.

Several of these points are highlighted in another attempt at community-based health delivery in the Philippines. Dr. Barrion (1980) describes three successive attempts to establish a viable program in the Makapawa district. While the structure and performance of the third and most successful attempt are interesting we shall instead focus on the reasons for the failure of the first two programs. The first attempt failed because of inadequate social preparation of the communities, which had a variety of negative effects: (1) the basic principles of the community-based program were ill-defined and hence not understood by the community itself; (2) as a result, the roles of the VHW and the health committees remained ill-defined; (3) the program failed to deal with health in the context of the economic, social, cultural, and political structures of the community; (4) the VHWs did not necessarily have leadership potential. The second major weakness of this program was "a fixation on health service activities." Consequently the program did not get to the "root causes" of illness in the community. Curative care became the operating norm and "health care [was] still seen as a dole out." Finally, Barrion tells us that the program remained "staff and leader centered," resulting in little commitment from the community and a dependent relationship of the villagers with the health project (1980: 3).

The next program which was set up tried to account for the problems of the first. In this case the focus was to decentralize the organization of the project and also to enter the community more as a religious service than a specifically "health" service. These efforts, however, were dysfunctional. Because there was only one Community Organizer (CO) per area, the CO tended to develop "a little kingdom" and the community became dependent on the CO (5). Secondly, because the project was not introduced as principally a "health" project, a long process ensued before "health" was voiced as a need, thus wasting health expertise.[1] Thirdly, Barrion tells us that the community participation which was achieved tended to come from the upper stratum of the community, thus undermining the "grass roots" goal of the project. (See also Rogahny et al., 1976.) The result was that the needs of the very poor were not articulated and hence not met. Finally, the decentralized nature of this attempt meant a lack of coordination (or linkages) between sub-units of the project. The result, then, was that the VHWs received too little supervision, and the health centers did not receive adequate medicines.

The failures of these two Makapawa projects point out some major obstacles to the establishment of a community-based health program. It seems to us that the problems in each of these projects can be seen as having two roots. The first program, from inception through implementation, was based on the "insight" of the program planners, not the community. The second attempt failed because its motive force was the CO, not the community. These cases highlight

[1]This is a point of major controversy in the field. See Behrhorst, 1974a and Storms, 1979.

problems in both a centralized and decentralized approach to implementing community programs. The fact that these actors had the interest of the community at heart was not enough. The problem is not one of defining the community and its interests, but rather of finding mechanisms which facilitate the community's own self-definition and the articulation of its own interests. Barrion concludes:

> There is no hard and fast rule in the implementation of a CBHP [Community Based Health Program] if it has to be people-oriented rather than programme-oriented. Instead, the programme must start at the present level of the people and respond to their needs in order to become relevant and acceptable to them. Failure to do so results in the people viewing the health programme as a commodity they can use in time of sickness or in an emergency. Many tend to feel and think of it, particularly the preventive aspect, as an outside imposition being forced on them rather than a help. Such programmes only create much dependency. What is important, therefore, is that the various processes employed are periodically evaluated and given direction. These evaluations, shared with other interested groups, will help them in their own search for a CBHP that is truly by and for the people (9; see also McGilvray, 1974: 14).

The Medex System. The Medex system is a prescriptive model which attempts to remedy the linkage problems of both the clinic and village systems while retaining the best aspects of each. The key to this model is the auxiliary health practitioner or Medex. This individual provides the institutional link between the M.D. and the VHW. The creators of this model, most notably Dr. Richard A. Smith, see this intermediary as essential because the communication gap between the M.D. and the peasant is too great to be bridged under normal circumstances.

The model assumes a set of premises which is instructive to anyone concerned with health care delivery systems in the Third World. First, the proponents assert that "primary health care must be integral to rural development" (Smith, 1978a: 19). Secondly, given political and economic constraints, a radical reorganization of most less developed countries' health care systems is practically infeasible. A broad-based foundation must be constructed using appropriately trained and deployed personnel. Third, though organizational change and adequate financing are essential, these are not the critical factors in initiating change. Rather the "development and deployment of appropriate manpower can be the most effective means to initiate change in the health system" (20). Fourth, "the community health program must be connected to the next larger governmental structure if a primary health care program is to survive" (20). Next, the auxiliary worker in the village must be connected through an intermediary to the presently established health system. This intermediary has two functions: to gain acceptance for the rural auxiliary by professionals at the center and to provide for supervision, training and patient referral. Finally, this system assumes that to get the support of the medical professionals the program must be seen as one which will *extend* the services of doctors to rural areas, not substitute for them. If the program is seen as a threat to medical authority there will be little or no help from the profession. This support is essential to any health program's long term survival—even in the bush.

Doctors have three roles in this model: (1) treatment of patients referred from less-trained auxiliaries, (2) management and supervision, and (3) development of curricula and teaching of curative medicine. "This will require retraining doctors in health planning, epidemiology, operations management and evaluation" (23).

The VHW is the agent of social change, whose role should be communicator-facilitator and promoter-educator. He/she should have a limited curative, but a strong preventive, role. The VHWs should come from the communities they serve; with the Medex system the location is determined before the VHW is trained. Workers should have "competency-based training" in rural areas by people with experience. "It is important not to overtrain these people, or they will tend to leave the village environment." (25). The VHW, then, is a "boundary spanner" who provides the linkage into the community.

Evaluation is a learning function and should be carried out on at least two levels. The first is the national or provincial level. Here a panel should be formed consisting of faculty of training institutions, private health practitioners, public health officials, evaluators, statisticians, and if possible health experts from other countries. This panel should ideally be made up of policymakers themselves, but where the national political system does not permit it, they can act as an advisory panel. This seems to us an extremely important point. What is being attempted here is to establish a linkage which will engage national elites in the program, secure their commitment to it and enable them to learn from evaluating it.

Secondly, there would be a "community panel" at the rural health unit level. This panel is to "assess traditional customs and practices affected by health unit activities and the acceptance of the new health practices by the community" (Bomgaars, 1978: 131). Though Smith and his colleagues do not detail who should participate here, it is clear that local elites as well as Medex representatives and VHWs should be included. Implicit in the discussion is that this level should make policy within the parameters of national or regional policy and should provide an information linkage to the center (see also Storms, 1979: 27). The most important information has to do with type and quantity of drugs and supplies.

This latter point, we should note, is somewhat controversial. Foege, for example, argues that the most important information which these local committees can provide is anthropological. Foege explains that effective health planning cannot leave out such important questions as what it means to be sick, where people go when they are sick, who gives them advice, what the significance is of foods and eating rituals and what the beliefs are about birth, death, and marriage. In other words, one must learn the traditions and customs of the people in order to understand their health attitudes and practices (cited in Storms, 1979: 31). Other analysts argue that these village communities should actually be the planners and decision-makers for their health programs.

To summarize, the most important linkages in the Medex system are those of training, evaluation, information communication, drugs and supplies. The most unique and attractive aspect of the system is the role of the Medex. The Medex is intended to be the personal as well as the social linkage between the modern medical system and the traditional environment of the village. He is both ideologically committed and professionally competent (both "red" and "expert," to use a Communist Chinese analogy) and clearly is intended to serve the function of "cadre" (see Smith and Powell, 1978: 13). Moreover, the Medex is intended to be the linkage which legitimizes the system as a whole to the medical establishment. The use of the term "Medex" or "medical extender" is well chosen. It is important to see that from the point of view of the medical establishment, the Medex is not intended to and cannot, in fact, replace the doctor. The function and even prestige of the doctor are somewhat upgraded in this system (see Smith, *et al.*, 1971).

We have spoken of the Medex model up to this point in a rather uncritical fashion. A few caveats should be added here. We have seen only one evaluation of Medex systems in operation (in Cameroon; see Gridley, Nzeussen and Teunissen, 1980). Plans, models and charts do not deliver health care, and Medex is a health plan which may be overly oriented toward organization structure as the crucial variable. We see this as a drawback because the Medex model does not at the same time allow for the redundancies which would help protect it from problems due to the poor linkages (communication or otherwise) which are perennial in the rural Third World. It is probable that in practice this system would be seriously hampered by linkage problems or barriers not foreseen in the model. The USAID evaluation supports this point of skepticism (Gridley, Nzeussen and Teunissen, 1980: i-iv, 1, 24).

LINKAGES

In Chapter I it was stated that the success of a program's implementation depends on four variables: the program's vulnerability to inequality; the nature of local elites and their interests; the nature and variability of interests among national agencies; and the distribution between national and local organizations of the capacity to meet the program's technical and administrative requirements.

Our examination of the various health care delivery modes most often used in the Third World illustrates these points. As we have seen, health care as traditionally delivered, like agriculture and public works programs, is highly susceptible to inequality on two levels. First, because of the high cost of modern curative care, modern Westernized hospitals consume a very high percentage of the LDCs' health care budgets, often leaving virtually nothing for rural health. Even at the village level, however, medical care is susceptible to inequalities which may hamper the long-run success of the program. For example, if high-cost and highly specialized drugs are available, often what little money the village has to spend on drugs will be used to finance the best for those villagers with power, resources or influence.

Curative medicine is consumed by the individual, rather than the community. It is reasonable to expect, then, that those with power at the local level will be able to ensure that they are treated first. In addition, demand far exceeds supply. Even in the modern industrialized countries of the West there seems to be no end to the demand for medical care. This problem is amplified at the village level many thousandfold. The reason, of course, is that the quality of care can be constantly improved. At the village level this means that the benefits for the few will be increased rather than spread out to the many. Finally, the delivery of high-quality medical care requires highly trained medical practitioners, which in most of the Third World simply do not exist in adequate numbers to meet the need. Moreover, highly trained practitioners are often unwilling to move into the bush and be separated from their own upper-class community.

On the other hand, the benefits of community-based health care, which focuses on low cost, low technology, preventive care, are much less divisible and more widespread. Moreover, because it is low cost and low technology, health workers can be trained in much greater numbers so that supply can approach demand. Since preventive care is an indivisible "public good," the supply-demand equation loses much of its relevance.

The nature of elites and their interests is clearly demonstrated here. The "successful" program is one which brings the interests of the local elite into some degree of harmony with the poor. Preventive care accomplishes this commonality of interest. Additionally, as Jamkhed illustrates, by incorporating the local elite one stands a better chance of mobilizing the community as a whole.

We cannot overstress the impact of national agencies on the long-term success of any health program (see Korten, 1976: 20). Without firm commitment of the MOH and the national medical profession, the programs are doomed either to failure or to total dependence on a donor agency for support, training and financing. Unless the national government or some agency is prepared to commit itself to a rural-health or simplified medicine approach, the donor is best advised to spend its resources elsewhere. We must remember that in a very high percentage of Third World nations the MOH and/or the national medical association are not interested in altering their approach to health care (see Ugalde, 1978). For this reason we are particularly interested in the establishment of public health agencies and schools throughout the Third World. These bodies bring with them a preventive orientation to medicine and are close enough to the rest of the medical profession to be able to have some influence on it.

Rarely are the technical or administrative capacities of an LDC sufficient to meet the rural poor's health problems. Though there are sometimes enough doctors to begin training and supervising auxiliary health workers, these doctors are themselves almost never trained in management—or for that matter in public health. Additionally, and of at least equal importance, rural villages are generally not organized politically in a manner which will readily facilitate the extension of preventive health care. In these cases such organizations must be established to provide a continuing linkage mechanism between the village and the external health care establishment. For the program to succeed it needs viable linkage mechanisms between a committed national government or its health agencies and an organized administrative body at the village level. Simply put, "it takes two to link."

Our analysis of innovative programs of primary health care delivery has indicated various linkage mechanisms which are more effective at promoting well-being in the village than is classic hospital-based medicine. Keeping in mind the very important caveat that a particular nation's political setting and stage of development will define the specifics of any successful program, we conclude this discussion with some general comments about linkages.

First, our examination of various health care delivery systems brings us to the same conclusions that Uphoff and Esman (1974) came to in their studies of rural development. Rural well-being, in this case, is best promoted when there are both strong local organizations and effective links between them and national agencies which can support them. Neither rural development (i.e., social change) nor its concomitant "well-being" can be "delivered" to a passive population.

Second, this chapter has emphasized above all that there must be a linkage between modern medicine and the traditional village in the form of an intermediary. Whether this role is performed by an auxiliary, Medex, extension worker, VHW or cadre, case after case demonstrates the inability of Western medicine to have more than transitory contact with the rural poor without such an intermediary. The most obvious reason for this is simply an economic one. Most Third World countries do not have the resources required to train an adequate number of doctors and to give them the incentives (facilities, salaries, drugs and supplies) necessary to sustain the M.D.'s presence in every village. The second reason is one of culture. Doctors come from the upper-middle or upper classes of their countries. This fact in itself presents immense barriers to communication between the villager and the doctor. With a training and socialization process in medical schools which inevitably is oriented toward high-cost curative care, the M.D. is often incapable of delivering more than curative medicine, for he is unable to affect the community's organization or to help facilitate the process of social change.

Third, having introduced the notion of auxiliary as intermediary, we see that we actually have two linkage issues rather than just one: between the intermediary and the medical system and between the intermediary and the village. The strengths of the linkage between the auxiliary and the rest of the medical system and the linkage between the intermediary and the village may be somewhat inversely related. There is clearly a tension between the notions of strong medical supervision or evaluation of the auxiliary and the notion of local control over health policy. The Jamkhed project points in this direction. The project itself altered goals according to the felt needs of the community. It seems likely that, had the linkage to the medical establishment been very strong, this sort of local innovation would have been impossible.

In the absence of leadership at the intermediate level, however, the center must establish relatively firm linkages to the intermediary. This is not to say that the dilemma above is false; rather that Jamkhed may have been a rather special case. All other cases we examined which used intermediaries stressed the importance of continued linkages of evaluation and supervision. This linkage is a subtly coercive one.

The simpler the task, the less central "control" is necessary, but supervision or guidance cannot be ignored. Still, if drugs and procedures are quite basic, there is less need to ensure against misuse (through elite usurpation or poor allocation by the auxiliary). The less developed and/or the lower the administrative capacity within a nation, the more basic the training and drugs of the auxiliaries should be.

Fourth, there are a variety of linkage mechanisms between the center and the periphery in health. The center can provide to the auxiliary: training (both initial and continued), instruction manuals, medical kits, transportation, continued supervision, periodic evaluation, and drugs (see Gish and Feller, 1979). The village links to the auxiliary can include: selection, policy committee (to set program priorities), pharmacy (to sell the drugs), financial support, facilities, and gifts (not necessarily but often the practice).

Finally, we have devoted little time to a discussion of linkages between structural units in these health systems, e.g., rural clinic to regional hospitals, because these linkages appear to exist only on paper. While every system studied has an organizational chart stating that patients should be referred from one level to the next, in only one case which we have studied does this actually happen (the Jamkhed project). People go to the facility nearest to them whether it is the VHW or a big city hospital. There are a variety of reasons for this: these countries often have very poor transportation networks, the villager is reluctant to leave the village especially when ill, leaving the village means loss of income, and limited training of auxiliaries or paramedics means lower quality care (than M.D. care).

The Jamkhed project is worth noting here because it is an exception: cases too complex for the auxiliary are brought to the attention of the doctor during his/her weekly visits. If there is a need for referral the doctor and the health team take the patient back with them. The linkage is direct and simple, so it tends to work better than when the problem is simply left to the patient.

COMMUNITY PARTICIPATION

Throughout this chapter we have advocated community-based approaches to health care in the Third World. Several problems with this approach have emerged during our analysis, however.

The literature on community health programs rarely specifies what "the community" is. Do we mean everyone in a particular village or district? Or do we mean just the poor? The problem with defining the community as "everyone" becomes apparent when we begin to grapple with the issue of community organization. Almost all villages have some form of social and political community organization, but by definition the local elites dominate these organizations. While there are cases of more or less egalitarian social and political structures in rural communities, one would be naive to assume that all traditional village elites are intrinsically more socially conscious than are elites in a modern setting. The experiences of rural cooperatives in most countries demonstrate that local village elites can, and often will, use programs for their own betterment irrespective of, and sometimes to the detriment of, the local poor (see Chapter III). What, then, is to prevent these same elites from using their power and influence in the community to direct the village health committee and/or VHW towards the delivery of curative care—which they can dominate or get the most benefit from—and away from preventive care? "Social change," as we have said, mandates a change in the social and economic well-being of the poorest segments of the village. The disappointing results of the "basic needs" approach to rural development draw attention to the difficulties of accomplishing this end. Local elites tend to dominate community organizations and manipulate the organizations' goals to meet their own ends (see Rogahny and Solter, 1973).

Furthermore, villages are often composed of several "communities" which can be ethnically, culturally, linguistically, and developmentally quite distinct (see, for example, Gridley, Nzeussen and Teunissen, 1980: 31; and Rogahny et al., 1976). The Indian experience highlights the point that the divisions in these villages may be highly inegalitarian. The problem, then, is: can you have a community organization which will speak for those elements which are at the bottom of the social hierarchy? Perhaps a viable solution is to have several such organizations in a village where there are several communities. At any rate, an across-the-board solution is not adequate; a much closer look at what "the community" is is clearly needed in each individual case.

A second problem with the community approach is that the primary felt need of the rural poor is certainly not preventive medicine. It is doubtful that even curative health care is high on the poor villagers' priority list. For example, Dr. Behrhorst, who participated in a community health project in Chimaltenango, Guatemala, writes that one of her first problems was to realize that the community did not necessarily want the things which she was trained to do. "We think they need triple vaccine and more protein in their diet, and while it is true that they need these things, they are probably much more interested in, and need other things altogether" (Behrhorst, 1974b: 296). Yet the very notion of village-based health care demands local planning and participation.

In addition, the major flaw in simply scaling down the technology and/or quality of health care delivery for rural villages is that it is still *delivering* health care. This is the problem we have seen in the clinic-based approach and the principal cause of failure in the first attempts in Mukapawa, Philippines. We suggest that the village-based approach—which we clearly favor—needs closer examination before it is universally applied. Just as planners saw the rural cooperatives as the cutting edge of the "basic needs" approach only to discover many years later some fundamental problems, community health care is being advocated uncritically. WHO, UNICEF, USAID, CMC and many other agencies are now looking to implementation strategies for this new "primary health care" alternative. While this model is unquestionably more "appropriate" than the hospital and task force models that we have described, little is really understood in terms of the processes of community organization and village participation other than a few cases led and described by a few highly motivated, altruistic and charismatic individuals.

The problem is that it is not easy to let someone else plan. As one Kenyan doctor has noted: "In theory everyone wants to support community participation but when it comes to the point, they only want it as a peripheral part of a health program. They do not see that to have real community participation, you cannot draw up a definitive program in advance" (Black, 1978: 2). A crucial question needs to be asked: Do the successful cases in fact represent true village participation in health planning and organization? Or, alternatively, are they in reality cases of villagers accepting the ideas spawned, pushed by and largely dependent upon professionals?

The most appealing aspect of the village-based models we describe is that they demand community organization and community participation in decision-making. They also demand linkages to the center, however, without which the program will flounder. Thus the community organization is to make policy within the parameters of national or regional policy. Moreover, training, retraining and supervision linkages imply that the community organization will have its agenda manipulated by the center, or at least by the intermediary. We must remember that almost all peoples, no matter how remote, have providers of health care—witch doctors, herbalists, spiritualists or quacks. We are not providing the rural poor with something they want but do not have, but rather we want to change their felt needs so they will want something different from what they now have. We want to replace some aspects of traditional health care with some aspects of modern health care, which includes modern notions of sanitation and preventive medicine. This is a process of social change.

We have seen how programs of placing clinics in the periphery (as in India or Thailand) or building water systems and latrines (as in Guatemala) have been failures. They have failed because they have induced no social change. These technologies are inappropriate when there is no concomitant social change.

If the VHW or Medex is to be an agent of social change, his or her role must balance between control from the top and participation at the bottom. He/she must be a cadre. The VHW must be a facilitative, not a regulative linkage. The only way we see of striking this balance is to give the VHW both technical training and some degree of ideological indoctrination in favor of the betterment of his/her community. It must be made clear that this "betterment" will occur with preventive medicine. This is precisely what socialist party systems have been so successful at doing. Once "indoctrinated," the VHW can work to channel local participation in the direction of his/her training. It is important to see that the health demands made on the VHW by villagers will be for curative care. Only after manipulation of the villagers' felt needs will there be much interest in preventive medicine and sanitation. This manipulation can come only after the VHW has established his/her worth in terms of curative care. On the other hand, the demands made on the VHW by the medical system must be in favor of preventive care if the objectives of rural health care are to be met. Since this end of the linkage is doing the manipulating, it must be sensitive to the VHW's dilemma (see Bedaya-Ngaro, 1972: 26).

We close with an old Chinese poem:

Go to the People
  Live among them

Learn from them
Love them.
Start with what they know
Build on what they have;

But of their best leaders
When their task is accomplished
Their work is done
The people will remark,
"We have done it ourselves."

REFERENCES

Arole, Maybelle, and Arole, Rajanikant S. 1975. A comprehensive rural health project in Jamkhed (India). In *Health by the people*, ed. K. Newell. Geneva: World Health Organization.

Banerji, D. 1975. Social and cultural foundations of the health services of India. *Inquiry* 12, 2 (June): 70-85.

Barrion, Leonard B. 1980. The Makapawa. *Contact* 56 (June): 1-9.

Bedaya-Ngaro, S. 1972. Preparing the future. *World Health Magazine*, June, pp. 26-28.

Behrhorst, Carroll. 1974a. The Chimaltenango Development Project: Guatemala. *Contact* 19 (February): 1-8.

__________. 1974b. The Chimaltenango Development Project: Guatemala. *The Journal of Tropical Pediatrics and Environmental Child Health* 20, 6 (December): 295-99.

Berliner. H. 1980. Whither public health? *Health Policy and Education* 1.

Black, M. 1978. Deciding in the daylight: community care in Western Kenya. *UNICEF News* 98: 1-8.

Blum, Henrick, 1976. *Expanding health care horizons*. Oakland: Third Party Association Corporation.

__________. 1979. The nature of health planning. Report of the International Conference of Health Planners, Copenhagen.

Boesch, E. 1974. Communication between doctors and patients in Thailand. In *Community health and health motivation in Southeast Asia*, ed. H. J. Diesfeld and E. Kroeger. Weisbaden: Steiner Verlag.

Bomgaars, Mona R. 1978. Primary health care program operations. In *Manpower and primary health care: guidelines for improving/expanding health services coverage in developing countries*, ed. R. A. Smith. Honolulu: University of Hawaii.

Bryant, J. 1969. *Health and the developing world*. Ithaca: Cornell University Press.

Christian Medical Commission. 1973. Position paper on health care and justice. *Contact* 16 (August): 3-6.

Clinton, J. J. 1978. *Health populations and nutrition systems in LDCs: a handbook*. Washington, D.C.: U.S. Agency for International Development.

Djukanovic, V., and Mach, E. P., eds. 1975. *Alternative approaches to meeting basic health needs in developing countries*. Geneva: World Health Organization.

Elliot, C. 1975. Is primary health care a new priority? Yes, but . . . *Contact* 28 (August): 1-8.

Fendall, N. R. E. 1972. Forerunners. *World Health Magazine*, June, pp. 4-8.

Flahault, D. 1972. The case for medical assistants. *World Health Magazine*, June, pp. 8-13.

Fournier, G., and Djermakoye, I. A. 1975. Village health team in Niger (Maradi Department). In *Health by the people*, ed. K. Newell. Geneva: World Health Organization.

Gish, Oscar. 1973. Dr. auxiliaries in Africa. *Lancet* 7840 (1 December): 1251-55.

__________. 1975. *Planning the health sector*. London: Croon Helm.

__________, and Feller, L. L. 1979. *Planning pharmaceuticals for primary health care: supply and utilization of drugs in the Third World*. Washington, D.C.: American Public Health Association. International Health Programs Monograph, Series No. 2.

Gonzalez, C. L. 1975. Simplified medicine in the Venezuelan health services. In *Health by the people*, ed. K. Newell. Geneva: World Health Organization.

Gridley; Nzeussen; and Teunissen. 1980. Mid-project evaluation; Medcan; USAID/Yaounde. Washington, D.C.: U.S. Agency for International Development; 25 March.

Hendrata, Lucas. 1976. A model for community health care in rural Java. *Contact* 31 (February): 1-7.

Hill, George. 1978. Project evaluation summary—rural potable water systems and construction. Washington, D.C.: U.S. Agency for International Development.

Illiach, Ivan. 1976. *Medical nemesis: the expropriation of health*. New York: Pantheon Books.

Korten, David. 1976. Management for social development: experience from the field of population. Paper read at the Conference on Public Management Education and Training, 11-15 August 1976, Bellagio, Italy.

Kroeger, E. J. 1974. Social change and family health in a plantation population. In *Community health and health motivation in Southeast Asia*, ed. H. J. Diesfeld and E. Kroeger. Weisbaden: Steiner Verlag.

Laib, A. Majib. 1972. Experiment in Algeria. *World Health Magazine*, June, pp. 16-21.

McGilvray, J. A. 1974. Motivation for community participation in health care delivery. In *Community health and health motivation in Southeast Asia*, ed. H. J. Diesfeld and E. Kroeger. Weisbaden: Steiner Verlag.

Navarro, Vincent. 1974. The underdevelopment of health or the health of underdevelopment: an analysis of the distribution of health resources in Latin America. *International Journal of Health Services* 4, 1: 5-27.

Newell, K., ed. 1975. *Health by the people*. Geneva: World Health Organization.

Pene, P. 1973. Health auxiliaries in Francophone Africa. *Lancet* 7811 (12 May): 1047-48.

Penido, H. M. 1965. Health objectives in Brazil. In *Health objectives for the developing society*, ed. Ernest C. Long. Durham: Duke University Press.

Ram, Eric. 1978. Integrated health services project: Miraj, India. *Contact* 44 (April): 1-15.

Rogahny, Hossain A.; Najazadeh, Ebrahim; Schwartz, Terry; Russel, Sharon Stanton; Solter, Steven; and Zeighami, Bahram. 1976. The front line health worker: selection, training and performance. *American Journal of Public Health* 66, 3 (March): 273-77.

Rogahny, Hossain A., and Solter, Steven L. 1973. The auxiliary health worker in Iran. *Lancet* 7826 (25 August): 427-29.

__________. 1974. Is the Chinese barefoot doctor exportable to Iran? *Lancet* (29 June): 1331-33.

Ross, David. 1979. The Serabu hospital village health project. *Contact* 49 (February): 1-8.

Selznick, Phillip. 1949. *TVA and the grass roots*. Berkeley: University of California Press.

Smith, Richard Alfred. 1978a. Designing an appropriate approach to improved health service coverage. In *Manpower and primary health care: guidelines for improving/expanding health service coverage in developing countries*. Honolulu: University of Hawaii.

__________, ed. 1978b. *Manpower and primary health care: guidelines for improving/expanding health service coverage in developing countries*. Honolulu: University of Hawaii.

__________; Bassett, G.; Markarian, C.; Vath, R.; Freeman, W.; and Dunn, F. 1971. A strategy for health manpower: reflections on an experience called MEDEX. *Journal of the American Medical Association* 217, 10 (6 September): 1362-67.

__________, and Powell, Rodney. 1978. The emerging role of health in development. In *Manpower and primary health care: guidelines for improving/expanding health service coverage in developing countries*, ed. R. A. Smith. Honolulu: University of Hawaii.

Storms, Doris. 1979. *Training and use of auxiliary health workers: lessons from developing countries*. Washington, D.C.: American Public Health Association. International Health Programs Monograph, Series No. 3.

Ugalde, A. 1978. Health decision making in developing nations. *Social Science and Medicine* 12: 1-7.

United States Agency for International Development. 1975. Health sector assessment for Bolivia. Washington, D.C. Report No. PNAAE-654.

Uphoff, Norman, and Esman, Milton J. 1974. *Local organization for rural development: analysis of Asian experience*. Ithaca: Rural Development Committee, Center for International Studies, Cornell University. Rural Local Government Monograph No. 19; November.

Chapter VI

CHOOSING AMONG FORMS OF DECENTRALIZATION AND LINKAGE

David K. Leonard

Rural development requires a new type of decentralization. What is needed is not power for either central government or local organizations but complementary strength in both. Central government agencies, intermediate organizations and local groups all possess resources and capabilities that are needed by the others. The challenge is to link these institutions together in such a way that their weaknesses are counterbalanced and their comparative advantages are used. By so doing, a contribution can be made to development which neither local nor national organizations could achieve alone. The process of rural development depends on combining the resources and skills which are scattered among organizations of different types and sizes.

The prospects of successfully implementing rural development programs for the poor and the way one goes about doing it are strongly influenced by four parameters: (a) the program's vulnerability to inequality; (b) the nature of the local elites and their interests; (c) the nature and variability of interests among national agencies; and (d) the distribution between national and local organizations of the capacity to meet the program's technical and administrative requirements. On the basis of their assessment of these four factors, the designers of a program should select an appropriate structure of decentralization and set of linkages.

Of course, those designing programs rarely have the opportunity to influence the constitutional or basic institutional structure of a society. When ideal choices imply changes at that level they generally are simply utopian. Nonetheless, very few, if any, societies manage all programs with a uniform structural format. The institutional heritage provides a certain latitude and within that realm of decision the program designers want to choose as well as possible.

The four factors we have advanced as influencing program implementation suggest four corresponding questions to use in deciding upon the best structural arrangements for it. We will proceed in turn to analyze the design criteria that follow from the answer to each of these questions.

THE CHARACTER OF INTERMEDIATE AND LOCAL ELITES

Congenial Elites, Inclusive Organizations and Devolution. The designer begins with an examination of the program's inherent vulnerability to inequality in the distribution of its benefits and of the way this vulnerability interacts with the social and political structure of the rural areas. This analysis leads to the answer to the first question—*For this particular program, do political elites at the intermediate level represent the interests of the rural poor?* If the answer is yes, then one is in the happy position of being able to devolve authority to inclusive intermediate representative organizations and to avoid major conflict. If the compatibility of intermediate elite and rural poor interests is fairly common across programs, then the appropriate choice usually would be the existing, generalist local government (i.e., devolution—types a, b, c in Table 2, Chapter I, page 32). If the program's compatibility of interests were an exception, however, devolution to functionally specialized units would be preferable (i.e., functional devolution—types d, e, f). The specialized organizations involved then would be spared the patterns of conflict or elite-oriented dominance that characterize the generalist structures.

With respect to both alternatives, central government assistance would be appropriate to overcome shortcomings in financial or administrative capacity at the intermediate level and to balance regional disparities in resources. Central government controls generally would be both unnecessary and dysfunctional, however. Since the intent of the intermediate organizations is to assist their poor, controls could only add to the complication of the task and make it more difficult to adapt the program on the basis of experience.

The second and closely related question concerns *the degree to which purely local political elites represent the interests of their poor.*

Most often the same elite structure will prevail at the local and the intermediate levels. There are exceptions, however. Intermediate organizations may be dominated by small-town or large-farm elites while undeveloped villages in the area still have inclusive interests. It also is possible for political struggles to have produced a progressive leadership at the intermediate level (particularly if they are aided from the center) while the purely local levels are still dominated by those unresponsive to the poor. The same general rule applies at the local as at the intermediate level. Where elite and poor interests are shared, inclusive organizations are used (column one in Table 2, Chapter I). Where they are different, alternative ones of the poor or the direct provision of services to the disadvantaged are preferred (columns 2 and 3). The difference between the intermediate level and the local one, however, is that the latter is too small and limited in its resources to be capable of much significant, sustained program activity by itself. To have an impact, the local level depends on assistance from central or intermediate organizations.

Conflict and Alternative Organizations. The cases in which both local and intermediate elites share the interests of the poor in a program are the easy ones for rural development, particularly when there is a committed central agency to assist them. Implementation is extremely difficult when the interests of either set of elites conflict with those of the disadvantaged. The "natural" leadership of a community is difficult to by-pass and it always puts strains on a program to attempt to do so (Ralston, Anderson, and Colson, 1981: 18-21). Where program alternatives exist that do not put the interests of the poor and the better-off in conflict, it usually is best to pursue them first. One always tries to incorporate the local elites whenever their interests can be made compatible with the program's objectives.

Nonetheless, in regions where serious rural inequalities exist, the time and the program come when the conflict of interest between the poor and their local elites is unavoidable. As long as these local elites dominate the intermediate organizations of the area, as they generally do, action by a strong and progressive central organization is necessary in order to accomplish anything (Ralston, Anderson, and Colson, 1981: 20). If organization does not exist, it must be created, probably through political action, before programs that are vulnerable to inequality can be safely attempted. The forms of decentralization needed in these circumstances are prefectorial or ministerial deconcentration and delegation to autonomous agencies (k, l, n, o, q and r in Table 2, Chapter I).

Even with the support of a strong, progressive central organization the program implementation problems and the linkage issues are difficult. After all, nothing less than social change is implied by action in this context. The combination of a progressive center and a local and intermediate leadership unresponsive to the poor probably is inherently unstable. Over time either the local socio-political structure or the progressiveness of the center will be transformed. The comparison of Egypt and China is instructive here. After their respective revolutions both supported programs of social change that would transform the economic and political structure of the rural areas. China succeeded (Schurmann, 1966). Egypt initially made great inroads but ultimately failed. The pre-revolutionary small landlords have re-emerged as the rural elite; the state under Anwar Sadat lost its former commitment to the rural poor; and programs of benefit to the less-advantaged majority sometimes seem as difficult as before the revolution (Harik, 1974; Adams, 1981). The consequences of the U.S. War on Poverty represent an intermediate case. Local elites have been made somewhat more responsive to the interests of the poor than they were before and the national government is no longer as progressive. All three cases suggest that over a fifteen to twenty year period of conflict the central and local political forces will converge on a common point.

The preceding analysis leads us to suggest the replication of what Dale Marshall has described as the implicit parallel linkage strategy of the U.S. poverty programs. Similar methods are employed in India, were used in the collectivization of Chinese agriculture and were attempted in Nasser's formation of cooperatives to consolidate Egyptian land reform (Schurmann, 1966; Harik, 1974). The strategy presumes both the need to use new organizations and national controls to avert benefit diversion by local elites and the inability of the center to sustain this effort forever. It creates alternative local and intermediate organizations to serve as channels for new program benefits for the poor and to place new demands on the intermediate political systems. (In other words, in addition to direct work with local alternative organizations, intermediate interest organizations of the poor are created—types g, h, i.) At the same time it pressures the elite-dominated inclusive local and intermediate organizations to change, implicitly recognizing that ultimately they will gain control over most of the new programs.

With the parallel strategy the links between the center and the new alternative organizations of the poor are extremely close. The assistance to these organizations must be ample. Most of them could not survive their early years without this support. With the exception of accounting, the control content of the linkages to the alternative organizations is low. These entities are being supported because of their affinity for the interests of the poor, and high degrees of control would inhibit their natural growth, adaptation and strengthening. These local and intermediate alternative organizations are the major channels for program benefits in the early years.

Simultaneously the established inclusive organizations at the local and intermediate levels are used as subsidiary channels for new programs for the poor. The financial assistance provided comes with very stringent formal controls aimed at assuring that the intended beneficiaries are reached and at stimulating a reorientation toward the new clientele. (In other words a restricted amount of devolution or functional devolution is accompanied with tight central controls.) Judging from the U.S. experience these formal controls will be less strict in practice than they are on paper. It will be difficult to be strict about them in the face of local political pressures. Nonetheless, they give the center something with which to bargain and enable it to maintain some influence. Accompanying the control linkages should be extensive assistance ones in the form of personnel, advice and training. The secondment of staff from a progressive center to an intermediate or local organization can be a powerful device for value transformation in the recipient unit. Training and advice have a less potent socializing effect but can be significant when accompanied by the pressures provided by central controls and the competition of alternative organizations.

The purpose of this parallel strategy is to create a change dynamic in the inclusive organizations. It recognizes that eventually they will gain power over the alternative organizations and their programs. It seeks to give the alternative organizations real bargaining strength in this ultimate relationship and to create internal changes in the inclusive organizations through the pressure of formal controls and the socializing influence of assistance linkages. The ultimate impact of this parallel strategy on the inclusive local and intermediate organization is political, producing a change in the responsiveness of its leadership to the rural poor. It is not an explicitly political strategy and sometimes not even a conscious one, however, for it works through administrative and programmatic channels. The strategy is not necessarily efficient at the delivery of program benefits in its early years. That is not its purpose. It is designed to assure that benefits reach the poor and to stimulate sufficient social change to assure that they continue to reach them in the future. Only once the conflict between the inclusive and the alternative organizations over the division of the program resources is stabilized can real efficiency be expected.

The foregoing paradigm of the parallel strategy draws heavily upon Marshall and the U.S. experience in the 1960s and 70s. Similar principles have been used in assaults upon inequality in developing countries as well. In the first years of collectivization in the People's Republic of China the wealthier small farmers were prohibited from joining the new Agricultural Producers' Cooperatives. Only after the collectives had been firmly established under the leadership of those committed to rural equality were the richer farmers incorporated. The skills, assets and guidance of the wealthier farmers have been important to the productivity of collective agriculture. It was critical to institutionalize the principles of equality in the new organizations before the local elites were incorporated, however. The center and the Chinese Communist Party have intervened periodically in the years since collectivization to reinforce the commitment to egalitarian development. The strategy clearly was first to organize the rural poor separately around their own interests, only later to incorporate the contributions of local elites, and then to use a progressive center as a counterweight to any inegalitarian pressures (Schurmann, 1966).

A similar strategy was used by Nasser in Egypt, although with a much more limited impact. Special cooperatives were created to serve those who received land in the reforms that followed the revolution. Only the landless received reform land and only those who had received such land could belong to the cooperatives. These coops thus became alternative organizations, with membership restricted to the rural poor. With the support of the state they became a vehicle through which the poor could press their interests in the local power structure (Harik, 1974). Unfortunately, however, the impact of land reform on rural Egypt was too limited to transform the social structure of most villages and when progressive support from the center waned, the traditional elite structures reasserted themselves in only a slightly less inegalitarian form (Adams, 1981).

Whether in the United States, China or Egypt, in its early stages the parallel strategy treats the poor as passive recipients. In this phase it is directed at rural poor who are in dependent client relationships with elite patrons, an all-too-common condition (Ralston, Anderson, and Colson, 1981: 20). Strong action is necessary to break through the initial reluctance of the poor to organize separately from their patrons. The parallel strategy aims to transform the disadvantaged from passive dependents into active members of their own strong interest organizations (types g, h, i). Once it has succeeded the poor are able to shoulder for themselves much of the burden of protecting their own interests.

In the early stages of working with the poor, alternative organizations are formed so that the views of the disadvantaged can at least be formulated, expressed and considered. It seems to us that such a step usually has to precede more explicitly political action. Where the poor are weak it probably is best for these early stages of organization to be as apolitical as possible so as to avoid repression (Chapter II). Program procedures that simply require consultation with groups of the poor are as much as is needed at this point. These at least promote organization of the poor and the formulation of their views.

Attempts to give the poor formal control over visible central or local government programs may be counterproductive when the poor are politically weak. Such control bodies then will be by-passed or manipulated by those who have real power. This is what ultimately happened in Egypt when the state's commitment to social transformation was seen to be weak (Adams, 1981). True consultation of the wishes of the politically unmobilized poor actually may be less when they have formal control than when the only requirement is that they be heard. Of course the grant of formal representation and program control to the poor does increase their influence when they already have sufficient power to use it and adequate organizational strength to protect themselves from co-optation. Our point is that apolitical organization and administrative consultation may be more effective in the first stages of progress toward this goal than are more explicitly political strategies.

Closely related to the issue of representation of the poor is that of the local elite. We have argued that the local leadership should be given control over those programs for which it does represent the interests of its poor. In those program areas where it does not, the appropriate degree of formal representation and control is less clear. Local elites will continue to have influence on decisions that affect them whether they have a formal role or not. When the Kenyan government took over several program areas from its county councils, local leaders simply pressed their influence with different actors (Colebatch, 1974). Nonetheless, formal representation generally does lead to an increase in such local influence. This is a disadvantage to the poor when these leaders are not responsive to their needs. On the other hand, elite representation offers the possibility of their being co-opted into support for a program, and such representation is essential if coordination is to be achieved between several programs.

On the latter point, coordination is possible only if agreement is reached among those with influence on the content of the programs. The elites are always among this number and their influence will undo the coordination if they are not consulted. Thus there is a trade-off between strengthening the voice of the disadvantaged, on the one hand, and co-opting elites and achieving coordination on the other. The appropriate choice can be made only in the context of a particular program. The parallel strategy of the U.S. War on Poverty suggests that both options be used simultaneously. Some programs formally incorporated the local leadership structures in order to achieve coordination and to nudge them toward responsiveness to their poor; others kept the elites at a distance. Both may have contributed to the increased political influence of the American poor that ultimately resulted (Chapter II).

A rural development program based on alternative intermediate and local organizations is heady and risky stuff. After all, nothing less than a non-violent social revolution is being attempted. Its success is dependent upon a strong and quite committed central government. We turn now to the all-too-common situation in which that requisite is missing.

THE NATURE OF THE NATIONAL GOVERNMENT AGENCY

National Support. The third major question is, *Does the central agency concerned have a positive commitment to this program's benefits' reaching the rural poor?* Obviously national support is dependent upon an affirmative answer. If such support is lacking, intermediate and local organizations must be able to implement the program by themselves (devolution and interest organization—a to i in Table 2, Chapter I) or they must surrender the field to philanthropic organizations or the market (privatization—s to x).

Central support for program benefits' reaching the rural poor may be general in the national government or concentrated in a particular agency. Where support is generalized the program gains strength, other things being equal, from supervision by a local coordinator, be it a prefect or a development corporation. Central government involvement then comes as prefectorial deconcentration (j to l). Such supervision may even be crucial if there is strong generalized support in the government for the program but the agency with the technical competence needed to implement it is lukewarm. Socialist party secretaries often find themselves in this position with respect to primary health care and the medical establishment. On the other hand, when support is concentrated in the implementing agency, it is best for the agency to be freed from oversight by indifferent or hostile generalist government coordinators (prefects). Deconcentration within that agency is then in order (ministerial deconcentration—m to o). When the supervision of a line ministry by the other generalist regulatory bodies, such as a civil service commission or a treasury, is inhibiting as well, the necessary freedom from oversight is often found by giving the agency parastatal status—delegation to an autonomous agency (p to r).

Where a supportive national agency and a congenial intermediate elite structure co-exist—the ideal situation—devolution (a to f) generally would take precedence over deconcentration and delegation. (The exception would come with administrative weakness at the intermediate level.) Central assistance to the intermediate organizations with devolved responsibilities would be helpful as long as it is either modest or stable and without significant conditions. The greatest degree of adaptiveness and local responsiveness is attained when such central assistance is administered through a deconcentrated or delegated structure.

Irresolute Central Support. An unprogressive center is defined by the absence of a national organization with both a positive commitment to deliver a particular service to the rural poor and the resources to do so. If there is any danger of opposition to the program by elites, simple willingness in an agency to help the disadvantaged will not be enough. A resolute commitment and ability to overcome the difficulties will be needed. A central agency that is well-meaning but infirm in its support is a weak ally.

In general one responds to such a constraint by devolving responsibility to lower, progressive entities (devolution or interest organization), by turning responsibility over to private businesses or philanthropies (privatization), or by giving up on this particular form of program intervention altogether. The last alternative is not to be ignored. A system that is uncongenial to one form of assistance for the poor majority may have adequate central support for another. The international aid merchant who travels from country to country with only one brand of assistance for the poor does a disservice by installing programs that cannot provide them with benefits in that context and by diverting attention from program possibilities that would.

When there are local and intermediate organizations that have a progressive orientation toward a program area and central organizations that do not, the autonomy of the former from the latter is quite important (devolution, functional devolution and interest organization—a to i). Nonetheless even here there are certain forms of links to the center that can be encouraged. It is the independence of the local and/or intermediate organizations which is critical. Control linkages will jeopardize that independence and are to be avoided, but some types of assistance do not.

Reasonable amounts of assistance for local capital expenditures are appropriate as long as they do not create dependence on the center for recurrent funds. Moderate capital fund assistance usually can be cut back or not repeated without threatening the ability of the organization to maintain its programs. A loss in assistance for recurrent expenditures almost always creates a crisis, however. Recurrent fund grants therefore create a dependence while capital assistance need not. Once the habit of recurrent fund subventions is established, the prospect of its withdrawal will be quite threatening and the recipient organization may give up its commitment to the welfare of the poor if that is a condition for continued aid.

Grants for capital expenditures that have large recurrent cost implications may be even more threatening to the independence of a local or intermediate organization. Once the facility is in place, funds will be needed to operate it. If the required level of expenditure is beyond the means of the organization, it will seek recurrent assistance from the center without having even the bargaining advantage of precedent. The danger of dependence on an unprogressive center will be especially great if the grant comes from an international donor and includes enough money to start the operation of the facility. The state then has no commitment to the support of the program and the local organization will be anxious to keep it going. Compromises that would be seen as unacceptable to local or intermediate leaders in other circumstances are likely to be made in these.

The most attractive form of capital assistance to an organization that needs to maintain its independence is one that creates a recurrent source of income. Most organizations and donors are keen to have someone else bear the recurrent cost implications of their program investments. Someone ultimately must pay the bill. When the YMCA in Kitwe, Zambia, conducted its campaign for building funds, it wisely raised more money than it needed for its program facilities. It built a block of shops and put its services above and behind them. The rent from the shops then produced much of the income that was needed to run the programs. This kind of creative use of capital assistance for local revenue generation is especially important when the center is not a reliable source. Services for which community health workers can charge, bridges on which villages can collect tolls, crop storage facilities for which local coops can charge rent, etc., are the kinds of ideas for capital assistance that should be promoted in this setting.

A related linkage question concerns the role of unprogressive professionals in programs for the poor. Engineers are inclined toward more capital intensive projects and doctors tend not to have a public health orientation (Tendler, 1979: 42-44; see Chapter V). Yet the exclusion of the relevant professionals from a project or their isolation on it seem to be dangerous. The rural works projects in Pakistan and Tunisia suffered because the engineers were kept in a peripheral role (Burki, 1969: 334-40; Grissa, 1973: 137-38).[1] In both cases large infusions of funds for public works were provided through the

[1]This and other analyses of rural public works projects in this chapter draw heavily on Garzon, 1981.

generalist prefectorial administration. In Pakistan, where the projects were carried out through elected local governments, the engineers had formal contact with the program content only through the prefects. In Tunisia most projects were administered by the centrally-appointed regional governors. In both cases the technical departments felt alienated from the programs and their main attempts at influence were futile efforts to regulate and control what the prefects and local governments were doing. The bureaucratic conflicts meant that engineers and other technical staff did not play the creative role in the *development* of technically sound and progressive projects that was needed. As a result much of the project money had no positive benefit beyond employment generation, especially in Tunisia. In a similar manner, a rural health project has to have doctors in supervisory and consultative capacities and the opposition of the medical establishment to such a program is usually enough to kill it (Chapter V). The secret is to put such professionals in the central roles they deserve but to do so by incorporating them into institutions which have the appropriate sets of values for the program. When professionals are surrounded by others who are oriented to the program's goals, they can be co-opted. Even sympathetic professionals, however, will undercut a program if they are situated in an organization which is dominated by their own profession and has values inappropriate for the program's goals. Thus one wants engineers on a labor-intensive public works program but probably in a Ministry of the Interior, Office of the President or county government, not a Ministry of Public Works. Similarly an M.D. probably will serve rural health needs better if he is situated in a separate Community Health Service than if he is in a conventional Ministry of Health (Chapter V).

THE DISTRIBUTION OF TECHNICAL AND ADMINISTRATIVE CAPACITY

The fourth question concerns *the technical and administrative capacities of the two levels potentially leading the implementation of the program—central and intermediate*. (We have not included the administrative capacity of local organizations in our assessment as it is almost never sufficient for them to play a lead role—as opposed to a contributory one—in a major program.)

Technical Assistance Linkages. Many failures in development programs can be attributed to weaknesses in the administrative capacity of one or more of the implementing organizations. As important as this factor is, however, it must be kept in perspective. It is less important than the commitment of the units and their personnel. The review of the U.S. literature in Chapter II indicates, for example, that staff that are "technically incompetent but dedicated" are more effective than those with the reverse attributes (Marshall and Godwin, 1971: 88). Training and technical assistance can substitute for administrative weakness more easily than controls can overcome a lack of commitment. Nonetheless, administrative problems are pervasive and serious in development. Technical assistance as a solution for them does presume that administrative capacity exists somewhere within the society. Programs also still have to be adapted to the capacity that does exist and the allocation of functions between organizations arranged so that it can be used where it is to be found.

Dale Marshall examined the evidence on the effectiveness and impact of technical assistance in the U.S. poverty programs. She found that through its use it is possible to compensate for low administrative capacity in the recipient organization in the short run and to build its competence in the long term. Close supervision and evaluation by a committed, competent central or intermediate unit can be an extremely effective form of assistance to a weak local or intermediate organization (Chapter II).

Nonetheless, such assistance is not easy for the superordinate body to provide. It makes intensive use of the provider's administrative and personnel resources; an assistance orientation has to be kept in the forefront; the temptation to invade the recipient organization's autonomy must be resisted; and resources have to be committed to long-term, low visibility efforts of diffuse impact even when immediate, readily apparent, focused results are being rewarded. These are demanding requirements and many central agencies have difficulty meeting them. One of the more difficult, but important, forms of international aid is that which institutionalizes a central organizational capacity to assist local and intermediate organizations. Donors have found it hard both to help local organizations and to teach national central agencies to do it too. This is one area in which American domestic experience may be especially helpful. In the War on

Poverty the national government funded intermediate organizations whose sole function was to provide technical assistance to weak local bodies (Finney, 1975). This model deserves further study for possible replication elsewhere.

The technical assistance model just described is based on the presumption that the local or intermediate organization will eventually develop its own trained staff. An alternative model is needed when this assumption does not apply. Sometimes discrete, decentralized governments offer too limited career opportunities by themselves. Good professional staff are reluctant to join them as they are afraid of being stuck in a small organization for the rest of their careers. The creation of a single national cadre from which local senior civil servants can be drawn then helps to overcome this barrier to recruitment. The Indian Administrative Service is a particularly famous example of this model of seconding national staff to state government use. This case also illustrates the danger that national assistance with personnel can have an element of control built into it when it is permanent and concerns the most senior, policy-making staff. The Government of India at times has suspended an elected state government and ruled through the I. A. S. officers it has posted there. National cadre schemes that provide for the secondment of teachers or accountants are less threatening to the autonomy of local policy in this regard.

Both technical assistance models do assume that administrative strength exists somewhere in the system and that administrative capacity can either be developed in the assisted organization or lent to it permanently. When these assumptions are not warranted, technical assistance is not the appropriate response.

Linking Apportioned Functions. Another strategy for dealing with administrative shortcomings is to move the more complex functions to those organizations or levels that have the capacity to handle them. Some organizations never will be able to develop certain forms of competence. In Brazil and India where there is a large supply, doctors resist working in rural clinics and their services are unavailable in the more remote villages (Chapter V). Similarly, small, rural cooperatives find it very difficult to retain adequate accountants for their needs (Chapter III). In circumstances of this sort, it is unwise to assume that these shortcomings can be remedied. If they are approached with professional training programs the organizations will simply lose their staff once they are qualified. Instead of pouring resources into a bottomless training bucket, one should move the function in question to an organization that can retain the relevant professional and then construct a link between it and the needy local organization. Thus many local cooperatives have their accounting provided by district level intermediaries (Chapter III). Sometimes the demand for accountants is so great that no public organization can retain an adequate supply of trained ones. This is the case in Kenya today. Then methods of linking public and cooperative bodies to the services of private accounting and auditing firms have to be created.

The linkage method has gained wide acceptance of late for dealing with technical weaknesses, especially for the local level. Primary health care systems have abandoned the attempt to place highly qualified medical staff in villages and are using them as the trainers, supervisors and back-up for those that are willing to work there. Linkages are being used within administrative hierarchies as well. The Training and Visit system, which the World Bank is promoting for agricultural extension services, is a good example. It uses sub-professionals as the farmer-contact agents and backs them up with very close management by professionals at the intermediate level (ministerial deconcentration with no local organizations – type o). These professionals assume full responsibility for the assembly of information, the design of technical packages and the adaptation of recommendations (Benor and Harrison, 1977). Somewhat similar methods have been proposed for extension via paraprofessionals as well (Colle et al., 1979 and Esman et al., 1980).

We have argued for such administrative methods ourselves in an earlier work (Leonard, 1977). Nonetheless, precisely because of the growing popularity of linking apportioned functions, we want to express three cautions about it. The method is quite demanding of the superordinate organization; it is not new and is difficult to maintain; and it poses real problems for maintaining local adaptability.

First, moving the more complex functions up a level in the organizational system reduces the technical demands on those at the base, but it more than proportionately increases them at the new level of responsibility. It requires greater professional skill to perform a technical task for someone else and then to help them put it to use than it does to do it for oneself. Thus an organization that uses linkages to support sub-professionals will be larger than one that uses only professionals. The former may even use almost as many professionals as the latter. The justification for paraprofessionals is not so much that they conserve professional staff as that they make technical skills indirectly available in rural areas where professionals are unwilling to live and provide for more intensive staff interaction with villagers. Thus in Madhya Pradesh (India) the World Bank's Training and Visit system for agricultural extension uses one professional at the district level and below to support every four sub-professionals working with farmers. When the system was introduced it required a 38 percent increase in the *proportion* of professionals employed (World Bank, 1977, Annex 2: 5). Linking apportioned functions can relieve local shortages of skilled personnel but it still requires substantial numbers of professionals in the larger support system.

Second, the support of local sub-professionals by professionals at the central and intermediate levels is not new. The idea is evident in the educational systems developed in the colonial era.[1] The role of the school inspector began as a monitor of instruction and examinations, to ensure minimal academic standards. As educational systems in the developing world expanded rapidly, trained teachers were in short supply and inspectors often assumed a new role. They came to serve as local curriculum consultants and to provide instructional advice and training for teachers, as well as continuing to act as agents of control. This combination of functions is similar to that of the professionals in the primary health care and Training and Visit agricultural extension systems. The historical experience with the educational inspectors sounds a note of caution. The inspectorates have generally been understaffed and hampered by poor transport. In most countries reviewed a school was fortunate to receive one visit a year, far less than needed. Given the pressures on the time of the inspectors which arise from their inadequate numbers, their control functions have tended to supplant their support ones (Inamdar, 1974; International Institute for Educational Planning, 1978, 1979, 1980; Olivera, 1979). The point is not that the apportioning of linked functions does not work; it does. Rather, we want to warn

[1]The following analysis draws upon Edelstein (1980).

that for it to work properly an investment of personnel and resources in support services is demanded that is hard to sustain. To do so requires foresight, attention and effort.

Third, the apportioning of linked functions poses problems for maintaining local adaptability. One of the attributes of professionals is that they have sufficient expertise to adapt their knowledge to local conditions. Good sub-professionals know the standard technical solutions but lack sufficient understanding of their basis to alter them when they do not work. The professionals not only have to develop and initiate the solutions for the sub-professionals to apply; they have to be constantly seeking signals of problems that the sub-professionals may be unable to recognize. Such feedback is difficult to maintain, for the professionals have to overcome administrative distance to receive the error messages. Hence one of the reservations often expressed about the Training and Visit system of agricultural extension is that it will not be adaptive and will lead to the mindless application of inappropriate technical packages (Lowdermilk, 1981). Doctors have a similar concern about misdiagnosis and misplaced simple cures in primary health care systems. The problem is serious and real. The ideal solution is to have professionals at the base of the system—but their unavailability was the origin of the apportionment of functions in the first place. Feedback and adaptation systems have to be designed and receive constant, high-priority professional attention instead.

The linking of apportioned functions is an attractive response to irremediable administrative weaknesses at the local and intermediate levels. It does depend on administrative strength at the center, however. There also are dangers of malfunction associated with it and attention is required to avoid them. Nonetheless it frequently is the best solution available.

Redundant Linkages. The solutions to administrative weakness that we have examined so far have presumed that there is compensating strength available at the center or from an international donor. Are there responses to administrative problems that would reduce their impact, rather than shifting them elsewhere? One is to build redundancy.

Especially when we are dealing with essential services or their component parts, organizational effectiveness—not efficiency—is the first criterion of performance. The important point is to do the job. Only after that is assured does attention turn to lowering the costs of doing it. "Efficiency" dominates the vocabulary of organizational virtues and it is easy to forget that its importance is subordinate to that of effectiveness. Effectiveness is especially important with regard to poverty programs, where failures may mean loss of life or exposure of change-oriented poor to retaliation by local elites whom they have been encouraged to challenge. No single mechanism is fail-safe, be it a machine or an organization. Thus protection against failure is needed in back-up systems, in redundancy.

Redundancy is most important when the solution to a problem is unclear. It then permits multiple approaches, with the chance that at least one will succeed. Rural development efforts are classic examples of "messy problems," ones in which the path from the present to the goal, and sometimes even the exact goal itself, is controversial or unknown (Johnston and Clark, 1982, Chapter 1). Multiple, redundant assaults on these "messy" problems greatly increase the probability that one will succeed.[1]

The preceding principles have implications not only for program design, where they suggest multiple strategies in the trial stages, but for organizational structure as well. When a program is tied to a single set of non-redundant organizations, then it will fail if any one of those units fails. In the Sudan, for example, the entire governmental health system is dependent on the Central Medical Stores for its pharmaceutical supplies. When that one unit recently lost its capacity to keep essential drugs and vaccines cold, most of the rest of the medical system was rendered impotent—no matter how well it was being run (Medical Service Consultants, Inc., 1977; U.S. Agency for International Development, 1980).

It generally is dangerous in development design to reduce functional redundancies in organizations. Let us take the example of cooperative organizations in East Africa. These began as a highly dynamic response to oligopolistic private marketing enterprises (Hyden, 1976). After a time some of them began to falter. To ensure their survival and to improve their efficiency they were granted monopoly rights over the marketing of certain export crops in their areas. Once this was done both the state and the peasant producers

[1]For the origin and best elaboration of these ideas, see Landau (1969).

became highly dependent on these coops. Farmers were reduced to the choice of using them or withdrawing from export production. Their "exit" options, to use Albert Hirschman's term, were limited (1970). The state was rendered even more dependent, however; it needed the foreign exchange revenues of these crops; it could not afford to let these coops fail. An unfortunate dynamic was thereby released. Since the state could not afford to let a coop fail, signs of weakness were met with new central controls. The peasantry then felt progressively alienated from "their" coops; they no longer controlled them; the state did. An institution which needs *responsible* local involvement to function well lost it (Hyden, 1970; Hyden, 1976: 17-19). This downward vicious cycle probably would have been broken if organizational redundancy had been permitted. Competition between coops in the same area or between traders and tax-advantaged coops (as in the United States) would have caused the weaker coops to disappear and would have made stifling government regulation unnecessary. In this way two important linkage principles could have been maintained—that the local organization be permitted some significant autonomy and that the credibility of withdrawal of central support be retained as a sanction. When there is no organizational redundancy in a critical sector, the center cannot withdraw and must instead exert control to protect its dependency (Landau and Stout, 1979).

Stephen Peterson's examination of the literature on agricultural marketing and input supplies suggests that organizational redundancies may be easier managerially and cheaper in resources than creating reliable organizations. In a resource-scarce environment agricultural services seem to be more reliable when provided by competing organizations. We need careful empirical research on this point. "Common sense" appears to suggest the opposite—that when skills are short they should be concentrated in a single organization to assure their most efficient use. Thus country after country has created parastatal or cooperative monopolies at various levels in their agricultural sectors. The weaker a country's administrative resources, however, the more likely these monopolies will break down, with negative consequences for production. Contrary to "common sense," competition (be it between private or public units) is less demanding of scarce administrative talent. The market is itself an administrative mechanism but one that does not use administrators (Chapter III).

One of the advantages of having structural redundancy is that failing organizations can be permitted to die. It is important to make reasonable efforts to assist weak organizations but when these are unsuccessful it is best to let the organization collapse. When malfunctioning organizations are kept alive by unending infusions of assistance, there are four negative consequences (Chapter IV). (1) The society must continue to endure poor performance in an organization from which it presumably needs good service. (2) The organization acts as a continuing, unproductive drain on central and local resources. (3) The example of assistance provided to an ineffective organization acts as a disincentive to others to perform well. (4) As long as the malfunctioning organization is kept alive, it inhibits the rise of an alternative, stronger one. Administrative problems often are institutionalized in a particular organizational structure. An alternative organization operating in much the same functional area might well not have the same problems. Indeed the collapse of a malfunctioning organization can be a positive learning experience for a community. The causes for its failure will be remembered and are less likely to be repeated in the next attempt. Organizational death helps to teach society how to administer and it releases scarce administrative resources to those agencies and groups that can use them more productively.

Redundancy also has its virtues looking upward in the organizational hierarchy. From the point of view of the peasant the existence of two or more local organizations providing a service (even if one is more conveniently located) assures him that he can alter behavior to depend on them, for at least one of them will be there when he needs it. He can grow a market crop knowing that if the coop collapses or becomes exploitative, there is another one or a trader there to turn to instead. The local organization also benefits from being linked to more than one central agency. If resources run down in one program area, then it can rely more heavily on those in another. When there are redundant channels of support available, dependency on the center need not end in loss of autonomy (for a South Korean example, see Korten and Young, n.d.). With upward and downward redundancies, strong interdependencies can be created among organizations without tight control by one over the other and with less danger that administrative weaknesses will cause the collapse of the whole service chain.

Administrative Simplification. The final response to administrative and technical weaknesses is to reduce the complexity of the program or its components to the capacity of the units that will implement them. Our research has indicated six maxims that can be followed in reducing complexity and administrative demands (Chapter IV). (1) Single-function organizations are less complex than multiple-function ones. (2) Small units are less complex than large ones. (3) The greater the number of hierarchical levels the larger the complexity. (4) The market is administratively simpler than a hierarchy. (5) It is much more difficult to administer benefits that are targeted for a specific clientele than those that are general. (6) When administrative capacity is in doubt, simplicity outweighs all other virtues in organizational and task design.

As trite as these maxims are, they frequently are ignored when their application would reduce the administrative problems of rural development. For example, they lead to a new look at large integrated rural development programs. It is one thing to argue that rural development requires many institutional components and that integration is therefore needed in analysis, planning and policy-making. It is another to create an *administratively* integrated, multifunctional program in an administratively weak environment. If the effective operation of each component is made dependent on the others, there is a high probability that the whole program will not work. This has happened with the World Bank's Integrated Agricultural Development Project in Kenya. It seems preferable to make components independent of one another—even at the cost of performance *potential*—in order to increase the probability that *actual* performance will meet minimum standards (Leonard, 1981).

Simplification is needed in administrative procedures as well as in organizational structures (Uphoff, Cohen, and Goldsmith, 1979: 277). Complex and lengthy procedures prevent poorer communities from administering their own programs and make even good administrators appear incompetent.

OVERWHELMING CONSTRAINTS

The theme of our analysis of constraints has been that problems in one area can be compensated by linkages to organizations with competence and commitment. Burdens can be shifted from the weak to the strong, however, only as long as strength exists somewhere. There are situations in which we have to accept that the constraints really are overwhelming and that nothing direct can be done to help the rural poor.

As difficult as it is, it is important to accept inaction in the face of the clear probability of failure. A program that fails in its objective to help the poor may well leave them worse off than before. If it has tempted the poor to form an alternative organization, it will leave them vulnerable to elite reprisals. If program benefits have been diverted to local elites, disparities in rural incomes and power may actually have been accentuated further. Even a harmless, ineffective program may persist by imposing a direct or indirect tax burden on the poor. When something is attempted against the odds, it is important to be able to shut the program down as soon as it is clear that it has aborted in its objectives.

What does one do for the poor in the face of overwhelming constraints? First, one looks for alternative programs that will not be as vulnerable to inequality or which make smaller demands on the society's administrative capacity. Just because one thing cannot be done for the poor does not mean nothing can.

As to the original area of action, the designer must leave it to charities and a competitive market (privatization—philanthropy and marketization—types s to x). As inadequate as these may sometimes appear to be to the redistributive needs of the poor, they are not as dangerous as uncommitted public agencies. The latter most often use their position to gain monopoly powers and force consumers to use inefficient, overpaid bureaucrats or otherwise become exploitative of the poor. There are large numbers of countries and many sectors in which a competitive market would represent a vast improvement for the poor over exploitation by public and quasi-public agencies (e.g., Bates, 1981). In this century of socialism it is easy to forget that Marx saw capitalism as a *progressive* force compared to the feudal and mercantilist structures that preceded it (Marx and Engels, 1959: 8-12). Many so-called socialist states in the developing world today would be more accurately labeled as mercantilist (Callaghy, 1979: 126-28). Socialist institutions placed in a hostile political environment often have most unsocialist consequences. A competitive market, for all its problems of maldistribution, is less exploitative than a rapacious government.

The foregoing argument for the use of the market needs to be distinguished from some of the current American demands for an expanded role for the private sector in economic development. The empirical evidence we have examined and the logical structure of the case we have presented support greater use of *indigenous, small competitive* entrepreneurs. Such enterprises are administratively simple, often use personnel with relatively low formal qualifications, are small enough to have strong, direct incentives to performance, and are strictly limited in their ability to exploit their customers by intensive competition in the markets they serve. Large multinational corporations are a wholly different entity from these small entrepreneurs, even if both are private. The multinationals are administratively complex, have highly trained personnel, are large, have bureaucratized incentive structures, and in less developed countries very frequently have monopolistic powers over the markets they serve. Just as the state has a role in keeping the market competitive and efficient for small entrepreneurs, an LDC government frequently has to use its regulatory powers as a substitute for the competitive forces of the market when dealing with multinationals. Multinationals may be more efficient than many state-run corporations in some developing countries, but both are equally capable of being exploitative when they have monopolistic powers. The general thrust of our argument and the evidence we have examined is to be fearful of monopoly, from whatever source it arises.

A major unanswered question remains about privatization as a device of rural development. Can an otherwise uncommitted or incompetent state do anything to promote the services offered to the poor by the private sector? Subsidies can sometimes be used to induce commercial interest in otherwise unprofitable ventures, as with nutritional supplementation of staple foods or the rural distribution of pharmaceuticals (Esman and Montgomery, 1980: 191, 199). In general, however, we know far too little about using the market to benefit the poor. Some attention has been given to the regulation of weights and measures as a mechanism for improving the prices received by poor farmers (Lele, 1975: 113-15). Considerable research also has been done on helping small businesses for the sake of their owners (e.g., Marris and Somerset, 1971), but little has been undertaken on assisting them to improve rural services. Overall, our understanding of the consequences for the poor of public control and assistance linkages to the private sector is in its infancy. We are more aware of the dangers than of the positive steps that can be taken.

THE ALLOCATION OF FUNCTIONS BY ORGANIZATIONAL PRIORITIES

The general theme of our studies is that different organizational units will tend to give priority to different aspects of a service sector. Thus we conclude that it is best to allocate primary responsibility for a task to that entity which treats it more seriously. Organizational value propensities are distinct from their technical capacities, although they sometimes are related. When the necessary technical capability to perform a task is to be found in more than one organization, even if it is only minimal in one of them, it generally is best to allocate that function to the unit which gives it the higher priority.

In education, for example, local school committees, in comparison with the levels above them, tend to be more concerned with physical plant facilities and manifest results, especially on standardized examinations. The educational professionals at the intermediate and particularly at the national levels, on the other hand, generally care more than the locals do about standards, curriculum development, and diffuse educational objectives. This suggests precisely the kind of division of responsibility between local school committees and super-ordinate units which has been adopted in most countries. The local community plays a major role in financing school buildings and can be trusted to press for teachers that will produce success by the more obvious educational indicators. At the intermediate and national levels the educational professionals set standards (and thus determine who can be hired as a "qualified" teacher) and define a great many of the success indicators (i.e., write the exams) on which communities rely. These higher levels also are best suited for the demanding support role of curriculum development.

With respect to health, local communities are likely to care most about the availability of curative health practitioners and pharmaceuticals. Elites and M.D.'s tend to give priority to the quality of curative medicine, at the expense of quantity if necessary. Public health professionals are oriented by their training to the promotion of healthful living conditions, to preventive medicine and to the wide distribution of health services. This latter set of issues are the ones which actually have the greatest impact on health status. Thus the interests of the rural poor are generally better served the greater the extent to which public health professionals are able to define the nature of the health care system and to influence the allocation of resources within it. Yet it is very rare for public health practitioners to control a national medical system. Usually the most they can do is to gain overall responsibility for rural health. There they can set program parameters such that there are adequate means for wide distribution. For example, the drugs that rural health centers are permitted to stock can be limited to the most critical, relatively inexpensive ones. This increases the likelihood that the poor will have access to the pharmaceuticals they most need. Otherwise the few would be likely to receive expensive drugs and the many, none at all. Similarly the training requirements for community health workers can emphasize the development of health promotion and preventive skills, so as to socialize them toward the benefits these offer. Within the parameters of such a system the demand of local communities for wide availability of curative services and the drive of M.D.'s for high quality are functional. Thus local governments and communities can be given responsibility for financing their facilities and M.D.'s can be allocated the role of supporting the work of paraprofessionals and handling referrals (Chapter V).

Unfortunately the literature on health care systems does not indicate whether this combination of guidance by public health professionals and a strong drive to expand the system is more likely to be found among intermediate local governments or national rural health services. Elected rural local governments have a history of pressing for the wide distribution of static health facilities and of doing battle with urban interests for the resources to support them. These intermediate organizations may be less receptive to the professional guidance which is needed to maintain a public health orientation, however. Further research is needed on this point.

The allocation of functions between local and intermediate cooperatives and the state poses somewhat different issues. Accounting is a nearly universal problem for cooperatives (Chapter III). In the larger and intermediate cooperatives there is the danger of misallocation of funds by the leadership. In small coops and alternative local organizations the members usually lack accounting skills. Thus the books are badly kept or are turned over to local elites—again raising the danger of misappropriation and perhaps forcing the poor to accept elite leadership unnecessarily. Only in coops with a membership that is both fairly sophisticated and relatively homogeneous is accounting not a weak point. In recognition of this problem the involvement of external agencies in cooperative bookkeeping is widespread and appropriate. Intermediate cooperative organizations usually have their accounts audited by or under the supervision of the state. The weaker primary cooperative societies and alternative local organizations generally are wise to obtain bookkeeping services from district cooperative unions or field officers of the state—both of which are intermediate organizations. This division of labor has several advantages. Those providing financial monitoring are in organizations that are more removed from the opportunities of profit from mismanagement; the state and secondary cooperative organizations often depend for their income on the performance of primary societies; accounting and auditing are provided at organizational levels where those skills are usually more easily found; and the assumption by an intermediate organization of the inherently bureaucratic accounting responsibilities permits the local organizations to be more infomal and therefore more accessible to control by their poorer members (Chapter IV).

The cooperative and primary health care examples suggest a more general rule. For those aspects of a program that are particularly vulnerable to inequality and where local elite interests are likely to diverge from those of the poor, external controls from the intermediate or central level are appropriate. Nonetheless, control over some aspects of a subordinate organization's performance should not mean control over all. *Appropriate* control is a service to the local organization's constituency and it is important to provide it only for those areas where the service is needed.

Effective control is based on four requisites: First, it depends on social distance. Where the controller is close to the people he is monitoring, he is likely to become a part of the problem. Where the center needs both to control an organization and to have good feedback from it, separate control and support agencies are implied. In the case of financial controls this can be done through the retention of private firms or separate government departments for auditing. The second requisite for effective controls is some political backing. If a problem is identified but nothing is done about it, the monitoring is for naught. Part of the problem in the Kenyan cooperative movement has been political protection for leaders identified by the Department of Cooperatives as having misappropriated funds. Third, controls must be accompanied by a deconcentration of authority to administratively competent field agents. Otherwise adaptability and the entire rationale for a decentralized structure is lost. Taiwan does this deconcentration well in monitoring its farmer associations (Stavis, 1974). Often the problem with controls is not that they exist but that the controllers have inadequate flexibility and discretion themselves. Fourth, external controls generally should be seen as a service to the organization's constituency, protecting it from its own internal weaknesses. Otherwise the controller loses sight of the purpose for which the organization exists and destroys its ability to function.

In assessing external controls special attention must be given to the needs of local organizations. These serve as a link between the formal governmental system and the face-to-face community. This tie between the formal and informal structures of society is what the state most needs from these local organizations. Generally there is a tension between the strength of the link to government and the tie to the community. Studies of primary health care and irrigation organizations particularly stress the need for local organizational autonomy (Chapters V and III). In general the greater the need for a close tie to the face-to-face community the more important it is to loosen government controls. To the extent that control is needed it often can be achieved indirectly through the intermediate organizations that provide services to the local ones. Thus Taiwan is able to guide local irrigation associations through its control over the intermediate, supply-providing, farmers' associations (Stavis, 1974). Generally intermediate organizations need less autonomy to preserve their downward links, as they already are more removed from the community.

When controls become too extensive any local sense of responsibility for the organization is lost and with it much of the ability of the organization to function well. One cannot define when controls become too tight in the abstract, for the issue is more subjective than objective. Some cultures, such as those in East Asia, expect high degrees of state control and will continue to feel responsible for a local organization under levels of external supervision that would quite discourage other peoples. "Too much control" then is a culturally relative concept but the point at which it is reached can be determined by observing organizational behavior in the society concerned.[1]

ASSISTANCE LINKAGES

Despite the need for supportive and equalizing controls in some areas, the basic emphasis should be on assistance from the center to intermediate organizations and from both to local ones. We have placed a great deal of stress on selecting organizations with the right set of institutional interests for a program. Nonetheless, a large proportion of appropriate local and intermediate organizations fail in implementation due to incompetence or a weak resource base. Assistance linkages are vital in overcoming these shortcomings. In our opinion, the need for the center to maintain a service orientation and to provide assistance beyond simply finances to intermediate and local organizations is the great decentralization lesson of our generation (see also, Esman and Montgomery, 1980).

One of the advantages of assistance linkages over control ones is that they facilitate the internalization of the basic value orientations of a program at the local level. This result emerges clearly from the U.S. experience with poverty programs. Central controls set up resistance and create an adversary relationship. Training, professional advice and the like are (properly) seen as assistance, are more readily accepted, create less psychological resistance and have a socializing effect on local program content. Thus assistance linkages that promote equalization or redistribution of services often produce more results among resistant organizations than controls do (Chapter II).

Despite its advantages, an assistance orientation is not an easy one for the center or intermediaries to maintain. It is costly for the unit providing it. Even non-material forms of assistance impose heavy

[1] For more on expectation levels and the related idea of relative deprivation, see Blau, 1964.

personnel and administrative burdens. While assistance internalizes costs for the providing organization, controls externalize most of the expenses and impose them on the receiving organization. Of course, the super-ordinate organization must still bear the expenses of administering the controls but most of the costs are borne by the subordinate one, creating the illusion for those above that controls are cheaper than assistance. For the system as a whole, however, they may actually be more expensive, for resources then are spent on interorganizational conflict as well as on getting the job done. Controls are frequently needed but often assistance is the better alternative and is discarded for reasons of false economy alone.

A footnote concerns the subtle boundary between control and assistance linkages. Certain forms of assistance have the potential for turning into controls—supply channels, marketing services, professional advice and services, etc. The clearest signal that the assistance may be turning into a control is the desire of the providing organization to monopolize it. The program designer and institutional analyst want to pay special attention to this transition and be sure that it is appropriate. Controls may well be needed and then their being clothed in the form of an assistance monopoly makes them more palatable. Where they are not truly necessary, however, this transformation of assistance lowers the effectiveness of the service system by imposing hidden, indeterminate costs and by reducing the redundancies in service channels that are so vital to organizational effectiveness.

There can be too much of a good thing. Assistance linkages can be enfeebling instead of supportive. When an organization is provided with too much assistance or receives it too fast, it becomes overwhelmed and the locality's administrative capacity and sense of responsibility are destroyed. The rural works program in Ayub Khan's Pakistan illustrates this problem particularly well (Sobhan, 1968: 89). The program's revenues were based on the sale of American gifts of grain. The bulk of the funds was channelled to elected local governments—the Union Councils.

> Paradoxically, the sudden flow of funds to the Unions, which overnight doubled their budgets, made them more, not less, dependent upon the central government and its district administrators. Often Unions responded to the windfall by lowering taxes

> or becoming more lax in collection . . . In this way, they incurred the favor of their constituents. For the same reason, the Unions devoted more attention to the Works Programme, and less to their traditional tasks of adjudication and tax collection. By reducing their own tax base, they became more dependent upon the grants, which were allocated yearly. Because they were entering new fields of endeavor, they also depended upon upper echelons for guidance (Garzon, 1981: 16).

The result of the assistance thus was a reduction in local government autonomy and capacity.

Emergency relief programs and large international donors are more likely to provide enfeebling assistance than other central organizations are. Their good intentions may need to be checked on occasion, in the long-term interests of development.

CONCLUSION

Equitable rural development is known to be central to balanced, sustained, national, economic growth (e.g., Johnston and Kilby, 1974). It also is extraordinarily difficult to achieve. Over the last decade a great many attempts have been made and only a few have succeeded. We believe that a large number of the failures derive from naivete about the importance and subtlety of organizational design. In retrospect we can see that a great many attempts to reach the poor majority were trusted to unsuitable organizations, where success would have been a miracle.

All too often programs to benefit the rural poor were implemented through organizations with little genuine commitment to them or with seriously deficient administrative capacity. As the international donor or the national government began to realize the inadequacies of the implementing organization, it moved to correct them through a series of controls. Most often these controls did not succeed in stopping the diversion of benefits to the more advantaged. Instead they made implementation even more complex and made any creative change impossible. Without the possibility of innovation, program success was even more unlikely. Rural development poses a notoriously "messy" set of problems;

creativity and adaptation are essential to their solution (Johnston and Clark, 1982).

The concern of this book has been to identify "appropriate" organizations for various types of rural development programs. We have seen decentralization as essential to efforts to reach the rural poor; no other course offers the possibilities for the adaptiveness and the participation of the poor themselves that are essential to success. We have argued, however, that decentralization can be achieved in a large number of different ways. The particular form of decentralization that is "appropriate" depends on the character of the program, the sociopolitical setting and the nature of the available organizations. We have developed a set of general analytic tools for identifying "appropriate" decentralization and have provided specifics about their application, particularly for the fields of agriculture and health.

It is our hope that program designers become sufficiently hard-headed about the choice of implementing organizations to avoid programs that are destined to fail and to make central-local relationships more of a partnership in those activities that are pursued. As long as control is the dominant, rather than the minor, theme in the interactions between donors, the national government and local organizations, tremendous amounts of effort will be expended in futile conflict. When central and local organizations are used that are congenial to a program's goals and requirements, mutually supportive relationships and program success become a probability.

This is not to say that we envision rural development without conflict. The welfare of the poor majority is frequently blocked by organizations responsive to the interests of elites. Controls over such organizations are necessary and are a key part of progressive change. We see these entities as the minor, not the major, instruments for implementation, however. In many settings new alternative organizations of the poor are the best vehicles for progressive programs. Here we favor a parallel strategy of assistance for alternative organizations (the major theme) and controls over elite dominated ones (the minor theme).

Thus we advocate a new type of decentralization as vital to rural development and the welfare of the poor majority. We see decentralization not as local power at the expense of the center but as a relationship in which linkages between local effort and central assistance produce a new partnership for progressive economic development.

REFERENCES

Adams, Richard H. 1981. *Growth without development in rural Egypt: a local-level study of institutional and social change*. Ph.D. dissertation, Department of Political Science, University of California, Berkeley.

Bates, Robert. 1981. *Markets and states in tropical Africa*. Berkeley: University of California Press.

Benor, Daniel, and Harrison, James Q. 1977. *Agricultural extension: the Training and Visit System*. Washington, D.C.: The World Bank.

Blau, Peter. 1964. *Exchange and power in social life*. New York: Wiley.

Burki, Shahid Javed. 1969. West Pakistan's rural works program: a study in political and administrative response. *The Middle East Journal* 23, 3 (Summer).

Callaghy, Thomas M. 1979. The difficulties of implementing socialist strategies of development in Africa: the "first wave." In *Socialism in sub-Saharan Africa: a new assessment*, ed. C. G. Rosberg and T. M. Callaghy. Berkeley: Institute of International Studies.

Colebatch, H. K. 1974. Government services at the district level in Kenya: roads, schools and health services. Brighton, England: Institute of Development Studies, University of Sussex. Discussion paper No. 38.

Colle, R. D.; Esman, M. J.; Taylor, E.; and Berman, P. 1979. *Concept paper: paraprofessionals in rural development*. Ithaca: Rural Development Committee, Center for International Studies, Cornell University; March.

Edelstein, Richard. 1980. Case studies of the rural school inspector. Berkeley: Project on Managing Decentralization, Institute of International Studies, University of California. Unpublished manuscript.

Esman, Milton J.; Colle, Royal; Uphoff, Norman; and Taylor, Ellen. 1980. *Paraprofessionals in rural development*. Ithaca: Rural Development Committee, Center for International Studies, Cornell University.

Esman, Milton J., and Montgomery, John D. 1980. The administration of human development. In *Implementing programs of human development*, ed. Peter T. Knight. Washington, D.C.: The World Bank. Working paper No. 403.

Finney, Henry C. 1975. *Problems of local, regional and national support for rural poor-peoples' cooperatives in the United States: some lessons from the War on Poverty*. Ann Arbor: Institute for Research on Poverty, University of Wisconsin. Reprint No. 142.

Garzon, Jose M. 1981. Small-scale public works, decentralization and linkages. In *Linkages to decentralized units*, ed. D. Leonard and D. Marshall. Berkeley: Project on Managing Decentralization, Institute of International Studies, University of California. Unpublished manuscript.

Grissa, Abdessatar. 1973. *Agricultural policies and employment: case study of Tunisia.* Paris: Development Center of the Organization of Economic Cooperation and Development.

Harik, Iliya F. 1974. *The political mobilization of peasants: a study of an Egyptian community.* Bloomington: Indiana University Press.

Hirschman, Albert O. 1970. *Exit, voice and loyalty: responses to decline in firms, organizations and states.* Cambridge: Harvard University Press.

Hyden, Goran. 1970. Government and cooperatives. In *Development administration: the Kenyan experience,* ed. R. Jackson, G. Hyden and J. Okumu. Nairobi: Oxford University Press.

__________, ed. 1976. *Cooperatives in Tanzania: problems of organization building.* Dar es Salaam: Tanzania Publishing House.

Inamdar, N. R. 1974. *Educational administration in the Zilla Parishads in Maharashtra.* Bombay: Popular Prakashan.

International Institute for Educational Planning. 1978. The organization of education in the Sankhuwa Sabha District of Nepal. Paris: UNESCO.

__________. 1979. The organization of education in the New Halfa District of the Democratic Republic of the Sudan. Paris: UNESCO.

__________. 1980. Problems of educational administration in remote rural areas. Paris: UNESCO.

Johnston, Bruce F., and Clark, William C. 1982. *Redesigning rural development: a strategic perspective.* Baltimore: Johns Hopkins University Press.

Johnston, Bruce F., and Kilby, Peter. 1974. The design and implementation of strategies for agricultural development. *Agricultural Administration* 1, 3 (July): 165-97.

Korten, Frances E., and Young, Sarah. n.d. The mothers clubs of Korea. In *Managing community based population programmes.* Kuala Lumpur: International Committee on the Management of Population Programmes.

Landau, Martin. 1969. Redundancy, rationality and the problem of duplication and overlap. *Public Administration Review* 29, 4 (July-August): 346-58.

__________, and Stout, Richard. 1979. To manage is not to control: the danger of type II errors in organizations. *Public Administration Review* 39, 2 (March-April): 148-56.

Lele, Uma. 1975. *The design of rural development: lessons from Africa.* Baltimore: Johns Hopkins University Press.

Leonard, David K. 1977. *Reaching the peasant farmer: organization theory and practice in Kenya.* Chicago: University of Chicago Press.

__________. 1981. Administrative issues in implementing Kenya's food policy. Paper read at the Ministry of Agriculture's National Food Policy Seminar, Nairobi, Kenya.

Lowdermilk, Max K. 1981. Promoting increased food production in the 1980's: approaches to agricultural extension in different production systems. Paper read at the Symposium on Promoting Increased Food Production in the 1980's, 5-9 January, 1981. Washington, D.C.: The World Bank.

Marris, Peter, and Somerset, Anthony. 1971. *The African businessman*. London: Routledge and Kegan Paul.

Marshall, Ray, and Godwin, Lamond. 1971. *Cooperatives and rural poverty in the South*. Baltimore: Johns Hopkins University Press.

Marx, Karl, and Engels, Friedrich. 1959. Manifesto of the Communist Party. In *Basic writings on politics and philosophy*, ed. Lewis S. Feuer. Garden City: Anchor Books, Doubleday and Company.

Medical Services Consultants, Inc. 1977. *Report of the health sector assessment team – Sudan*. Washington, D.C.: U.S. Agency for International Development.

Olivera, Carlos. 1979. *The administration of education in Latin America*. Paris: International Institute for Educational Planning, UNESCO.

Ralston, Lenore; Anderson, James; and Colson, Elizabeth. 1981. *Voluntary efforts and decentralized management*. Berkeley: Project on Managing Decentralization, Institute of International Studies, University of California.

Schurmann, Franz. 1966. *Ideology and organization in Communist China*. Berkeley: University of California Press.

Sobhan, Rehman. 1968. *Basic democracies rural works programme and rural development in East Pakistan*. Dacca: Bangladesh Bureau of Economic Research, University of Dacca.

Stavis, Benedict. 1974. *Rural local governance and agricultural development in Taiwan*. Ithaca: Rural Development Committee, Center for International Studies, Cornell University. Rural Local Government Monograph No. 15; November.

Tendler, Judith. 1979. *New directions for rural roads*. Washington, D.C.: Office of Evaluation, U.S. Agency for International Development.

United States Agency for International Development. 1980. Sudan health sector support project paper. Washington, D.C. No. 650-0030.

Uphoff, Norman T.; Cohen, John M.; and Goldsmith, Arthur A. 1979. *Feasibility and application of rural development participation: a state-of-the-art paper*. Ithaca: Rural Development Committee, Center for International Studies, Cornell University.

World Bank. 1977. India: Madhya Pradesh agricultural extension and research project. Washington, D.C. No. 1442a-IN; 2 May.

AUTHOR INDEX

Aaron, Henry, 46
Adams, Dale, 91-92, 94-95, 96, 97, 98-99
Adams, Richard, 19, 196, 199
Alford, Robert, 53
Almond, Gabriel, 15
Altshuler, Alan, 50
Ambrecht, Biliana, 64
Anderson, James, 3, 15, 66, 199
Arnstein, Sherry, 63
Arole, Maybelle, 168-72
Arole, Rajanikant, 168-72

Banerji, D., 158, 162, 164
Bardhan, P. K., 74, 75
Barrion, Leonard, 175-77
Bates, Robert, 214
Bedaya-Ngaro, S., 187
Beer, Samuel, 43
Behrhorst, Carroll, 173, 176, 185
Bellin, Seymour, 50, 51, 55, 57, 60, 64
Benor, Daniel, 207
Benson, Jonathon, 63
Berliner, H., 152
Berman, Paul, 51, 57
Berry, R. A., 74
Black, M., 186
Blackton, John, 104
Blakely, Edward, 45
Blau, Peter, 58, 220
Blum, Henrick, 152, 174
Boesch, E., 166
Bomgaars, Mona, 179
Bottral, A. F., 102
Bradshaw, Ted, 45
Braun, Eugene, 131-34
Brown, Anthony, 44, 61
Browning, Rufus, 51, 64
Bryant, J., 160, 165, 166
Buccola, Steven, 49, 60
Burki, Shahid, 203

Caetano, Raul, 156, 157
Callaghy, Thomas, 214
Carroll, Thomas, 91, 107-8
Chayanov, A. V., 140
Chitere, Preston, xii
Christian Medical Commission, 155
Clark, Kenneth, 65
Clark, William 2, 3, 16, 73-76, 127, 140, 210, 223
Cline, Robert, 42
Cline, W. R., 74
Clinton, J. J., 151
Cloward, Richard, 64
Cohen, John, xii, 3, 17, 18, 63, 139, 213
Cohen, Stephen, 28, 31, 34
Colebatch, H. K., 200
Colle, R. D., 207
Colson, Elizabeth, 3, 15, 66, 199
Conway, Richard, 63
Council of State Community Action Agencies, 49, 51
Coward, Walter, 129
Cunningham, Clark, 165
Cunningham, Paul, 106-7

Davis, Karen, 50, 51, 52, 56, 64
Derthick, Martha, 51
Djermakoye, I. A., 158, 160
Djukanovic, V., 153, 172, 174
Dommell, Paul, 59
Donovan, John, 49

Eagle, Eva, 27, 28
Edelstein, Richard, xii, 208
Elliot, C., 153, 155
Engels, Friedrich, 214
Esman, Milton, 2, 3, 4, 16-17, 46, 63,

115-16, 117, 118, 121, 135-37, 182, 207, 215, 220

Farkas, Suzanne, 43
Feller, L. L., 184
Fendall, N. R. E., 151, 157
Finney, Henry, 60, 61, 206
Flahault, D., 153
Foege, 179
Fournier, G., 158, 160
Fox, Roger, 84, 85, 88-89

Gamson, William, 52
Garzon, Jose, xii, 6, 23, 203, 222
Gentil, 86
Gershman, Carl, 65
Gish, Oscar, 153, 157, 184
Gittel, Marilyn, 50, 52, 63
Godwin, Lamond, 49, 51, 60, 205
Goldsmith, Arthur, 3, 17, 18, 63, 213
Gonzalez, C. L., 173
Gotsch, C. H., 74
Greenstone, J. D., 64
Gridley, 180, 185
Grissa, Abdessatar, 101, 109, 203

Haider, Donald, 43
Harik, Iliya, 15, 196, 198
Harrison, James, 207
Haveman, Robert, 46, 47, 51
Healey, D. T., 73
Heath, Billie, 49
Heiby, James, 4
Hendrata, Lucas, 174-75
Hill, George, 159
Hirschman, Albert, 113, 211
Hollinsteiner, Mary, 128
Hollister, Robert, 50, 51, 55, 57, 60, 64
Honadle, Beth, 45
Howse, C. J., 96
Hyden, Goran, 20, 113, 114, 210, 211

Ilchman, Warren, 2, 24
Illiach, Ivan, 152
Inamdar, N. R., 208
Inayatullah, 36, 78, 115
Ingram, Helen, 51
International Confederation of Free Trade Unions, 31
International Institute for Educational Planning, 208

James, Jr., Thomas, 63
Jiggins, Janice, xii
Johnston, Bruce, xii, 2, 3, 8, 13, 16, 73-76, 127, 140, 210, 222, 223
Jung, Richard, 59
Justice, Judith, 163

Khan, Azizur, 80, 93, 97
Kilby, Peter, 16, 73-74, 222
King, Anthony, 43
King, Roger, 86, 89-90, 93, 95
Kirst, Michael, 59
Korten, David, xii, 125, 126, 128, 130, 141, 142-45, 161, 162, 181
Korten, Francis, 212
Kramer, Bernard, 50, 51, 55, 57, 60, 64
Kramer, Ralph, 51
Kroeger, E. J., 152, 166-67

Ladman, Jerry, 97
Laib, A. M., 157
Lamb, Curt, 51
Landau, Martin, xi, 27, 28, 210, 211
Lau, L. J., 74
Lele, Uma, 87, 89, 215
Leonard, David, 207, 213
Levin, Henry, 50, 55, 56, 60, 64
Levine, Robert, 51
Levitan, Sar, 46, 47
Long, E. C., 22
Long, Norman, 100-1
Lowdermilk, Max, 209

Mach, E. P. 153, 172, 174
Magagna, Victor, xii
Mann, Fred, 131-34
Marcus, Isabel, 57
Margen, Sheldon, 161, 163

Marris, Peter, 62, 215
Marshall, Dale, 51, 64
Marshall, Ray, 49, 51, 60, 205
Marx, Karl, 214
Mazmanian, Daniel, 51, 57, 59, 64
McGilvray, J. A., 151, 160, 164, 177
McLaughlin, M., 51
Medical Services Consultants, Inc., 210
Mellor, J. W., 73
Migdal, Joel S., 2, 15
Montgomery, John, xii, 45, 46, 215, 220
Moore, M. P., 105
Morawetz, D., 73
Moynihan, Daniel, 46
Murphy, J. T., 51
Myrdal, Gunnar, 152

Nathan, Richard, 51, 59
National Academy of Public Administration, 46
Navarro, Vincent, 157
Ness, Gayl, 4
Newell, K., 153, 174
Nzeussen, 180, 185

Olivera, Carlos, 208
Orden, David, 49, 60
Oyugi, Walter, xii

Pene, P., 157
Penido, H. M., 157
Peterson, Paul, 64
Pillsbury, Barbara, 4
Piven, Frances, 64
Plotnick, Robert, 44
Powell, Rodney, 179
Pressman, Jeffrey, 44, 47, 51

Ralston, Lenore, 3, 15, 66, 199
Ram, Eric, 163
Reagan, Michael, 47
Rein, Martin, 62
Rochin, Refugio, 60
Rogahny, Hossain, 156, 160, 167-68, 176, 185
Rondinelli, Dennis, 34, 57
Ross, David, 158
Rudra, A., 75
Rusch, William, 131-34

Sabatier, Paul, 51, 57, 59, 64
Sanzone, John, 47
Schattschneider, E. E., 66
Schoen, Cathy, 50, 52
Schurmann, Franz, 15, 18, 19, 196, 198
Scott, Richard, 58
Seers, Dudley, 1-2
Selznick, Philip, 62, 175
Skidmore, Felicity, 44
Smith, R. A., 151, 177-80
Sobhan, Rehman, 221
Sokolow, Alvin, 44, 45, 59
Solter, Steven, 156, 160, 167-68, 185
Somerset, Anthony, 215
Stavis, Benedict, 81, 97, 103-4, 106, 219
Storms, Doris, 153, 176, 179
Stout, Richard, 211

Tabb, David, 51, 64
Taggart, Robert, 46
Tendler, Judith, xii, 5, 8, 19, 23, 97, 98, 125-30, 138, 145-47, 203
Teunissen, 180, 185
Thoden van Velzen, H. U. E., 22
Thompson, James, 4, 26

Ugalde, A., 182
United Nations Centre for Regional Development, 34
United Nations Research Institute for Social Development (UNRISD), 114-16, 136, 141, 147-48
United States Advisory Commission on Intergovernmental Relations (USACIR), 42, 44, 45, 47, 51, 56, 61, 63, 64
United States Agency for International Development (USAID), 155, 210
Uphoff, Norman, xii, 2, 3, 4, 16-17, 18, 21, 24, 63, 115-16, 117, 118,

121, 135-37, 182, 213

Van Horn, Carl, 51, 64
Verba, Sidney, 15
Viau, A. D., 22
von Freyhold, Michaela, 100, 108, 118

Washnis, George, 53
Wells, Miriam, 61
Whitman, Ray, 42
Wildavsky, Aaron, 44, 47
Williams, Walter, 41, 47, 51, 57, 58, 62
Wilson, Frank, 87-88, 89
Wirt, Frederick, 51
World Bank, 208

Yates, Douglas, 51, 52, 64
Yin, Robert, 51, 64
Yotopoulos, P. A., 74
Young, Sarah, 212

Zimet, Melvin, 50
Zone, Martin, 45

SUBJECT INDEX

Accounting, 5, 86-87, 108, 111, 116, 117, 119, 126, 130, 197, 206-7, 217-18
Actionable hypotheses, xi
Adaptability, 3, 55, 76, 77, 209, 219, 223
Administrative capacity, ix, 3, 8, 24-27, 45, 52, 59, 65, 102, 119, 120-21, 182-84, 204-13, 214; local, 83, 128, 136, 201; national, 84, 86, 156
Africa, 87, 96, 114, 157, 162, 210-11. *See also* Algeria; Cameroon; Egypt; Ethiopia; Kenya; Lesotho; Malawi; Niger; Nigeria; Rhodesia; Senegal; Sierra Leone; Sudan; Tanzania; Tunisia; Zambia
Agricultural: pricing policies, 75-76, 89, 91-92; programs, ix, 10, 13, 16, 48, 49, 73-121, 125-49; research, 75. *See also* Credit; Extension; Marketing
AID. *See* USAID
Aid agencies. *See* Donors
Algeria, 157
Alternative organizations, x, 15, 17-20, 29, 30-34, 45, 48, 50, 51-53, 55, 56-59, 66, 77, 78, 98, 114, 125-49, 195-200, 214, 218, 223
Ascriptive conflicts, 19-20
Asia, 87, 96, 115, 220. *See also* China; India; Indonesia; Iran; Korea; Pakistan; Philippines; Taiwan; Thailand; Sri Lanka
Assistance. *See* Linkages, assistance
Auditing, 86-87, 115, 117, 130, 207, 219
Autonomy, organizational, 219
Ayurvedic medicine, 162

Bangladesh, 79-80, 83-84, 93
Barter system, rice/fertilizer, 82, 118
Basic Needs, 2, 185, 186
Benefits, indivisible, 12, 44. *See also* Elites, local: benefits for
Bimodal agriculture, 16, 74, 79
Bolivia, 155
Brazil, 94-95, 156-57, 160, 206

Cameroon, 180
Capacity. *See* Administrative capacity
Capital expenditures, 202-3
Carter, Jimmy, 44, 59
Centralization: need for, 3-4, 31; defined, 27
China, 18, 32, 74, 110, 167-68, 187-88, 196, 198-99
Christian Medical Commission, 155, 168, 186
Client demand, 9, 12, 14
Clinic models, 159-60, 161, 162-67, 186
Cohesion, social, 126, 130
Comilla, 79-80, 83-84, 93
Commitment: agency, 3, 6, 8, 21-23, 50-52, 61, 104, 181, 205, 221; local, 45, 119, 205, 221; national, 21, 45, 65, 84, 86, 102, 113, 120-21, 195-96, 198-200, 201-4, 214; staff, 60-61, 203-4, 205. *See also* Values, professional
Competition, 79, 81, 84, 90, 96, 99, 103, 113, 114, 119, 214, 215; for leadership, 15, 17-18
Complexity, administrative, 25-26, 86, 100-1, 112, 116, 127, 137, 213
Constraints, overwhelming, 213-16
Context of implementation, 136-37. *See also* Political, context
Continuity, institutional, 127, 133, 134

SUBJECT INDEX

Control. *See* Linkages, control

Cooperatives, x, 5, 20, 31, 32, 33, 60-62, 73-121, 136, 140-42, 147-48, 185, 196, 206-7, 210-12, 217-18; communal production, 100-1, 107-11, 126, 141-42, 198; conditions of success of, 113-14; formal, 78-79, 125, 127, 133-35; marketing, 84-90; production, 99-111; supply, 79-84; traders', 89-90; U.S., 60-62

Co-optation, 62-63, 199-200

Coordination, 63, 200. *See also* Integration

Corruption, 96, 108, 112, 117, 118, 129, 137, 149

Costa Rica, 86

Credit, 9, 10, 76, 80, 81, 90-99, 108, 118, 120; default on, 93, 97, 129, 130; group, 97, 126, 128-35, 147; informal, 91-96, 97, 99

Decentralization: defined, 4, 27-28; need for, 4, 76; types of, 27-34, 76-77

Deconcentration, 28, 31, 77, 201, 219; prefectorial, 32, 34, 196, 201, 204; ministerial, 33, 34, 76, 196, 201, 207

Delegation to autonomous agencies, 33, 34, 76-77, 196, 201

Demand/supply, 9, 12, 14, 181

Development, defined, 1

Devolution, 28, 30, 32, 194, 197, 201, 202. *See also* Functional devolution

Differentiation: institutional, 127; socio-economic, 2

Donors, ix, 23-24, 128, 138, 144, 145-46, 149, 152, 181, 202, 203, 205, 221-22

Dual strategy. *See* Parallel linkages

Economic infrastructure, 75-77, 89, 103

Ecuador, 126

Education, xi, 5, 9, 10, 14, 31, 32, 48, 49, 50, 51, 53, 58, 64, 208, 216. *See also* Elementary and Secondary Education Act; Head Start

Effectiveness: of groups of poor, 126-27; organizational, 143-45, 209-10, 221

Efficiency, organizational, 143-45, 198, 209-10

Egypt, 196, 198-99

Ejidos, 107-8, 116

Elementary and Secondary Education Act (ESEA), 49, 55, 56, 58-59

Elites, local, x, 8, 44, 62-63, 113, 179, 194-200, 218, 223; benefits for, 92-93, 94-95, 118; congenial, 194-95; domination by, 17-19, 78, 79-80, 86, 91, 106, 116, 139, 149, 185; interests of, and poor, 2, 15-20, 125, 128, 136-37, 181; opposition by, 140-42, 210, 214

England, 160

Ethiopia, 118, 120

Exit, 79, 141

Extension, agricultural, 2, 10, 12, 22, 33, 51, 59, 60, 76, 120, 129-30, 207-9

Failure, organizational, 110, 127, 128, 141, 147-48, 212

Family planning, 11, 14

Feedback, 209

Ford, Gerald, 42

Form vs. function, organizational, 127-28, 137, 140

Function, organizational, multiple vs. single, 105, 126-27, 135-40, 144, 147. *See also* Specialist

Functional devolution, 31, 32, 48, 76-77, 194, 197, 202

Fundacion del Centavo, 131-35, 145

Generalist: officials, 45; organizations, 29, 30, 32-33

Grant system, U.S., 41-44, 55, 58; block, 42-44; categoric, 42-44, 55; general revenue sharing, 42-44, 58

SUBJECT INDEX

Groups of poor. *See under* Effectiveness
Guatemala, 22, 131-35, 159, 173-74, 185-86, 187

Head Start, 50, 53, 55, 56
Health, xi, 11, 14, 49, 50, 51, 53, 60, 64, 151-88, 201, 204, 206, 208, 209, 210, 216-17, 219; budgets, 155-56, 157, 180; costs, 160
Health workers, community (paraprofessional, village), 5, 153, 157, 159-61, 170-72, 173, 177-79, 182-83, 184, 187, 217
Homogeneity, social, 15-17, 19-20, 86, 105-6, 111, 112-13, 115, 127, 130, 136-37, 185, 218
Honduras, 126
Hospital systems, 154-58, 186

Immunizations, mass, 158
Incentives, 106-7, 108, 109, 117, 130; for organizing, 131, 140-42, 149
Inclusive organizations, 17, 18, 19, 20, 29, 30-34, 73-121, 125, 136, 139, 194-95, 197-98
Incrementalism, 3
India, 31, 32, 46, 85, 125, 158, 160, 162-64, 168-72, 175, 181, 183, 184, 185, 187, 196, 206
Indonesia, 174-75
Inequality, vulnerability to. *See* Vulnerability
Inputs, 10, 12, 75. *See also* Cooperatives, supply
Institutional development, phases of, 142-43
Integration, administrative, 137, 139-40, 213. *See also* Coordination; Vertically integrated production
Interest organization, 31, 32, 48, 77, 196, 199, 201
Interest rates, 91-92, 94-95, 97, 98-99, 129, 133-34
Interests, homogeneity of, 20. *See also* Elites, local, interests of
Intermediate organizations, 29, 30-34, 36, 37, 49, 60, 61, 77, 110-11, 117, 131-35, 138-39, 183, 194-96, 202, 219
Iran, 160, 167-68
Irrigation, 10, 25, 33, 75, 81, 101-6, 110, 112, 120, 121, 126, 129, 142, 219

Jamkhed, 168-72, 175, 181, 183, 184
Johnson, Lyndon, 42

Kennedy, John, 42
Kenya, 5, 20, 32, 33, 85, 87-88, 186, 200, 213, 219
Khan, Ayub, 221
Korea, 212

Labor intensive, 10, 13, 73-75, 103, 120, 129
Land purchase, 128, 133, 135, 147
Land reform, 2, 75, 82, 104, 107, 118, 128, 196, 198
Latent organizing strategy, 140-42
Latin America, 96, 125. *See also* Bolivia; Brazil; Costa Rica; Ecuador; Guatemala; Honduras; Mexico; Venezuela
Leadership, 15-18; effective local, 105-6, 108; role, 24
Learning model of institutional development, 128, 142-45
Lending quotas, 98
Lesotho, 96
Linkages: assistance, 6, 36, 54, 57-62, 64, 80, 103, 108-13, 115, 132, 134-35, 143-49, 154, 163, 178, 184, 187, 197, 201, 202, 208, 220-22; control, 36, 54-58, 62, 64, 80, 81, 96-98, 102-4, 109, 110, 112-13, 115-18, 144-49, 154, 163, 183, 187, 197, 202, 208, 211, 218-21, 223; costs of, 221; defined, x, 6; facilitative, 36, 110, 114-15; parallel, 48-54, 61, 65, 196-200,

223; political, 156, 157; professionals to paraprofessionals, 167, 173, 175, 178, 183; purpose of, 116-18; redundant, 209-12; regulative, 6, 35, 36, 88, 89, 110, 114-15, 215; sequence of, 89, 119, 142-49; types of, 35, 118-20; upward, 41, 43, 62, 83, 104, 121, 138-39; village, 159, 161, 165, 167, 178-79, 183, 184. *See also* Technical assistance
Linking apportioned functions, 5, 206-9
Local government, elected, xi, 40-66, 104, 204, 217, 221-22

Malawi, 96
Market, free, x, 2, 10, 30, 125, 214, 215
Marketing, agricultural, 76, 81, 84-90, 126, 129, 210-11
Marketization, 33, 34, 77, 201
Medex health system, 177-80
Medical referrals, 162-63, 184
Medicine, human: curative, 9, 10, 22, 152, 164-65, 169, 176, 181, 183, 185, 187; preventive, 10, 22, 153, 157, 164, 170, 181, 185, 187, 217; traditional, 162, 165, 169, 170, 187
Medicine, veterinary: curative, 9, 10; preventive, 10
Mercantilism, 214
Messy problems, 210, 222
Mexico, 107-8, 111, 116
Ministerial deconcentration. *See* Deconcentration
Monopoly, 10, 12, 78, 79, 83-84, 85, 87, 88, 95, 99, 113, 119, 210-11, 214, 215, 221
Multinational corporations, 215
Multiple function organization. *See* Function
Mutual dependence. *See* Partnership

Nasser, Gamel Abdel, 196, 198
Niger, 86, 158, 160
Nigeria, 86, 89-90, 93-94, 95, 117
Nixon, Richard, 42
Nyerere, Julius, 1

Office of Economic Opportunity (OEO), 48, 49, 50, 55

Pakistan, 203-4, 221-22
Parallel linkages, 48-54, 61, 65, 196-200, 223
Paraprofessionals, 207-9, 217. *See also* Health workers, community
Parastatals, 34, 76-77, 201
Participation, community, 3, 4, 6, 17, 29, 51-52, 62-64, 83, 131, 137, 139, 142, 168-70, 172, 173, 175, 176-77, 179, 184-88, 199-200, 223. *See also* Representation
Partnership for Health, U.S., 50, 56
Partnership of central and local organizations, x, 4, 6, 41, 47, 182, 193, 223
Philanthropy, x, 30, 33, 34, 77, 131-35, 145, 146, 201, 202, 214
Philippines, 125, 175-77, 186
Political: action, 195-97, 198, 199; context, ix, 21, 23, 43, 45, 48, 56, 57, 113, 128, 140, 145, 149, 153, 155, 156, 157, 163, 164, 174, 177, 182, 197, 214, 219; strategy, 47, 52, 65-66, 118, 131, 140, 149, 178-79, 200
Prefectorial deconcentration. *See* Deconcentration
Private entrepreneurs. *See* Traders
Privatization, 30, 33, 34, 77-78, 201, 202, 214, 215
Professional staff requirements, 206-9
Progressive center. *See* Commitment
Public goods, 181
Public health, 22, 169, 174, 182, 203, 217
Public works, xi, 11, 13, 23, 33, 203-4, 221-22

Quality vs. quantity, 9, 156

Reagan, Ronald, 44
Recurrent expenditures, 202-3
Rediscount spreads, 98
Redundancy, 54, 81, 96, 110, 120, 137, 141, 147, 162, 180, 209-12, 221; upward, 212
Regional inequalities, 4, 82
Regulation. *See* Linkages, regulative
Representation, 7, 17-18, 62-64, 83, 111, 121, 138, 199-200. *See also* Linkages, upward
Rhodesia, 96
Roads, 5, 11, 12, 22, 75, 88, 126, 128, 142
Rural savings, 91-93, 96, 98-99

Sadat, Anwar, 196
Sanitation, 11, 12, 14, 159, 166, 187
Savings clubs, 96
Scale, economies of, 14, 84, 86, 100, 103, 109-10, 112-13, 136-37
School inspectors, 208
Secondment of technical personnel, 119, 197, 206
Senegal, 160
Sierra Leone, 158
Simplicity in organizational design, 127, 213
Single function organization. *See* Function
Small farmers. *See* Unimodal agriculture
Social change, 47, 149, 152, 153, 160, 167, 175, 183, 185, 187, 196, 198, 200
Social distance, 161, 165, 170-71, 183
Socialist economies, 9, 74, 100-1, 107-11
Socialization. *See* Commitment: agency, staff
Specialist: agencies, 29, 30, 32-33, 49; officials, 45. *See also* Function
Sri Lanka, 102, 104-6, 111, 121, 166
Standard of living, 152, 153
Stimulating local organizations, 141
Stimulating new efforts, 42, 61
Subnational government. *See* Local government
Subsidies, 9, 215
Sudan, 210
Supply. *See* Demand; Inputs

Taiwan, 96-97, 102, 110, 111, 117, 118, 121, 219; farmers' associations, 80-83, 103-4, 118
Tanzania, 1, 100-1, 108, 110, 111, 118, 119
Targeting, 13-14, 42, 48, 49, 80, 87, 92, 97, 98, 120, 129, 131
Task-force health interventions, 158-59, 186
Technical assistance, 35, 36, 59-62, 102, 130, 135, 143-45, 205-6
Tenant farming, 75
Termination: of organization, 127, 128; of support, 110, 119, 145-49, 211. *See also* Failure, organizational
Thailand, 102, 106-7, 160, 165-66, 187
Traders, 77, 79, 83-84, 85, 87, 89-90, 112, 114, 125, 202, 211, 212, 215
Traditional medicine, 162, 165, 169, 170, 187
Training and Visit System, 207-9
Transaction costs, 92, 97
Transportation problems, 208
Tunisia, 109-10, 117, 203-4

Ujamaa, 100-1, 108
Unimodal agriculture, 16, 73-76, 79, 120, 149
Union of Soviet Socialist Republics, 74
Unit of consumption, 9, 12
United Nations Children's Fund (UNICEF), 152, 158, 186
United States, 40-66, 155, 160, 164, 165

Urban bias, 155, 164, 165
U.S. Agency for International Development (USAID), 138, 146, 152, 155, 158, 159, 180, 186

Values, professional, 22-23, 216-17. *See also* Commitment, staff
Venezuela, 172-74
Vertically integrated production, 85, 86
Village-based health systems, 160, 161, 167-77, 186
Vulnerability of a program to inequality, 8-15, 44, 46, 180-81, 193, 194, 214, 218

War on Poverty, U.S., 18, 22, 31, 32, 37, 40-66, 196, 198, 200, 204-5, 220; assessment of, 46-47
Water systems, 9, 11, 14, 159
Weights and measures, regulation of, 88, 89, 215
Well-being, 152, 162
World Bank, 207, 208, 213
World Health Organization (WHO), 152, 158, 186

Zambia, 96, 203

NOTES ON CONTRIBUTORS

DAVID K. LEONARD is an Associate Professor of Political Science at the University of California, Berkeley. He has spent ten years living and working in four African countries. Most recently he served as an advisor to the Ministries of Agriculture and Livestock Development in Kenya. He also is author of *Reaching the Peasant Farmer.*

DALE ROGERS MARSHALL is a Professor of Political Science at the University of California, Davis. She has been monitoring and doing research on U.S. poverty programs since 1965. Her most recent book is *The Struggle for Political Equality: City Government Responsiveness to Blacks and Hispanics* (forthcoming) with Rufus Browning and David Tabb.

STEPHEN B. PETERSON is an Assistant Professor of Political Science at Pepperdine University. His doctoral dissertation was on "The State and the Organizational Infrastructure of the Agrarian Economy: A Comparative Study of Smallholder Agrarian Development in Taiwan and Kenya."

SVEN STEINMO holds a Masters of Public Health from the University of California, Berkeley. He is currently doing a comparative analysis of health care politics in industrialized societies for his Ph.D. dissertation.

INSTITUTE OF INTERNATIONAL STUDIES
UNIVERSITY OF CALIFORNIA, BERKELEY

215 Moses Hall Berkeley, California 94720

CARL G. ROSBERG, *Director*

Monographs published by the Institute include:

RESEARCH SERIES

1. *The Chinese Anarchist Movement.* R.A. Scalapino and G.T. Yu. ($1.00)
7. *Birth Rates in Latin America.* O. Andrew Collver. ($2.50)
15. *Central American Economic Integration.* Stuart I. Fagan. ($2.00)
16. *The International Imperatives of Technology.* Eugene B. Skolnikoff. ($2.95)
17. *Autonomy or Dependence in Regional Integration.* P.C. Schmitter. ($1.75)
19. *Entry of New Competitors in Yugoslav Market Socialism.* S.R. Sacks. ($2.50)
20. *Political Integration in French-Speaking Africa.* Abdul A. Jalloh. ($3.50)
21. *The Desert & the Sown: Nomads in Wider Society.* Ed. C. Nelson. ($5.50)
22. *U.S.-Japanese Competition in International Markets.* J.E. Roemer. ($3.95)
23. *Political Disaffection Among British University Students.* J. Citrin and D.J. Elkins. ($2.00)
24. *Urban Inequality and Housing Policy in Tanzania.* Richard E. Stren. ($2.95)
25. *The Obsolescence of Regional Integration Theory.* Ernst B. Haas. ($4.95)
26. *The Voluntary Service Agency in Israel.* Ralph M. Kramer. ($2.00)
27. *The SOCSIM Microsimulation Program.* E. A. Hammel et al. ($4.50)
28. *Authoritarian Politics in Communist Europe.* Ed. Andrew C. Janos. ($3.95)
29. *The Anglo-Icelandic Cod War of 1972-1973.* Jeffrey A. Hart. ($2.00)
30. *Plural Societies and New States.* Robert Jackson. ($2.00)
31. *Politics of Oil Pricing in the Middle East, 1970-75.* R.C. Weisberg. ($4.95)
32. *Agricultural Policy and Performance in Zambia.* Doris J. Dodge. ($4.95)
33. *Five Classy Computer Programs.* E.A. Hammel & R.Z. Deuel. ($3.75)
34. *Housing the Urban Poor in Africa.* Richard E. Stren. ($5.95)
35. *The Russian New Right: Right-Wing Ideologies in USSR.* A. Yanov. ($5.95)
36. *Social Change in Romania, 1860-1940.* Ed. Kenneth Jowitt. ($4.50)
37. *The Leninist Response to National Dependency.* Kenneth Jowitt. ($4.95)
38. *Socialism in Sub-Saharan Africa.* Eds. C. Rosberg & T. Callaghy. ($12.95)
39. *Tanzania's Ujamaa Villages: Rural Development Strategy.* D. McHenry. ($5.95)
40. *Who Gains from Deep Ocean Mining?* I.G. Bulkley. ($3.50)
41. *Industrialization & the Nation-State in Peru.* Frits Wils. ($5.95)
42. *Ideology, Public Opinion, & Welfare Policy: Taxes and Spending in Industrialized Societies.* R.M. Coughlin. ($6.50)
43. *The Apartheid Regime: Political Power and Racial Domination.* Eds. R.M. Price and C. G. Rosberg. ($12.50)
44. *Yugoslav Economic System in the 1970s.* L.D. Tyson. ($5.50)
45. *Conflict in Chad.* Virginia Thompson & Richard Adloff. ($7.50)
46. *Conflict and Coexistence in Belgium.* Ed. Arend Lijphart. ($7.50)

47. *Changing Realities in Southern Africa.* Ed. Michael Clough. ($12.50)
48. *Nigerian Women Mobilized: Women's Political Activity in Southern Nigeria, 1900-1965.* Nina Emma Mba. ($12.95)
49. *Institutions of Rural Development for the Poor.* Ed. D. Leonard & D. Marshall. ($11.50)
50. *Politics of Women & Work in USSR & U.S.* J.C. Moses. ($9.50)
51. *Zionism and Territory.* Baruch Kimmerling. ($12.50)
52. *Soviet Subsidization of Trade with Eastern Europe.* M. Marrese & J. Vanous. ($14.50)
53. *Voluntary Efforts in Decentralized Management.* L. Ralston et al. ($9.00)
54. *Corporate State Ideologies.* C. Landauer. ($5.95)
55. *Effects of Economic Reform in Yugoslavia.* J. Burkett. ($9.50)

POLITICS OF MODERNIZATION SERIES

1. *Spanish Bureaucratic-Patrimonialism in America.* M. Sarfatti. ($2.00)
2. *Civil-Military Relations in Argentina, Chile, & Peru.* L. North. ($2.00)
9. *Modernization & Bureaucratic-Authoritarianism: Studies in South American Politics.* Guillermo O'Donnell. ($8.95)

POLICY PAPERS IN INTERNATIONAL AFFAIRS

1. *Images of Detente & the Soviet Political Order.* K. Jowitt. ($1.25)
2. *Detente After Brezhnev: Domestic Roots of Soviet Policy.* A. Yanov. ($4.50)
3. *Mature Neighbor Policy: A New Policy for Latin America.* A. Fishlow. ($3.95)
4. *Five Images of Soviet Future: Review & Synthesis.* G.W. Breslauer. ($4.50)
5. *Global Evangelism Rides Again: How to Protect Human Rights Without Really Trying.* E.B. Haas. ($2.95)
6. *Israel & Jordan: An Adversarial Partnership.* Ian Lustick. ($2.00)
7. *Political Syncretism in Italy.* Giuseppe Di Palma. ($3.95)
8. *U.S. Foreign Policy in Sub-Saharan Africa.* R.M. Price. ($4.50)
9. *East-West Technology Transfer in Perspective.* R.J. Carrick. ($5.50)
10. *NATO's Unremarked Demise.* Earl C. Ravenal. ($3.50)
11. *Toward Africanized Policy for Southern Africa.* R. Libby. ($5.50)
12. *Taiwan Relations Act & Defense of ROC.* E. Snyder et al. ($7.50)
13. *Cuba's Policy in Africa, 1959-1980.* William M. LeoGrande. ($4.50)
14. *Norway, NATO, & Forgotten Soviet Challenge.* K. Amundsen. ($2.95)
15. *Japanese Industrial Policy.* Ira Magaziner and Thomas Hout. ($6.50)
16. *Containment, Soviet Behavior, & Grand Strategy.* Robert Osgood. ($5.50)
17. *U.S.-Japanese Competition in Semiconductor Industry.* M. Borrus et al. ($7.50)
18. *Contemporary Islamic Movements in Perspective.* I. Lapidus. ($4.95)
19. *Atlantic Alliance, Nuclear Weapons, & European Attitudes.* W. Thies. ($4.50)